Advertising as Multilingual Communication

Also by Helen Kelly-Holmes

MINORITY LANGUAGE BROADCASTING: Breton and Irish (*editor*)

EUROPEAN TELEVISION DISCOURSE IN TRANSITION (*editor*)

Advertising as Multilingual Communication

Helen Kelly-Holmes
Research Scholar
University of Limerick, Ireland

165101

First published in hardcover 2005

First published in paperback 2008 by
PALGRAVE MACMILLAN
Houndmills, Basingstoke, Hampshire RG21 6XS and
175 Fifth Avenue, New York, N.Y. 10010
Companies and representatives throughout the world.

PALGRAVE MACMILLAN is the global academic imprint of the Palgrave Macmillan division of St. Martin's Press, LLC and of Palgrave Macmillan Ltd. Macmillan® is a registered trademark in the United States, United Kingdom and other countries. Palgrave is a registered trademark in the European Union and other countries.

ISBN-13: 978–1–4039–1725–6   hardback

ISBN-13: 978–0–230–21706–5   paperback

This book is printed on paper suitable for recycling and made from fully managed and sustained forest sources. Logging, pulping and manufacturing processes are expected to conform to the environmental regulations of the country of origin.

A catalogue record for this book is available from the British Library.

Library of Congress Cataloging-in-Publication Data

Kelly-Holmes, Helen, 1968–
    Advertising as multilingual communication / Helen Kelly-Holmes.
        p. cm.
    Includes bibliographical references and index.
    ISBN 1–4039–1725–6 (cloth) ISBN 0–230–21706–0 (pbk)
        1. Advertising. 2. Advertising – Language. 3. Multilingualism – Economic aspects. 4. Multiculturalism – Economic aspects. 5. Intercultural communication. I. Title.

HF5823.K346 2004
659.1′042—dc22   2004054891

10 9 8 7 6 5 4 3 2 1
17 16 15 14 13 12 11 10 09 08

Transferred to Digital Printing in 2008

For my parents, and for Kevin and Jennifer

Contents

Acknowledgements

I would like to thank the following people for their help in the writing of this book: Jill Lake and all the staff at Palgrave Macmillan for their assistance; my colleagues in the Department of Languages and Cultural Studies and the Centre for Applied Language Studies in the University of Limerick, in particular Dr David Atkinson for his careful reading and valuable criticism; my former colleagues in the Department of Languages and European Studies, Aston University, in particular Dr Sue Wright, Professor Rüdiger Görner, Professor Nigel Reeves and Dr Gertrud Reershemius; the University of Limerick Foundation for its generous funding; the companies and individuals who cooperated in the research for this book; and, finally, my parents, family and friends.

HELEN KELLY-HOLMES

Introduction

It is breakfast time, I am listening to a national commercial station in Ireland, and the presenter is announcing details of a competition to win a holiday in Italy. The competition is sponsored by *Buittoni* pasta. Competitors have to complete two tasks on the air: first of all they have to say an Italian phrase in the most convincing accent they can; secondly they have to judge whether or not different celebrities are 'real' or 'fake' Italians, defined in this context as being born in Italy or elsewhere, based on their names. The competition is followed by a commercial break. This can be seen as the explicit market text section of the programme; however, since the product being sold is commercial radio, the programmes are an intrinsic part of this and also constitute, in my opinion, a type of market discourse. During this particular break there is an advertisement featuring men speaking what is to most listeners an incomprehensible language in an excited fashion. The narrator of the advertisement, in an Irish male media voice, tells the listener that these Japanese people were very surprised by 'the result'; the listener then hears calmer, more laid-back people speaking what sounds like Italian, and the narrator intervenes once again to tell the listener that the Italians were not surprised at all by 'the result'. The result in question is then explained: namely the triumph of *Hyundai* – a Korean car, the listener is told – in being named car of the year. In the next ad break, a 'French' accent advertises holidays in Paris. This is followed by the sports report in which the presenter switches to Irish in order to congratulate a Gaelic football team on its victory. This is the cue for the sports presenter and the morning-show disc jockey to indulge in some language play using '*go raibh maith agat*' ('Thank you') and '*slán*' ('goodbye'), before reverting to the default, the commonsense norm against which all these eccentric and exotic excursions into other languages take place, the English language.

An early morning breakfast show on a national commercial station in Ireland is hardly something that springs to mind as a piece of multilingual communication. However, the cumulative experience of listening every day to such a programme, on the one hand, exposes the listener to different voices, accents and languages, while on the other hand reinforces impressions of language and languages that are part of the culture within which the listener lives and the radio programme as text functions. Pierre Bourdieu, commenting on his own work, wrote of the difficulty of managing 'to think in a completely astonished and disconcerted way about things you thought you had always understood' (Bourdieu, 1991, p. 207). His words lay down the challenge and point the way forward for all of us who are concerned with investigating the mundane, banal omnipresence of the market, its texts and its languages, its presentation of the other and of the self, of the other's and our own language and languages in our everyday lives. This book represents an attempt to meet this challenge, with two main objectives in mind: firstly, to examine how advertising and other market discourses use languages and exploit and hyperbolize linguistic difference in order to sell products and services; secondly, to explore how advertising responds to situations that are bi- or multilingual in nature, and to attempt to assess the effects of language choices made by advertisers and the producers of market discourses in general in these situations in order to sell products and services.

In Chapter 1, various traditions of looking at multilingualism are examined, with the objective of finding ways of treating and analysing multilingual, market-driven media. First of all, there is an attempt to define the language and role of advertising in a market society. Following this, the discussion centres on the notion of 'foreign' words: how these manifest themselves in various types of discourse and what methods have been used for examining their effects. Sociolinguistic theories of code-switching are then examined and compared with translation theories for dealing with foreign words. Finally, in recognition of the fact that much of this use is symbolically driven and related to the market, a notion of linguistic fetish is proposed.

Chapters 2, 3, 4 and 5 present four different case studies of advertising as multilingual communication. The main concern in Chapter 2 is how advertising and other commercially-driven messages use nationalities and languages, and how ethnocentric marketing techniques such as the country-of-origin effect provide the paradigms within which a type of linguistic fetish operates. It is argued in this chapter that the use of languages in country-of-origin-based market discourses is primarily symbolic. The two main case studies focus on the German and French linguistic fetishes in Europe, but there will also be examples from other languages.

Chapter 3 examines the special case of English and its use in advertising discourses in a number of countries. Unlike the examples discussed in Chapter 2, where the respective languages are used because of their association with a particular country of origin or country of competence in a particular domain, English has acquired a variety of fetishized meanings internationally, many of which are detached from the countries in which the language is spoken as a first or major language. The first part of the chapter discusses the presence of English words in German advertising texts, in an attempt to explore these various associations. The Internet is often seen as just one more medium in which English will push out other languages, and so the second part of the chapter looks at linguistic choices made by global brands and corporations on their various international and local websites. Finally, the issue of English in advertising discourses in Central and Eastern Europe is examined using examples from a number of countries.

In Chapter 4, the issues of minority languages, accents and dialects in advertising are dealt with in an attempt to give an overview of these many and varied developments and their implications. The use of minority languages, accents and dialects in advertising can be seen to be the result of advertisers attempting to speak to people 'in their own language'. First of all, the issue of allochthonous minority languages and advertising is explored. Such a phenomenon automatically assumes an everyday multilingual context for the recipients of these advertising messages. The remainder of the chapter is then devoted to a case study of the Irish context, which highlights many of the issues of concern here, namely the uses and abuses to which accent, dialect and indigenous minority languages are put in advertising.

Chapter 5 examines the functioning of multilingual or heteroglossic advertising within a pan-national framework. The new media paradigms that make possible pan-national advertising are first examined in an attempt to define what pan-European media and markets actually mean in cultural and linguistic terms, before going on to look in detail at *Eurosport*, a pan-European television channel, to see the functioning of a multilingual market and media context.

Finally, Chapter 6 restates the main findings of the various case studies, discussing them under the broad themes of how the market simultaneously 'creates' while at the same time attempts to combat multilingualism.

The examples discussed in the book come from a variety of media and sources: magazines, television, radio, the Internet, newspapers, billboards, labels and packaging spanning a considerable period of time, from the late 1980s to the early 2000s, a collection that has been put together opportunistically through my own encounters with advertisements in a variety of media. A qualitative approach to analysing the individual advertising texts and contexts is employed. The objective, here, is not to decode the advertisements and get to the 'heart' of their meaning. With a few exceptions, there is no attempt to go beyond the resources that are available to the general advertisee, and to present information that is not generally available in the intertextual field within which the advertisements presented operate. It is hoped, in this way, to avoid falling into the 'decoding' mode that Guy Cook (2001) among others has criticized, whereby the academic decodes advertisements for an ignorant public. Instead, the book is intended to be about observing these texts as examples of multilingualism in a market context, and attempting to assess their impact on the wider issue of multilingualism; observing and commenting on the presence of different languages in the linguistic landscape of the market; and evaluating them as contributions to multilingual or multi-voiced contexts. I would also not want to claim that the range of contexts presented is either comprehensive or universal. Instead these are the contexts that I know best and feel most confident in evaluating and assessing, namely the European context and the English-speaking world in general, and the Irish, British and German contexts in particular. Although this limited selection of contexts cannot represent a global survey of advertising as multilingual communication, I would argue that many of the examples and findings have relevance beyond their linguistic and geographical frontiers.

Finally, it may strike the reader as strange that graphics and visuals from the various advertisements discussed are excluded from the book, although the accompanying images are, in the main, described. There are a number of reasons for this decision. First of all, it would have been too difficult to pick a limited number of examples, these becoming necessarily privileged in the eyes of the reader in the process. Secondly, when advertisements are reproduced in books like this, in black and white, their visual impact is invariably reduced, in the sense that colour is omitted, and also, and more fundamentally from my point of view in writing this book, the textual component of the advertisement becomes even harder to read. Thirdly, the ads presented and discussed in the book come from a range of media, print being only one of these, and so it would seem disingenuous and slightly unbalanced to reproduce these simply because it is possible to do so given the nature of the medium in which they appear. The final point is that the book is about different languages in advertisements, and so the focus is necessarily on text as well as the aural and visual paralinguistic features of that text. There are many excellent books that focus on the visual aspects of advertisements more, and also on the interplay of graphic and text. Here, however, I have chosen to keep the focus on the text by reproducing this and not the images in the book. The extracts from the collection of market-driven texts should then be seen as citations from primary texts, in the same way that in a book on a historical or literary theme, citations are made from relevant political speeches or works of literature by selected authors to support a particular argument, rather than being reproduced in their entirety.

1
Defining Multilingualism in a Market Context

> **Shhh! Don't letta the kids know what goes into it. When'sa your Dolmio day?**

Extract from advertisement for *Dolmio* pasta sauce in *Woman's Own* magazine

From the point of view of most linguists, the term multilingualism has an invariably positive ring. It conjures up associations of pluralism, cultural enrichment, diversity and the expression of linguistic rights and freedoms. It is a phenomenon to be celebrated, a cause that is, generally, championed. In this scheme of things, multilingualism has little or nothing to do with the market. In the natural order of things, it is the market that is the great enemy of multilingualism. Its Darwinian disregard for precious but non-dominant codes and languages appears only to hasten the demise of a linguistically diverse world. It may therefore come as something of a surprise to realize that the market is also a place of multilingualism. And, the dilemma then is how to investigate this phenomenon. Are the terminologies and taxonomies of sociolinguistics, language rights, eco-linguistics, bilingual education and so on appropriate for such a non-natural, manipulative type of multilingual communication? Are these developments to be applauded and seen as heralding a richer, more culturally pluralistic world or are they to be condemned outright and languages afforded greater protection from marketers and copywriters?

The main purpose of this chapter is to look at ways of treating multilingual communication in advertising, but before exploring the specific nature of multilingual advertising communication, it is first of all necessary to examine advertising as communication, as such. Therefore, the first half of the chapter looks at how advertising functions in a consumer society and what the specific characteristics of advertising discourse might be. The second half of the chapter is then concerned with providing theoretical frameworks that enable an examination of multilingual texts, borrowing from disciplines such as cultural studies, sociolinguistics, translation theory and philosophy.

The functioning of advertising in a consumer society

The quote at the beginning of this chapter is taken from an advertisement for *Dolmio* pasta sauce that appeared in the UK women's family magazine *Woman's Own* on a regular basis throughout 2003. The advertisement features the familiar *Dolmio* man, a gentle Italian in puppet form. The full text goes as follows:

> Shhh!
> Don't letta the kids know what goes into it.
> If the kids knew all the natural things that go into Dolmio, they'd probably be horrified: juicy sun-ripened tomatoes, not to mention basil and Italian olive oil.
> But that's our little secret, eh?
> When'sa your Dolmio day?

The functioning of this advertising text relies on a number of different relationships. There is the immediate relationship between the reader of the advertisement, who could be called the advertisee, and the text itself; between the advertisee and the advertiser, who, although they do not meet in person, do interact via the advertising text; between this text and the ones that appear before and after it in the magazine, both articles and advertisements; between the brand, *Dolmio*, and the consumer; between *Dolmio* and other competing brands; between human beings and food; between the UK, the country where the advertisement is received, and Italy, the country alluded to in the advertisement; between mothers and their children; between food shopping and money, and so on. Underlying this and other advertising texts, then, are multilayered, multidimensional relationships between individuals, companies, brands, products, services and texts. These relations are socially, economically, culturally, linguistically and politically constructed. The political dimension may not seem immediately obvious, but when the ethnocentric nature of much marketing, such as this approach by *Dolmio*, is considered, then it becomes clear that the realms of history, international relations and politico-economic relations between countries and regions underpin many market-driven messages in contemporary consumer society. Such relationships are also two-way: on the one hand, in order for this advertising text to function, the advertiser needs to assume a common culture or communicative context. Otherwise, it could not be assumed that these relationships would work. On the other hand, this advertising text helps to reinforce all of the relationships upon which it is founded. As Norman Fairclough has pointed out, 'discourse and practice in general ... are both the products of structures and the producers of structures' (2001, p. 39).

The habitus or cultural context of advertising

There are many ways of describing these relationships, how they are created and maintained, and the common communicative or cultural context upon which they are based. Habermas (1993) has talked about the 'lifeworld', Foucault (1986) of a culture that is 'the sum of its orders of discourse'. Raymond Williams (1981) used the termed 'signifying system', while Gert Hofstede (1983), more pessimistically, has spoken of 'collective mental programming'. Perhaps the most complete description is offered by Pierre Bourdieu's notion of a habitus: 'a set of dispositions which incline agents to act and react in certain ways. The dispositions generate practices, perceptions and attitudes which are "regular" '. In Bourdieu's scheme, these 'dispositions' are 'inculcated, structured, durable, generative and transposable' (Thompson in Bourdieu, 1991, p. 12). The inculcation, analogous perhaps to socialization, takes place through structures – in the case of the market society, the structures and institutions of that society, not just ones directly linked to the market, and much of this takes place through texts. These 'dispositions' are durable because they are inculcated and reinforced by the structures – and language – of the market society. They are generative and transposable because they give individuals a set of tools and language with which to operate in different situations within the habitus, in this case the habitus of the market society, upon which market discourses such as advertising rely – discourse being understood as text within its context or within these sets of relationships outlined above (cf., for example, Foucault, 1986; Cook, 1989, 2001).

The creators of the *Dolmio* advertisement, for instance, have assumed a habitus or common communicative culture in which Italians are viewed as knowing about and producing good food, particularly pasta products. Other common-sense assumptions underlying the text include the idea that children do not want to eat healthily, that olive oil is a product for which Italians have cultural competence, that Italians speak English with a particular accent, that mothers are interested in their children eating healthy food, and so on. All of these assumptions are based on the various relationships within the particular habitus assumed by the advertiser, and, in turn, the advertisement creates a context within which future advertising, not just for this particular brand or food type can function, but within which such relationships can be assumed again.

Advertising and consumerization

The knowledge the advertisee has about these relationships and about common-sense assumptions in the advertisement is acquired through experiencing the particular habitus on an everyday basis. Consumerization or socialization into consumer society happens, primarily, through example and through language. Children learn the rituals of participating in the market and its language through being with their parents and they also learn it through market discourses like advertising. It is worth keeping in mind here that advertising is more than simply explicit advertising messages: it encompasses a whole range of texts and objects, such as toys, books, television programmes, packaging and so forth. On average, children in the developed world are exposed to 20,000 commercial messages per year (Leonhardt and Kerwin, 1997, cited in Dotson and Hyatt, 2000), while in Europe, the number and frequency of television advertisements targeting children is growing by 15–20 per cent per year (Stewart-Allen, 1999 cited in Dotson and Hyatt, 2000). By the age of four or five, children can differentiate between programmes and advertisements, but they cannot decipher the persuasive intention (Roedder John, 1999), this being the reasoning behind the banning or curtailment of advertising during the broadcasting of some children's programmes in different countries. Before children learn to read they can recognize brands (Roedder John, 1999 and Schlosser, 2002), so it is thus hardly surprising that 'children are storehouses of commercial information' (Dotson and Hyatt, 1994, cited in Dotson and Hyatt, 2000).

As children move into their teenage years, their enjoyment of advertising decreases, and they become more aware of the persuasive intention (cf. Dotson and Hyatt, 2000). This all sounds healthy, until one considers the level of brand awareness among teenagers in consumption-driven societies, which would seem to prove that inculcation is complete.

Many people protest that advertisements have no effect on them, and research frequently reports that people's recall of advertisements – in terms of the products/brands being advertised, rather than the texts or scenarios of the particular advertisements – is very poor. Likewise, from the other side, marketing managers invariably find it very hard to link advertising expenditure with increased sales. However, decreasing or abandoning advertising usually leads to a fall in sales. It seems, therefore, that advertising simply confers authenticity and legitimacy. Following inculcation, for the rest of one's 'consumer life', brands simply need to be present, they do not really need to persuade, since by being present through advertising messages – and, again, this means not only explicit advertisements, but also the products themselves – they have their legitimacy. As Bourdieu puts it, it is 'the belief in the legitimacy of words and of those who utter them' (1991, p. 171) rather than the words themselves that gives power and authority to advertising texts and slogans. Although this process of consumerization or consumer socialization[1] appears to happen seamlessly, naturally even, it is in effect, in Gramscian (1971) terms, a form of hegemony, whereby partaking in consumption becomes a substitute for partaking in democracy. Indeed, it is often those people who do not insist on their rights as workers and voters who gain empowerment through their role in consumption. Likewise, children in most contemporary consumer societies know more about the market than they do about their system of democracy – they need to be taught the latter explicitly, whereas the former is imbibed from an early age.

A final point about the functioning of advertising is that it is absolutely flexible and adaptable. As changes occur in the structures and texts of the particular culture or society, then advertisements too will respond to this. A good – if rather tasteless – example is a *McDonald's* campaign from 2002. As Eric Schlosser (2002) points out in his book, *Fast Food Nation*, *McDonald's* built its brand around the fact that families could eat out together cheaply. *McDonald's* was about families and family values. In this particular campaign, however, a child of separated parents is shown playing them off against each other so that he can manipulate their feelings of guilt to his own end – two trips to *McDonald's*. Thus, *McDonald's* is responding to changing structures and changing texts in society, within which families are defined differently.

Advertising and intertextuality

As well as being embedded in society through consumption and its rituals, and through relationships between individuals and products, market discourses are also embedded in a system of texts. 'Intertextuality', as defined by writers such as Roland Barthes (1981) and Julia Kristeva (1986), or 'heteroglossia' in Bakhtin's (1981) terms, means that in every advertisement an individual comes across, there are other texts present. Fairclough (1992) distinguishes between manifest intertextuality – which can be described as the form of a text – and constitutive intertextuality – which can be described as the content of a text. The *Dolmio* advertisement is found in what would best be described as a family women's magazine, and in terms of form or manifest intertextuality, it not only looks like other food advertisements, but it looks like advertisements that appear in this particular type of publication. By using the familiar figure of the *Dolmio* man, the brand's graphic and the same slogan, the advertisement links intertextually with other *Dolmio* advertisements, and so builds on the advertisees' knowledge of these other texts.

More than this, however, in constitutive terms, there are many other texts – or voices as Bakhtin (1981) called them – that are present in any given advertisement, although not in such an explicit way. In the *Dolmio* ad, the intertextual links are not just to the other advertisements in the magazine and in other media, but also to texts defining and pre-scribing motherhood in society, from legal, constitutional and religious texts, which deal with gender roles in society, to works of literature, journalistic texts, television programmes, films and so on which all pro-vide the intertextual sphere within which this particular advertisement operates.

Within this overarching relationship between texts, commodities and individuals, the particular advertisement will then, necessarily, select and create its own specific context, choosing from ingredients such as age, gender, location, income, education, linguistic factors and others to form a particular mix. By choosing this particular context, the advertiser can target a composite advertisee who best represents the main charac-teristics of the group being addressed or targeted. Consequently, the advertiser can rely on the advertisees sharing what Sperber and Wilson (1986) have called 'common knowledge', which helps to ensure that the communication is successful. For example, the advertisement for *Dolmio* was featured in a women's magazine aimed primarily at women with children, and this creates the context within which this kind of message can work. The same advertisement would, for example, not be used in a men's magazine, since men are not generally assumed to be as interested in their children's nutrition as women. Similarly, the adver-tisement would not feature in a women's magazine aimed primarily at women without children or more 'career-oriented' women, since the target advertisee is not assumed to share these contexts. More than this, however, the advertisement assumes a broader cultural context in which children are assumed to be fussy eaters, to not want to eat what adults are eating, to not want to eat anything healthy or nutritious. Again, this does not apply universally, since one only has to look at the difference between two geographically close countries such as Britain and France to see massive differences in terms of what is expected of children in terms of eating habits. All of this means that the advertiser can take for granted that a female of a particular age, living in a certain country, speaking a certain language, with a certain income, reading a particular magazine or watching a particular programme, will, by virtue of consumer socialization and sharing the texts of a particular habitus or cultural context, have a certain amount of common knowledge.

Any advertising communication will contain 'new' (Halliday, 1985) or 'entropic' (Shannon and Weaver, 1949) information alongside 'given' (Halliday, 1985) or 'redundant' (Shannon and Weaver, 1949) information, that is known or available through encounters with previous texts in the particular cultural context. This context may be very volatile – it may change on a regular basis, from one advertisement to the next – or it may be relatively stable. In general, the more generic the appeal of the particular medium (for example a national television station) in which the advertisement appears, the more the cultural context of individual advertising messages will be subject to change. The parameters of a national television station will probably be drawn very widely, at the national level or lowest common denominator, for some programmes, whereas for others highly specialized interest groups will be targeted.

The same is true for the advertising on such a channel. Thematic channels (such as MTV, QVC – the shopping channel – and Eurosport) and specialist or subscription-only magazines are, for this reason, highly attractive for advertisers, since a high degree of common knowledge can be assumed. In looking at what constitutes redundancy or shared knowledge and assumptions, the definition of the particular culture concerned is crucial. For example, if a highly abstract advertisement is only made available to and viewed by a highly specialized and homogeneous group of people, then in the particular culture which those people constitute at that particular time, the advertisement may contain a very high degree of redundancy for most members of this culture, much more so than if the advertisement had been featured in a mainstream channel or publication. Communicative cultures are not exclusive, they exist side by side. For example, different advertisements will assume and convene different communicative cultures: at times these will be national, at other times highly specific, class, education, occupation or interest-based cultures.

Advertising and language

The language of advertising has been described as a 'functional dialect' (Smith, 1982, p. 190), a term that describes the product of a process whereby language is chosen and used for a particular purpose (hence, 'functional'), and consequently becomes a variety (hence, 'dialect') of its own because it becomes associated with this particular function. Such a definition implies that the language of advertising is somehow different to normal, everyday language. Although the distinction between advertising language and 'ordinary' language is blurred in the sense that advertisers attempt to speak to consumers 'in their own language', and advertisements, particularly slogans, come into everyday conversations, one of the things that does distinguish advertising language is the degree to which it is planned in advance. Words cost money, in terms of visual and aural space, and so the text used in advertisements that have been printed, recorded, uploaded and so on is there for a purpose, and because other words have been deemed unsuitable for this particular purpose. Language choice in commercially driven discourses is rarely, if ever, random, and this statement applies even more, the higher the production qualities and costs in terms of space and time involved.

Many studies of advertising discourse have focused on the language used in advertisements (for example Vestergaard and Schroder, 1985; Geis, 1982; Myers, 1994; Goddard, 2002; Cook, 2001). Language can, of course, have various functions and may be used for a wide variety of purposes: for example, to express feelings and emotions (the expressive function); to offer advice and recommendations or to persuade (the directive or vocative function); to inform, to report, to describe or to assert (the informational function); to create, maintain and finish contact between addresser and addressee, for example small talk (the interactional or phatic function); to communicate meaning through a code which could not otherwise be communicated (the poetic function) (Crystal, 1997). Although it might be expected that the informational and directive functions would dominate in advertising discourse, because advertisements are frequently multitype, hybrid discourses, examples of all these functions can be found in individual advertisements.

Along with a consideration of the actual language and words used and their purpose, any analysis of advertising language must also take into account how that language is presented to the addressee. This is because 'the substance which carries language is also the vehicle of another kind of meaning ... conveyed simultaneously by voice quality, or choice of script, letter size and so on' (Cook, 2001, p. 64). Paralanguage can be seen as the texture of language, and advertising 'carries a heavy proportion of its meaning paralinguistically' (Cook, 2001, p. 74), something that, as Cook points out, is intended to aid the process rather than the product of a text or communication. The paralanguage of an advertisement links visually to other texts (manifest intertextuality) and has significance and meaning because this visual aspect, for example the choice of a particular font or the use of italicized script, 'is positioned in relation to other signifiers in this system to which they belong' (Bonney and Wilson, 1990, p. 188). Through careful design of the paralanguage of an advertisement, the advertiser can give printed words both symbolic and iconic meaning in order to reinforce the advertising message. When considering the effectiveness of paralanguage in advertising it is important to remember that its interpretation is ' ... not a process of decoding. It depends on knowledge of the world and will vary from one language user [and culture] to another' (Cook, 2001, p. 74). Thus, the paralanguage of advertisements and other market-driven discourses is not only linked into the society or habitus in which the texts take place and have meaning, but knowledge of this meaning is acquired in much the same way as the acquisition of knowledge about consumption and its language takes place. According to Barthes (1977), the denotation of a sign or message, that is its literal meaning, is not necessarily culturally determined. However, the connotation of a message or sign, that is its implied or indirect meaning 'can in large measure be regarded as being common to all members of a culture' (Vestergaard and Schroder, 1985, p. 43) and as such the addressee would require a certain level of cultural knowledge in its interpretation. Not surprisingly, given the nature of advertising discourse, 'in advertisements, it is usually the connotation rather than the denotation of a signification which is important' (Bonney and Wilson, 1990, p. 192).

Another 'paralinguistic phenomenon' is prosody, that is 'the patterning of sound' (Cook, 2001, p. 96), involving rhyme, alliteration, assonance and so on. In later chapters it will be argued that accents, dialects and foreign words are to a large extent part of the paralanguage of advertising discourse. For example, in the *Dolmio* advertisement an attempt is made to write down an 'Italian' accent speaking English ('When'sa'; 'letta'). This visual representation of an Italian speaking English is linked intertextually to other texts in which this 'accent' is heard aurally, principally the mafia film genre. Such film texts give the language choices in this particular advertisement authenticity. In the *Dolmio* advertisements, the representation of this accent functions as part of the visual texture of the advertisement rather than being part of the content or information contained in it, and these words must therefore function more at the connotational rather than the denotational level, since in terms of the latter, without recourse to culturally-specific intertextual links, they are meaningless.

Advertising texts and different languages

In his study of the use of English and other foreign languages in Japanese advertising, Harald Haarmann (1989) confined his classification of advertisements as bilingual or multilingual to the particular speech act. In this book, however, multilingual advertising communication is seen in broader terms. Multilingual communication as a phenomenon in advertising and other market discourses is defined here as the appearance of a number of languages or voices in a market-discourse situation. This can be manifested in a variety of ways: an advertisement with both English and Spanish lexical items; an advertisement with only French language items in an otherwise English publication; a setting in which a television advertisement in the German language is followed by one in English; a setting in which the 'other' language of an advertisement is known to one group but not to others in a particular cultural-communicative context; a text in which the 'language' is in fact an accent or a dialect, used to represent either the self or the other, as in the case of the *Dolmio* advertisement.

Code-switching

Switching between different languages or dialects has long been recognized and studied by sociolinguists, mainly under the term 'code-switching'. In the words of Gumperz (1996, p. 365), code-switching can be defined as 'alternation among different speech varieties within the same event'. Holmes (1992, p. 42 ff) lists manifold possible reasons for code-switching – some or all of which may also be used in combination. The switch may, for instance, be specific to a particular situation, in terms of the participants concerned and their linguistic knowledge, or may perhaps be motivated by the desire to greet or include speakers of other languages. Equally, code-switching may be topic-related, where individuals are most at home discussing a particular topic in a different code or language. The use of English in an advertisement that is primarily in another language or directed at another language community may often be motivated by this, particularly where technical products are concerned (cf. Chapter 3 for examples of this).

Code switches may also be motivated by the desire to mark, assert or adopt an ethnic or regional identity, and this is known as tag or emblematic switching. In such a case, the speaker(s) need not be proficient in the particular language. Analogous to the concept of emblematic or tag switching is the notion of 'crossing' (Rampton, 1995, 1999). The switch from one code to another may also function as speech marks, signalling the start of a quote in a different language. Affective switching is of particular interest in the context of multilingual advertising texts, since the switch between codes is used primarily to create a communicative effect – for paralinguistic purposes – rather than to bring across referential meaning. In other words it is used for effect or form rather than information or content, and as such it is perhaps better viewed, in some cases, as part of the form or manifest intertextuality rather than part of the content or constitutive intertextuality. Finally, and also of relevance, code-switching may be employed for dramatic effect or variation, using the associations of both codes to produce, for example, an amusing or provocative result.

Gumperz (1996, p. 366) sees code-switching strategies in terms of contextualization, 'providing information to interlocutors and audiences about how language is being used at any one point in the ongoing stream of talk' and about the context within which to interpret a particular message. Code-switching and other indirect contextualising or signalling mechanisms are 'for the most part culturally or subculturally specific' (*ibid.*) – in other words, they provide a shorthand to fill in the context and intended meanings around the explicit, direct and overt information in a particular exchange. At this point, a valid argument could be made for the use of code-switching in the analysis of multilingual advertising; however, there are a number of reasons why a different way of looking at such texts seems desirable, albeit using many of the basic ideas of code-switching. Firstly, code-switching theories have largely been the product of research driven by oral data, in other words from 'spontaneous' and 'natural' communication, something advertising certainly is not. Secondly, as Holmes (1992) points out, simply borrowing a particular lexical item from language 1 when speaking language 2 is 'very different from switching where speakers have a genuine choice about which words they will use in which language' (Holmes, 1992, p. 50). It is clear from the use of 'foreign' or 'other' languages in the advertising texts that are examined later in the volume that, in many cases, in-depth and familiar knowledge of the foreign language is neither displayed by the advertiser nor assumed on the part of the advertisee. Finally, the commercially-driven dimension to the use of foreign languages in advertising texts would seem to demand special treatment.

It is worth noting that code-switching as a multilingual phenomenon is not always seen as a positive thing, something that enriches languages – an argument often put forward, as shall be pointed out below, by those writing about lexical borrowing. In fact, for threatened languages, it can often be the harbinger of language death rather than of language evolution or change. Nancy Dorian (1992), for example, sees code-switching as associated with dying languages and a lack of corpus planning.

Developing code-switching

The concept of 'crossing' (cf. Rampton, 1995, 1999) is a very useful way of analysing situations where individuals are free to pick and choose from various identities without being stuck in a straitjacket. Instead, they can simply play with elements from other languages in their particular repertoire, which may be known to a greater or lesser extent by the particular individual, repeating them as they would a favourite tune. In such a scheme, this repertoire of borrowed words forms part of the soundtrack of individual lives.

Eastman and Stein's term 'language display' (1993) represents an attempt to point at the use of language that is not linked to the ethnic identity of the speaker. In fact, they argue that language display, or what might colloquially be termed 'showing off', is most successful in a situation where there is at best minimal contact with or knowledge of the language being displayed. Thus, language display, perhaps more than crossing, 'represents symbolic rather than structural or semantic expression' (Eastman and Stein, 1993, p. 200).

In all of these various scenarios, what is required, however, is a common 'habitus' in which there are shared ideas and beliefs about 'other' languages, and even other words. This seems obvious when considering the *Dolmio* example, which relies on a common, shared notion of what an Italian speaking English sounds like, and the particular code that represents this, whether aurally or visually. Allan Bell's (1984) notion of 'initiative shifts' in style also relies on community norms (or media community/audience norms) about language. He distinguishes between 'responsive style', in which the relationship between language and social setting is predictable and established, and 'initiative style', in which these regular associations may be subverted for effect and language elements from a different social, cultural, linguistic situation may be imported in order to create an effect. In a media context, initiative style achieves its objective by using language to refer to or identify with a group – not necessarily the group being addressed, but, for instance, a group being referred to by the use of a particular accent or particular vocabulary, as in the case of the *Dolmio* advertisement, which refers to a composite 'Italian' identity.

Eastman and Stein (1993) also argue that the intentional use of 'politically correct' vocabulary or shifting from a formal to an informal style within one and the same speech act are instances of language display, since the speaker is attempting to construct themselves in a particular way. They also hint at the power relations involved, asserting that successful language display or style-shifting are dependent on the speaker being in a more powerful position than the audience, in the particular context.

Bourdieu (1991) also alludes to this when he discusses the notion of condescension. It is only those who are sufficiently confident of their position in society – such as advertisers – who will risk using the 'common touch'. In fact, on the surface, advertising with its soundbites and use of popular and easily understandable slogans and language could be seen in contrast to the legitimate language, in opposition to the official, correct usage which is propagated by the education system and other agents of official socialization. However, the superficial appearance of popular speech offered by advertising may in fact only serve to reinforce a hierarchy of languages, accents and dialects:

> the symbolic negation of the hierarchy (by using the 'common touch', for instance) enables the speaker to combine the profits linked to the undiminished hierarchy with those derived from the distinctly symbolic negation of the hierarchy – not the least of which is the strengthening of the hierarchy implied by the recognition accorded to the way of using the hierarchical relation. (Bourdieu, 1991, p. 68)

As Androutsopoulos (2000) points out, although research such as that done by Hill (1995, 1999) on 'Junk Spanish' and Rampton (1995) on crossing and stylized Asian English does point to the link between code-switching or the use of foreign or other words in the context of oral or everyday speech on the one hand and the context of the mass media on the other, there has not been much in-depth research devoted to the latter phenomenon alone. A number of studies have, however, focused specifically on the issue of lexical borrowing and bilingualism in advertising texts (for example Haarmann, 1989; Bhatia, 1992; Piller, 2001; Grin, 1994). In the main, the borrowed language that has been studied has been English. Some specific examples include the study of English in advertising in Switzerland (Cheshire and Moser, 1994); English and also other European languages in Japanese advertising (Haarmann, 1989); English (and French and Italian) in German advertising (Piller, 2001); English in French advertising (Martin, 2002); and English in Korean advertising (Lee, 2004). In all of these studies, the symbolic functioning of the borrowed language has emerged as the primary motivation for its inclusion in the particular advertising texts.

Defining 'foreign' words

The attribute 'foreign' is used here with inverted commas to attest to the disputed nature of the concept and the fact that the definition or categorization of a word as foreign is not a straightforward process. It is instead rather laden with potential pitfalls. Lexical borrowing of foreign words is an accepted and established practice among translators, and David Crystal defines a loan word as 'a linguistic unit (usually a lexical item) which has come to be used in a language or dialect other than the one where it originated' (Crystal, 1997, p. 227). Transference, what Peter Newmark describes as 'the process of transferring a source language (SL) word to a target language (TL) text' (Newmark, 1988, p. 82) is also recognized as a standard translation strategy, and results in the production of texts that are not fully monolingual.

Whether a word is a loan word, an internationalism, or a domesticated foreign word depends on a great number of factors. A cursory glance at the etymological entries in any dictionary serves as a quick reminder of how many English words originally come from Latin, Greek and a whole host of other mainly Indo-European languages. Usage, spelling, phonology and other factors all combine to make a word more or less 'foreign'. The evolution of the usage of certain words can be traced, starting from a point at which a word is explained or an equivalent or general term is given, to the use of the term as self-evident. '*Bundesbank*' is a good example of this. No longer explained as Germany's central bank in many English texts, it generally stands alone now in media texts. This appears to be an obvious, logical and even welcome progression. After all, is it not a good thing for the reader to be confronted with 'foreign' words, to have to learn what they mean, to have to realize that the world is not monolingual? On the surface, the answer seems to be, yes, of course. However, looking at the motivations behind the choice of such a foreign word and the context in which a word like this is used, prompts a questioning of this seemingly self-evident truth. For example, the notion of the 'unfindable', 'untranslatable' word may in fact perpetuate misunderstanding and stereotype in intercultural communication, the idea that 'our' language is simple, while 'their' language is unnecessarily complicated, so much so that it cannot be translated. There was an interesting example of this generally suspicious attitude towards foreign words in the UK-based *Prospect* magazine, a monthly publication that deals with, in its own words, 'politics essays and argument'. In an essay about French secularism, the author discusses the French term *'laïcité'*, and comments that 'the very word seems dangerous to me, because it defies definition and translation' (King, 2004, p. 64).

The degree of tolerance for foreign words and lexical borrowing can vary greatly, not only between languages, but also between different linguistic cultures and political and historical eras. As George Steiner points out in his book *After Babel*:

> At certain moments, languages change at an extraordinary pace; they are acquisitive of lexical and grammatical innovation, they discard eroded units with conscious speed ... At other moments, languages are strongly conservative. (1975, pp. 19–20)

Languages also earn – deservedly or not – reputations as being 'open' or 'closed' to foreign words. For instance, English is seen as flexible, German too is seen as more open to English words than French, which has a reputation for purism and intolerance (particularly in the light of the Toubon laws[2]). It is also important to remember that the notion of being open to foreign words may vary over time, and it is not a fixed truism that certain languages are and always will be open to foreign words. Even more significant perhaps is the attitude that is betrayed by labels such as 'open', 'flexible' and 'tolerant', which attach value statements to languages.

Foreign equals elitist

In his discussion of the practice of transference, Peter Newmark cites possible reasons why the translator may opt for using the source language word rather than finding a target-language equivalent, and in doing so sheds light on what appears to be a commonly held notion, that foreign words are elitist:

> In regional novels and essays (and advertisements, e.g. gites), cultural words are often transferred to render, to give a sense of intimacy between the text and reader – sometimes the evoked image appears attractive ... terms are transferred for snob reasons: foreign is posh, the word is untranslatable ... The argument in favour of transference is that it shows respect for the SL country's culture. The argument against is that it is the translator's job to explain. (Newmark, 1988, p. 82)

These sentiments are partly echoed by Theodor Adorno in his essay 'On Foreign Words', in which he argues that 'foreign words should not be protected as one of the privileges of education' (1974, p. 290). However, there is a difference here. One suspects that Newmark is arguing for the translator to popularize in favour of the reader, whereas Adorno is urging the translator to challenge the reader. Eastman and Stein (1993), too, point out that language display is used where speakers want to appear sophisticated and to imply the achievement of a higher educational standard. There is, therefore, this idea that 'foreign' words give a text an elitist flavour. This is, in and of itself, an interesting attitude, particularly in relation to the Anglophone worlds. While it is of course true that only those with access to a certain level of education have the opportunity to acquire a second language, this is really only the case in the industrialized world – since the vast majority of the rest of the world grows up bilingually if not multilingually. The comments reveal an underlying cultural resistance to 'foreign words' and, indeed, a related resistance to foreign languages. They are something used by people wishing to show off, to display superiority: using foreign words and speaking foreign languages are not part of everyday normal life, what Adorno describes as the 'dreary imprisonment in preconceived language' (1974, p. 289).

Lawrence Venuti (1994) alludes to this attitude when he remarks upon 'the misunderstanding, suspicion and neglect that continue to greet the practice of translation, especially in the United States and the UK' (p. 219). What is interesting to note here, however, is that the United States and the UK are far from being monolingual; in practice multilingualism thrives on the ground in both countries. This is not, however, the 'posh' version, the language of *gites*; instead it is the language of immigrants and allochthonous minority groups. And, it is worth pointing out that this everyday, lived multilingualism does not necessarily impact on a greater openness to foreign languages. Something that made a huge impression on me as someone who regularly visited secondary schools in the English midland counties around the industrial heartland of Birmingham was, on the one hand, the overwhelming sense of multilingual practice in terms of speaking languages other than English such as Urdu, Gujarati, Bengali and so on, which gave the context an unmistakably multilingual aural texture; and, on the other, a similarly overwhelming sense that foreign words and languages – particularly those of continental Europe – were something 'posh', pointless and difficult, a perception shared by monolingual and multilingual pupils alike.

Venuti goes on to argue that in, particularly, the Anglophone world, people do not even want to know that a text is a translation, such is the level of resistance to foreign words. Instead the desire is for such a text to be recognizable and familiar, 'seemingly untranslated'. This is best achieved by 'suppressing the linguistic and cultural difference of the foreign text, assimilating it to dominant values in the target language culture' (1994, p. 218). This conclusion further points to the need for an exploration of the use of foreign words in the context of the market society, in order to link their use to the omnipresent concept of the market, that pervades everyday attitudes to many factors, including languages, in such societies.

Domesticated foreignness

In such a context, the treatment of the foreign, its presentation and 'sale' to the consumer, must be couched in domestic terms. As Venuti also points out in relation to the translation of advertising:

> when [the] products are foreign, the significance must be domestic but its reverberation will be intercultural: a translated ad can simultaneously create or revise a stereotype on a foreign culture, while appealing to a specific domestic constituency, a specific segment of the domestic market. (1994, p. 220)

It is, then, not an Italian product that is being advertised to the British advertisee in the *Dolmio* advertisement, but a British idea of an Italian product. As Roland Barthes (1972) has pointed out, advertising texts mythologize products for consumers, and this mythologizing includes the supposed national culture of the particular product, alluded to by the language. Numerous examples of this phenomenon abound, but one in particular springs to mind: the British television advertising for the *Renault Clio* car of a number of years ago. *Renault* is of course a French brand, and for many years a standard of British advertising was the interplay between Papa and Nicole amidst the tourist idyll of a *château* in a generic French location. The highly successful advertising sketches were in fact the product of a London-based agency; they were shot on location in the 'home-counties' around London. Papa and Nicole, neither of whom uttered more than each other's names in a 'French' accent, were in fact both English actors. The UK-based advertising agency Publicis – which has a French parent – had discovered in its pre-campaign research that the French way of life was perceived as 'desirable' by the British public, and so this enviable lifestyle became the theme for the sketches that ran for eight years and made *Renault* one of the top-selling brands in the UK (Yan, 1995, cited in Jaffe and Nebenzahl, 2001, p. 90). This 'French' lifestyle, again the product of perception rather than reality, was summed up by the rustic country-side, the flirtatious relationship and the 'French' accents, just as the 'Italian' accent conjures up notions about Italian food in the *Dolmio* advertisement.

Lawrence Venuti, in his study of translation, points out that such practices can in fact have a negative effect. This has prompted him to call for 'an ethics of change in which the translator calls attention to what domestic norms enable and limit, admit and exclude, in their encounter with foreign texts and cultures' (Venuti, 1994, p. 221). This is seen as necessary because the indiscriminate and unconsidered use of such terms and foreign words can mystify the culture concerned even further, making it more different, more exotic. In the end, such practices may lead to the reinforcement of the very prejudices that translators and those concerned with cross-cultural communication are trying to challenge. As Venuti points out:

> Nonethnocentric translation reforms cultural identities that occupy dominant positions in the domestic culture, yet in many cases the reformation subsequently issues in another dominance and another ethnocentrism. (1994, p. 221)

Thus, it could be argued that advertising strategies involving foreign words, taken out of their original contexts and domesticated for commercial purposes contribute to – or at least play into – an ethnocentric view of 'foreign' languages. As Bourdieu points out, 'strategies of assimilation and dissimilation' (1991, p. 64) can often reproduce systemic power imbalances in the legitimate language, in other words they may reinforce stereotypes about otherness. Furthermore, rather than being something challenging, such borrowed words can become 'neutralized' (*ibid.*, p. 96).

One of the interesting things about many of the examples of multilingual advertising texts cited in the chapters that follow is that they challenge many of the truisms of loan words and lexical borrowing; for instance, the idea that foreign words are something elite. Newmark advises translators that if they do use foreign words, they need to give 'a functional descriptive equivalent for less sophisticated TL [target language] readerships' (1988, p. 147). However, this is clearly contradicted by the use of foreign words in the tabloid press and in advertising for products far more lowbrow and mundane than *gites*.

What is also significant about the use of foreign words in commercial contexts is that it appeals to a lowest-common-denominator type of language knowledge and ability. Indeed it is intended to glorify the communal ignorance of foreign languages: the joke is shared, initially between advertiser and advertisee, ultimately among the public at large, thus reinforcing a sense of language as part of identity. As Bourdieu (1991) points out:

> In order for one mode of expression among others to impose itself as the only legitimate one, the linguistic market has to be unified and the different dialects (of class, region or ethnic group) have to be measured practically against the legitimate language or usage (p. 46)

What is also interesting is that although there may be recognition of these words and because of the close relations between European language families there may also be understanding of simple slogans like Renault's '*Créateur d'Automobiles*', there will, in Bourdieu's terms, be 'very unequal knowledge of this usage' (1991, p. 62). Thus, there may be a certain level of 'competence', in Chomsky's (1965) terms, in the ability to comprehend passively, but this does not correspond to an ability to perform. This highlights a further dimension of foreign words, namely how they affect the individual's own linguistic competence, and, perhaps more importantly, their feelings about their own competence. As Bourdieu puts it: 'The sense of value of one's own linguistic products is a fundamental dimension of the sense of knowing the place which one occupies in the social world' (1991, p. 82). Thus, the ability to interpret German, French or Italian words or phrases in an advertisement that is otherwise in English and is encountered in an English-language medium may make the particular individual feel better about their linguistic abilities and meta-linguistic knowledge, while failure to 'get it' may have the opposite effect. As Piller (2001) rightly points out, the employment of English words in German texts makes the young, educated elite targeted by such strategies feel good. However, this can also alienate other groups, for example, elderly German people for whom the meaning of the 'friends and family tariff', and other English linguistic decorations, offered by *Deutsche Telekom* in a German-speaking context, is not immediately apparent. Consequently, the employment of foreign words in advertising has the potential to create in-groups and out-groups, all of which, it can be argued, contribute both directly and indirectly to societal attitudes to languages, otherness and multilingualism.

Heteroglossia and impersonal bilingualism

Mikhail Bakhtin's concept of heteroglossia or multi-voicedness in texts is particularly useful in looking at the employment of languages in advertising discourse. Bakhtin coined the term mainly in relation to literary language and more in reference to dialect, accent and register than to other languages, but his ideas are very relevant to this discussion. According to Bakhtin, borrowed words lose the 'quality of the closed sociolinguistic system; they are deformed and in fact cease to be that which they had been'. However, if they preserve their 'otherlanguagedness', they then affect the borrowing language; 'it too ceases to be that which it had been, a closed socio-linguistic system ... what results is not a single language but a dialogue of languages' (1981, p. 294). Bakhtin, the anti-purist and lover of hybridity, would thus see this as having a positive effect on the language. As he puts it, 'the dialogic contrast of languages creates a feeling for these boundaries, compels one to sense physically the plastic forms of different languages' (*ibid.*, p. 364). Taking the *Dolmio* advertisement again, at first glance it does not appear to be a multilingual text. However, applying Bakhtin's notion of heteroglossia to the text reveals the many other voices present, for example the 'Italian' voices heard in mafia-genre films.

Bakhtin himself acknowledges the ethnocentrism involved in the process, mentioned by Venuti. In Bakhtin's terms:

An intentional hybrid [i.e. the mixing of two languages or the appropriation of lexical items from another language] is precisely the perception of one language by another language, its illumination by another linguistic consciousness. An image of language may be structured only from the point of view of another language, which is taken as the norm. (1981, p. 360)

Thus, rather than being concerned with communication, heteroglossia in a text is a fetish: borrowed language is not present

> in the capacity of another language carrying its own particular points of view, about which one can say things not expressible in one's own language, but rather in the capacity of a depicted thing. (*Ibid.*, p. 287).

Thus, the appearance of a German or French word or phrase is not really telling the individual addressee anything *in* German or French – at least that is not the intention – it is instead telling him/her something *about* German or French, from his/her own linguistic point of view (or more accurately the prevailing societal one), about the characteristics and symbols summoned up by those languages in individual's own sociolinguistic environment (just as in the *Renault Clio* and *Dolmio* advertisements discussed above). Its symbolic nature takes precedence over its referential or informative nature.

Based on the conclusions of his study of the symbolic use of foreign languages in the Japanese media, Harald Haarmann (1989) talked about a phenomenon of 'impersonal multilingualism'. This type of mass media multilingualism is not really 'normal' multilingualism or bilingualism. It is not about people using languages 'naturally' and it does not generally reflect societal multilingualism. For example, he cites Japan, which is not, contrary to its image, a monolingual country. According to Haarmann (1989), there is a substantial minority language group constituted by Korean speakers. If mass media multilingualism in Japan were normal and merely a reflection of a multilingual society, then one would expect to find numerous instances of Korean in Japanese advertising, rather than the large amount of English – and to a lesser extent French, German and other European languages – that is found. This is similar to the situation in many European countries. In neither Belgium nor Germany do native English speakers from the UK, the USA or Australia, for example, make up a sizeable ethnic or linguistic minority; instead, the most significant linguistic minorities are constituted by speakers of Arabic, Turkish and Slavic languages. Thus, the disproportionate dominance of English words and phrases in advertising does not reflect the true multilingualism of these countries. Because of this, as Haarmann points out in the Japanese context, the language used does not link in with normal usage and involves instead the 'verbal strategies of impersonal multilingualism' (p. 54). This is similar to Cheshire and Moser's (1994) findings about the use of English in

French-speaking Switzerland. They, like Haarmann, concluded that this usage had very little to do with 'normal' English usage in the context of native speakers, but was instead a special culture- and media-specific type of usage, particular to the respective situation. One of the main arguments of this book is that much of the use of languages in advertising today is symbolic, something that is upheld by Haarmann (1989), Cheshire and Moser (1994) and Eastman and Stein (1993), having little to do with 'normal' everyday communication in that particular language or in that particular sociolinguistic context, and so this dimension, something that will be termed 'linguistic fetish', will now be examined.

Linguistic fetish[3]

Marxian paradigms are particularly useful in the analysis of foreign words in advertising. Since the collapse of communism, there is today almost a need to defend Marx in the light of writers like Francis Fukuyama, who declared in his 1992 thesis that the events in the Soviet bloc effectively meant the end of history, the end of historical materialism and Marxian and Hegelian dialectics in the sense of a search for answers in the form of thesis, antithesis and synthesis. In Fukuyama's scheme, the answer has been found, and it is the 'free' market capitalism. However, Marx has never stopped being relevant. He was one of the first sociolinguists, although not really thought of in this way. In 1845/6, about 70 years before Saussure's *General Course in Linguistics* was published, he wrote:

> Language is as old as consciousness, language is practical, real consciousness that exists for other men as well, and only therefore does it also exist for me; language, like consciousness, only arises from the need, the necessity of intercourse with other men. (Marx and Engels, 1989, p. 33)

Marx's range of influence, too, is enormous, encompassing Bakhtin and Bourdieu. There are very few analyses that rival Marx's for the combination of the market, society, culture and the symbolism of all of these. Finally, contemporary cultural theorists who are producing the most useful analyses of the culture of consumption (for example, Frederic Jameson, 1991) and ideas about fetishizing of cultures (for example, Edward Said, 1991, in his analysis of the phenomenon of Orientalism) are all profoundly influenced by Marxian ideas.

For Marx, fetishization involved 'the capacity of creating [symbolic] value – a value greater than it contains' (Marx and Engels, 1959 [1894], p. 392). To quote from the first volume of *Capital*,

> Hence we bring the products of our labour into relation with each other as values, it is not because we see in these articles the material receptacles of homogeneous human labour. Quite the contrary: whenever, by an exchange, we equate as values our different products, by that very act, we also equate, as human labour, the different kinds of labour expended upon them. We are not aware of this, nevertheless we do it! Value, therefore, does not stalk about with a label describing what it is. It is value, rather that converts every product into a social hieroglyphic. Later on, we try to decipher the hieroglyphic, to get behind the secret of our own social products; for to stamp an object of utility as a value, is just as much a social product as language. (1954, pp. 78–9)

The consumer does not therefore see in the advertising message or the branded article the production process that may, for instance, involve sweatshops, meagre wages, large profits, poor working conditions, health implications, enormous environmental impacts and so on; instead the brand appears as social hieroglyphic, this production process being mystified by symbolism. It becomes, as Marx put it: 'the meaningless form of capital, the perversion and objectification of production relations in their highest degree' (1959 [1894], p. 392). Through such a process, use values become obscured and it is symbolic value that becomes all.

Beyond this, however, the notion of fetishism is particularly useful and relevant in explaining how foreign words and phrases are used in advertising. Marx claimed that the process of fetishization mystifies the social relations by which commodities have been produced. They come to be independent things in themselves and are simply accepted as part of the natural order, with a seemingly naturally ordained value and existence, with the ability to reproduce, to have properties inherent in themselves, to exist independently (and uncontestedly). Indeed, through fetishization, the use-value becomes 'the capacity of creating [symbolic] value – a value greater than it contains' (Marx, 1959 [1894], p. 392).

This leads to a situation where there is 'form without content', in other words, the separation of essence and appearance (*ibid.*, p. 393). Through the fetishization of commodities, the utility or use value of the commodity becomes secondary to its symbolic value. Commodities become instead 'social hieroglyphics' (Marx, 1954 [1867], pp. 78–9), signifiers of socially and culturally determined (and commonly shared) meanings, which are themselves the products of social and production relations. As Wellmer (1981) points out:

> When Marx criticizes commodity-fetishism, he discovers behind the apparent natural qualities and the apparent social relations of things, the social relations of men, produced historically and both mediated and repressed from consciousness by coercive conditions. (Wellmer, 1981, p. 58)

Applying Marx's ideas to the use of foreign or other languages in advertising today, the use-value of languages can be seen to have become obscured by their exchange or symbolic value. The use-value of a language can be equated with its referential function, its utility as a means of communication. Where the utility value of the language is not 'mystified', then the content, the meanings themselves are the essence. In much, though not all multilingual advertising texts, however, language seems to be used primarily for its symbolic value, while the communicative or utility value of the particular words has come to be obscured or mystified through the process of fetishization to the point where it becomes irrelevant. The language appears to achieve value independently and this value is not the product of its communicative value, but rather of its symbolic value in the process of advertising communication. Although this symbolic value appears part of the natural order and is accepted as a thing in itself, it is in fact the product of social, political, economic, historical and linguistic relations between different countries, relations which – as Marx pointed out – are obscured, masked or even repressed from consciousness by fetishization.

Although no foreign words are used in the text, the *Dolmio* advertisement, nonetheless, combines the fetishizing of language and the fetishizing of cultures. The approach is about investing the attribute 'Italian' with a whole range of associations, which are then symbolized when the advertisee 'hears' the Italian speaker. The 'foreign words', in this case English phrases written in an Italian accent, are meaningless on their own, without recourse to this symbolism. And, they more properly function as part of the graphic, the visual and aural paralanguage of the advertisement, rather than as any meaningful type of information. The fetishized, symbolic nature of this 'Italian' accent becomes even more clear when it is considered that *Dolmio* is part of the *Mars* Corporation, which also owns, to name but a few, *Uncle Ben's* rice and sauce products, *Pedigree* dog food, and *Snickers* bars – a reality and identity that seem very far removed from the easy-going Italian family image of the product.

Conclusion

Multilingual advertising communication is, in this book, defined as the appearance of a number of different languages or voices in a market-discourse situation. This appearance may be minimal, consisting of only one word, or it may be fairly extensive, consisting of entire texts or blocks of text. The words may come from an entirely different language, unknown to the native speaker of the default language of the medium or text within which they appear, or they may be familiar, coming from his/her everyday linguistic repertoire. The market discourse situation is used here in preference to alternative terms such as 'speech act' or 'text'. The market-discourse situation covers a range of possibilities from advertising texts to television channels and Internet sites with their associated links.

In the chapters that follow, various types of multilingual advertising discourses from various contexts are examined. In all of these texts, examples of the various phenomena discussed above can be found; for instance, emblematic and affective code-switching, lexical borrowing, heteroglossia, linguistic fetish and so on. At times the language usage appears to be purely symbolically driven, at others multilingual choices appear to be primarily driven by referential functions. This distinction between the mainly referential/informative and the mainly symbolic is problematic, since most communication consists of both symbolic and communicative/informative aspects. However, such a distinction, albeit a crude one, does make possible an analysis of the way in which foreign languages are used in advertisements. As Juliane House (2003) has argued, it can be useful to try to disentangle the use of 'language for communication' from the use of 'language for identification', as she puts it. What is argued here, then, is that the choice, use and functioning of these foreign words, accents and languages is primarily driven by symbolism, by connotation rather than denotation, and by the way the visual/aural aspect or the form of the advertisement – rather than the informational or the content aspect – is formulated and understood.

The effect of these multilingual advertising communications may be to challenge monolingualism by, for instance, introducing a different point of view, by normalizing bi- and multilingualism, or by raising the status of a different language and its speakers. They may, on the other hand, have the effect of reinforcing this monolingualism by making speakers of another language the object of humour in advertising, and by constructing them as an out-group. In all cases, however, the examples of multilingual advertising communication discussed in the following chapter have two things in common: they are driven by the market, and have meaning within the context of the society and culture ('habitus') posited on the market; and, they do not permit a purely monolingual communication experience.

2
Foreign Languages in Advertising Discourse

> **Neutrogena Norwegian formula hand-cream**
> (On a tube of hand cream with a Norwegian flag)
>
> **Designed in consultation with Swedish dental expertise**
> (On a packet of toothpicks)
>
> **Richmond Irish recipe sausages**
> (On packaging of sausages)
>
> **Opel cars are German-engineered**
> (Extract from advertising text)

The list preceding is just a very small selection of the abundance of references to countries, cultures and languages found on products and in advertising texts in Western Europe. How does a nationality become a product attribute or even, to use marketing jargon, a 'unique selling proposition', the key variable that differentiates the product from its competitors and that becomes the core of the advertising message? And, why are consumers apparently more reassured by the expertise of Swedish dentists than that of their Italian or Turkish or Indian colleagues? It would seem that much of this knowledge about the apparent expertise of particular countries, the so-called 'country-of-origin effect', is acquired through consumerization, as discussed in Chapter 1, through exposure to the language and rituals of the market. And, the process is, of course, not simply one-way. Through advertising and other commercially-driven messages and their use of nationalities and languages, such conceptions and perceptions are created, strengthened and maintained. This, in turn, provides the context within which the use of languages in advertising is interpreted. In this way, marketing techniques such as country-of-origin effect provide the paradigms within which a type of linguistic fetish (cf. Chapter 1) operates, and the use of languages in country-of-origin-based market discourses is, it will be argued in this chapter, primarily a symbolic one. This chapter looks at how country-of-origin-driven advertising creates multilingual texts. The two main case studies focus on the German and French linguistic fetishes in Europe, but there are also examples from other languages.

Ethnocentric marketing and linguistic fetish

Ironically, while the examples shown seem to be all about the other – Norway, Sweden, Ireland, Germany – some exotic image that the consumer apparently wants a part of, the starting point for this kind of marketing is inevitably the self. Such a marketing strategy is therefore best described as ethnocentric. Ethnocentrism literally means seeing oneself or the group to which one belongs as the centre, the standard against which all others and other groups are judged, the filter through which information, texts, individuals and products from outside that group must be measured (cf. Kottak, 2003). More than this, however, it also implies viewing one's own group in a particular way, using a particular snapshot rather than accepting that this group, too, inevitably changes and evolves. There is of course an identity aspect to this, since it is impossible to have a group identity, if this cannot be measured against a notional out-group. Thus, notions about the self are inevitably linked to notions about others, and vice versa.

In the world of marketing, it is not only products and brands that have images, but also countries. As Wolff Olins, an international branding consultant who has been involved in studies of how to improve the 'Great Britain' and 'Germany' brands claims, 'all countries can be branded, provided one can find the essence of the nation' (1999). This brand or image is necessarily an external phenomenon, it is how the country is viewed from outside even though it may have been formulated domestically, and it is necessarily a simplified view. It is important to differentiate a country's or a company's identity from its image. Identity can be seen to 'comprise the way a company [or country] aims to position itself', in other words its understanding of itself, whereas image can be seen as 'the way the [external] public perceives the company [or country] or its products' (Jaffe and Nebenzahl, 2001, p. 13). Country image is also something of which companies are acutely aware. For example, a survey carried out by branding consultancy Wolff Olins in 2000 'found that 72% of *Fortune 500* companies see national image as an important influence on their purchasing decisions' (Edwards, 2002).

The country-of-origin effect

Country-of-origin, in terms of market discourses, can be defined as 'the country which a consumer associates with a certain product or brand as being its source, regardless of where the product is actually produced' (Jaffe and Nebenzahl, 2001, p. 27). Here again this knowledge would seem to be acquired in the process of consumerization (discussed in Chapter 1), since 'prior knowledge that a given country is associated with a certain brand' ensures that 'exposure to the brand name triggers recall of that country and its attributes' (*ibid.*, p. 61). This prior knowledge is then reinforced by experience with the brand and exposure to the brand name. It is important to point out here that this experience may not actually result in a purchase, and it may in fact have nothing to do with any purchase decision whatsoever. It may take place purely in the realm of experiencing and processing, consciously or subconsciously, advertising messages about brands, countries and languages to which the individual is exposed every day.

So, for example, an individual may have a very well-developed sense of what a 'French' product is, without ever having bought or ever intending to buy products, services and so on that conform to this notion. In fact, purchase decisions may even be based on the degree of difference between the product and the perceived notion of a 'French' product – in other words the individual may use this knowledge as a type of anti-identity in making purchase decisions. As Jaffe and Nebenzahl point out, the country-of-origin effect

> is generally understood to stand for the impact that generalizations and perceptions about a country have on a person's evaluations of the country's products and/or brands. (2001, p. 41)

Since Schooler's seminal study of the concept, published in 1971, country-of-origin marketing has long been recognized as an important tool in advertising. What such an approach involves is exploiting the brand's or product's 'nationality' or 'regionality' in an attempt to extend existing, and hopefully positive, stereotypes associated with that particular country or region to the brand or product in question. As Marr and Prendergast (1992) point out:

> The effect of country stereotype will be to shift the position of the product in the perceptual space vis-à-vis its competitors' offerings and alter the overall evaluation of its merits. (p. 37)

The products and brands should take on the attributes of the countries and regions, and, for this reason, it is proposed, a person confronted with a bottle of French wine will be more likely to favour this than wines from other countries. As someone responsible for constructing and promoting a national image abroad, the director of the British Council for the Baltic States sums up this common-sense assumption:

> We know as consumers that we'll pay extra for engineering from Germany, food from France or clothes from Italy. Successful companies capitalise on this. (Edwards, 2002)

Country-specific competence

One consequence of the country-of-origin approach would appear to be a fairly well-developed sense, or perhaps better, a fairly widespread consensus, among those who formulate and those who receive market discourses about the particular competences a country or region does or does not have – and this applies in particular to Western Europe. Any brief survey of advertising in a number of countries in Western Europe shows how competences have been assigned to nations and regions based on deep-rooted conceptions and perceptions about these nations and regions, many of which have nothing at all to do with the market or with the products in question. What is also interesting, if somewhat depressing, is the extent to which such notions are commonly held. For example, a study of country image reported in Jaffe and Nebenzahl (2001) shows surprisingly similar images of different countries. According to the study, France and Italy have an image of 'style, design and refinement', whereas Germany's image is associated with 'reliability, solidity and quality'. Interestingly, the UK and Spain appear to have the least positive images (cited in Jaffe and Nebenzahl, 2001).

It is also important to point out when discussing country image, that, like identity, it too is subject to different levels of definition at different times. So, for example, just as multiple levels of national, regional or local identities are possible, so too does this knowledge about image exist in different ways. It may be relevant to the immediate locality or region, or it may be commonly held throughout a particular country, between different countries or within a larger union such as Europe, or it may be held between different parts of the world. The larger the area within which these common-sense assumptions about competence and image are shared, the less detailed, more superficial and probably less product-related they will be.

While the notion of competence being linked to a particular country may seem questionable, it is worth considering whether an advertisement in which a Portuguese person was praising an Irish-made car would really convince most advertisees in Western Europe? Or, an advertisement in which a Briton enthuses about a Swedish cordon bleu sauce? These are not the expectations commonly and externally shared about these cultures, and thus, they are not what can be said. There is, in Bourdieu's terms, a form of self-censorship

> which determines not only the manner of saying, that is the choice of language or the level of language, but also what it will be possible or not possible to say. (Bourdieu, 1991, p. 77)

And

> the definition of acceptability is found not in the situation but in the relationship between a market and a habitus, which itself is the product of the whole history of its relations with markets. (*Ibid.*, p. 81)

This issue of acceptability is a complex one. Jaffe and Nebenzahl go so far as to say that it is very hard to counteract 'the effect of a low image country' even with a strong brand (2001, p. 20). Likewise, 'a highly favourable country image' does not, as Jaffe and Nebenzahl point out, 'guarantee a highly favourable country image as a source of a certain product line' (p. 53). An example here would be the fact that the positive image of Ireland created in tourist discourses has provided a favourable context within which to market Irish food products; however, this context would not support the marketing of Irish cars, for instance. Likewise, the widespread consensus in Europe that Germany is the continent's engineer (Head, 1992) does not help the image of German-origin food products. While German food, drink and beauty products may 'hide' their 'nationality' (see below), these are the very products best left to their neighbours, the French, generally accepted in advertising discourse as the European cooks and culinary experts. For example, the slogan of one campaign for *Perrier* mineral water in the UK read 'What the French drink, when they're not drinking'. The French are generally presented as the wine experts in market discourse and are expected, stereotypically, to drink wine. Thus, Perrier's credibility comes not only from its country-of-origin, France, a culinary expert, but also from the assertion in the ad, that when French people are not drinking wine (as would be expected), they choose *Perrier*. This example also shows that country-of-origin image is subject to change. With changes in the habitus, for example, the increasing emphasis on moderate drinking, as well as the stringent penalties for driving under the influence of alcohol in the UK, this particular positive country-of-origin image can be used to market new alternatives. Again, however, the impetus for changing the image comes from an ethnocentric base. It is not the object itself (France) that needs to see itself differently, but the 'beholder', the UK.

The other area of common-sense French cultural competence is that of beauty and cosmetics, and the centre of origin here is the French capital, Paris. Thus, perfume advertisements almost always include 'Paris' under their brand. For example,

> Lancôme, Paris
> Guy La Roche, Paris
> Van Cleef & Arpels, Paris
> Lagerfeld, Paris
> Guerlain, Paris

The city has not only become part of these brands, but almost part of the product too, and certainly a key part of a product's identity and credibility. The unacceptability, in Bourdieu's terms, of certain statements is particularly applicable to this whole area of country-of-origin. For example, the following slogan would not work at the end of a perfume advertisement even though it is, perhaps, a more accurate description of the production process, as pointed out by Schlosser, 2002:

> Lancôme, Daytona, New Jersey

Countries and categories

Where a particular country's image is not firmly established in the advertisee's culture, then, as Jaffe and Nebenzahl (2001) point out, the construction of an image of that country will be influenced to a large extent by the 'country category in which it is classified' (p. 17). A good example here is Spanish product-specific cultural competence, which is perhaps harder to identify instantly for Anglophone consumers.[1] However, as *Seat* cars' television advertising slogan of the early 1990s showed, it is perhaps easier to identify what it is not:

> German engineering, Spanish design.

In other words, engineering is too serious a business to leave to the Spaniards, who, it seems, can be trusted with the less-practical, more abstract and 'fluffy' aspects, such as design and appearance. Likewise, in a German advertisement (from German news magazine *Der Spiegel*, 1994) for Spanish brandy, reference is made to two aspects of 'Spanishness' that may be known to the advertisee and that allow the use of a country category in order to classify competence in the product. The references made are to the Spanish painting tradition, more specifically the Spanish artist Goya, and to Spain's main area of cultural competence for many Europeans, namely its weather and the package holiday product, neither of which has anything to do with brandy.

This country category approach is also found in an advertisement for Portuguese wines in the UK (in the *Observer* Sunday newspaper magazine from the late 1990s), in which the following text was used:

Discover what these people have in common ...

The reader is then presented with pictures of three leading chefs and restaurant owners based in London, and the punch line:

... they are all new Portuguese wine explorers. Are you?

The categorization and associations intended are clear: Portugal was known for its explorers and 'discoveries' in previous centuries. This cultural competence is used here to advertise a product now seen as or wanting to be seen as stereotypically Portuguese, namely wine. Likewise, in an advertisement for Greek wines in the German news magazine *Der Spiegel* from the early 1990s, the cultural association exploited is not competence in winemaking, but Greek antiquity. The image is that of Zeus leading Europa to Crete, encircled by the stars of the European flag, and this myth also forms the content of the advertisement, Greek wine being constructed as 'a gift of the Gods for Europe today'.

In addition to this strategy of alluding to a different type of cultural competence or categorization altogether when advertising products outside their cultural competence, brands can also use an approval strategy by appealing to the accepted cultural competence of another. An example of the former was the re-launch of the Czech *Skoda* brand, following its takeover by German car manufacturer *Volkswagen* in the early 1990s. The whole message of the campaign was that *Volkswagen* approved of *Skoda* and had supervised a complete overhaul of the factory and the product. Clearly it was felt that the testimony of the European carmaker (Germany) was necessary, in order for the Czech *Skoda* brand to be taken seriously. This type of approval strategy can also be used in intracultural advertising. For example, in a campaign from the early 1990s on British television, a German *Mercedes* engineer is driving a British *Rover* car with Stuttgart number plates, Stuttgart being the headquarters of *Mercedes*. So, German cultural competence in car-making is used to reassure British consumers about buying a British car.

As was clear in the *Perrier* example cited above, an important point about country image and the country-of-origin phenomenon is that, as Jaffe and Nebenzahl point out, it is wrong to assume that this is somehow static. David Head (1992), for instance, has shown comprehensively how the once shameful and embarrassing brand 'Made in Germany', which was imposed by British authorities in the late nineteenth century to mark inferior German products, has in time come to encompass exactly the opposite. Likewise the image of goods manufactured in some parts of the Far East has improved greatly in the minds of Western consumers.

Individual advertisees respond to country-of-origin appeals in a variety of different ways, and Jaffe and Nebenzahl have identified four different types of consumer. First of all 'patriots', who, as the name suggests, will prefer appeals based on locally-made products, in contrast to the second group, 'cosmopolitans', who are more open-minded in evaluating appeals. 'Traitors' prefer to buy imported rather than home-produced goods and so should be more susceptible to exotic country-of-origin appeals. Finally, 'hostiles' will automatically reject goods from certain countries and may even impose boycotts on produce from others. Thus, this group would be very receptive to country-of-origin information. Patriots can be defined as ethnocentric consumers, and a study by Shimp and Sharma ((1987) reported in Jaffe and Nebenzahl, 2001) found higher levels of ethnocentrism among patriot-type consumers, who 'held more favourable attitudes towards domestic-made products and negative, stereotyped attitudes towards imports' (2001, p. 75). Consumer ethnocentrism may result from factors such as education, income and social class. However, it can be argued that ethnocentric attitudes do not mean that consumers only buy locally/nationally-produced goods or only have favourable attitudes to them. What it does in fact mean is that their responses to foreign country-of-origin appeals will necessarily be ethnocentric and their images of countries will be determined primarily by internal, domestic factors. So, a patriot consumer may in fact have a positive response to exotic appeals, albeit from an ethnocentric base.

Country-of-origin as fetish

The final point worth keeping in mind is that brands are the ultimate fetishes. They are the triumph of form over content, the reason why the market will demand anything from €5 to €500 for a white shirt, the reason why a brand like *Nike*, which as Klein (2001) has pointed out, in content terms, means nothing, simply a holding company, can have so much symbolic meaning. And, the 'nationality' of a brand – together with the language associated with that nationality – is part of that fetish. Country-of-origin is generally fetishized and symbolic rather than real. As Eric Hobsbawm (2000, p. 65) pointed out, *Ford* cars are manufactured using Japanese and European components, yet they are still branded as American. The scents for 'French' perfume brands, *Lancôme's Trésor* and *Clinique's Happy*, are manufactured by International Flavors and Fragrances located in Dayton, New Jersey, off exit 8a of the New Jersey Turnpike (Schlosser, 2002, p. 120). In adjoining rooms, the flavours for *McDonald's* fries are concocted. It is hard to imagine a more contrasting environment to the image of a Paris fashion house.

The beer market in the UK is another example. *Guinness*, fetishized with all that is perceived to be Irish is brewed in the Park Royal brewery outside London. *Budweiser*, marketed as the 'all-American brew' is also brewed in Greater London. Belgian beer *Stella Artois*, whose advertising is reminiscent of French films such as *Jean de Floret*, is brewed in South Wales. Interestingly, in a print campaign directed at readers of the UK *Observer* Sunday newspaper 'Food Monthly' supplement, *Stella Artois* took over the entire cover (outer and inner pages) to provide guidelines to readers for telling a real *Stella Artois* glass – indicated by the fact that the hunting horn featured in the logo is 'clearly Belgian, circa 1366' – from a fake one. *Kronenbourg 1664* 'which claims to embody the French spirit is in fact brewed somewhat closer to the M25 [London orbital route] than Marseilles' (Lane, 2002), and *Carlsberg Export* beer, whose slogan is 'So good, the Danes hate to see it leave', is brewed in Northampton (Lane, 2002). According to Mark Hastings of the British Beer and Pub Association, less than 10 per cent of beer consumed in the UK is actually imported. In his words, 'it's the taste of the country being sold as much as the taste of the beer' (in Lane, 2002). Thus, in a highly competitive market, the association of foreignness proves to be a key product attribute, and the way to differentiate beers for the consumer in advertising is not through taste but through a fetishizing of cultures and languages that has little to do with the reality of production. As Jaffe and Nebenzahl (2001) highlight, 'for the individual, the image represents the object, or even is the object' (p. 13). Perception, then, is everything here. It is, in Sperber and Wilson's (1986) terms, assumptions about the world rather than the actual state of the world that is paramount in the realm of market discourse.

Country-of-origin and linguistic fetish

A shared language is seen by many as one of the key defining aspects of identity in many countries and cultures (Wright, 2000; Smith, 1991). Parallel to this, the language of the other is a key marker of another group, part of its image as viewed externally. To put it another way: speaking French is seen as a key part of being French (identity) *and* being seen as French (image). It is therefore not surprising that companies wishing to maximize the country-of-origin effect employ language for this purpose. The presence of a word or phrase from the language associated with the country of origin reinforces both the visual and/or aural texture of the advertisement, working with the paralanguage, the graphics, the particular scenario, use of colour and so on, to reinforce the message. This presence may be only minimal, but its effect should not be dismissed. As was highlighted in Chapter 1, language choices in advertising are not the result of a random process; they represent the attempt to use language to achieve a particular market-oriented goal, and the words present in the advertising text are there because a very conscious decision has been taken to put them there and not to put other words there.

Linguistic fetish approaches

One example of the minimal fetish type of approach is the decision as to whether to localize the particular country or place of origin for the audience, or leave it in its original. In general, where a linguistic fetish approach is adopted, the country-of-origin is given in the original, adding even more to its authenticity. So, for instance, in print advertisements for Swiss-based *Raymond Weil* watches, *'Genève'* instead of Geneva is printed under the brand name in an otherwise English-language advertisement. Something that is more obviously a fetish is where the original (that is foreign) product name is used rather than a local or domesticated version. So, for example, an advertisement on German television for Dutch cheese states *'Kaas, nicht nur Käse'* – 'not just cheese, but *Kaas'*, *Kaas* being the Dutch word for cheese. In such a context, the Dutch word becomes fetishized with the symbolic associations and cultural competence of the Dutch. *'Kaas'* then becomes a brand name, superior to simple cheese which does not have the same cultural credibility (Kelly-Holmes, 2000a).

Sometimes the linguistic fetish may be confined simply to the brand name, as in the case of the international ice-cream brand *Häagen-Dazs*. In the 1950s, when New Jersey-based ice-cream manufacturer Reuben

Mattus needed to find a competitive edge, he moved into what he called the 'super-premium' ice cream niche. His way of telling customers that this ice cream was super-premium was to give it a European-sounding name, since European ice creams had the association of quality. Rather than being the name of a Danish ice cream-producing family or having some other heritage association, the name was invented by Mattus to make the brand appear Danish, since a leading quality brand at the time, *Premium Is*, was in fact Danish (Ullmann, 1993, cited in Jaffe and Nebenzahl, 2001, p. 109).

The linguistic fetish may be extended to the whole range of a company's products, and to the consumer's experience of them. A good example here is the *Ikea* furniture shopping experience – designed to be a celebration of 'Swedishness' – that can be seen to be a highly successful example of linguistic fetish. The Swedish product names emphasize that the products are made by Europe's furniture maker/designer. Throughout *Ikea* outlets, the bilingual signposting and Swedish product names add to the authenticity of the products on display. The Swedish lexical items used in the restaurant menu are not there to highlight or complement any notional Swedish competence in the area of fine cuisine. Instead, the wholesome, sturdy sounding names and meals they identify reinforce the sturdiness, simplicity and 'Swedishness' of the furniture products. The Swedish linguistic fetish is continued on *Ikea's* country websites, where, for example, '*Hej*' is used in the children's furniture section. The term is accompanied by the explanation: 'This little word is how friends greet each other in Swedish' (www.ikea.de).

Non-product-specific linguistic fetish

As in the case of *Ikea*, linguistic fetishes are generally employed because the language in question is associated with a particular product category, or a culture that has expertise in the relevant area. However, as was seen with the country categorization approach discussed earlier, there are many instances where this is not in fact the case, and where, instead, the language is used to allude to stereotypes about the particular culture of the language. In such cases, then, the language is not linked specifically with product-related cultural competence. For example, in an advertisement for brandy, which appeared in German news magazine *Der Spiegel* in the mid-1990s, the graphic consists of a starkly beautiful naked woman lying on a bull – clearly alluding to a key marker of Spain's external image, namely the tradition of bullfighting. This is accompanied by a few easily comprehensible Spanish lexical items in the slogan, in and of themselves stereotypically associated with the country:

> Un poco macho un poco ángel.

This 'passion' theme links intertextually to the market discourses of other Spanish products. For example, *Seat* cars' current (2003) slogan for its advertising is '*Auto emoción*' (www.seat.com). On the UK website, the slogan is set against a background of a heart in flames, presumably invoking the Spanish reputation for passion. The *Seat* range also features names that have resonance with famous or familiar Spanish settings such as the Alhambra, Toledo and Ibiza. All of these tactics de-emphasize the engineering competence that is of course 'owned' by the German language.

Eastern European brands, which wanted to break into Western markets in the 1990s, had to create a new type of cultural competence and linguistic fetish. Some, like the *Skoda* example cited earlier, relied on a Western testimonial to accredit their competence, while others, like Czech beer *Staropramen* played on the communist heritage of their brand, in terms of competence and, consequently, language. A print advertisement, from the *Observer* Sunday newspaper magazine from 1996, when the beer was first launched on the UK market, contains the following text:

> In the fever-pitch excitement of a game of shove-drobáky only one beer will do. The good citizens of Prague are fond of a beer. In fact, they're very fond of a beer. And the beer they're fondest of is Staropramen. They'd tell you that the secret of Staropramen's unique flavour and texture lies in our double brewing technique ... They'd tell you, that is, if you could prise the bottle from their lips. Staropramen 100% Czech.

The graphic opposite the text comprises a picture of a run-down bar/café, ostensibly in Prague. The plasterwork on the wall needs redoing, and on top of a dresser there is an old bottle with what looks like dead flowers. Two men are playing a game of *shove-drobáky*. '*Shove-drobáky*' is not the only Czech word to appear in the advertisement. On the wall of the bar are two old signs in Czech, one an ad for *Staropramen*:

> Staropramen
> Ležák

The other is an ad for a bank:

Slavia
Vzájemně pojišťovací banka
Zastupitelství

The Czech words here have the flavour and function of image rather than language, since it is probably safe to assume that the target readership encountering the advertisement will not understand their meaning; or, perhaps more importantly, it is not the intention of the advertiser that these words should be understood. However, the choice of signs and the language in them is interesting. By using an old sign advertising *Staropramen* in an authentic Prague bar, the image adds greater credibility to the beer as a traditional Czech beer, '100% Czech'. Similarly the choice of '*slavia*' in large bold letters, identifiable to non-Czech speakers as something like 'Slavic' also adds to the beer's credibility, its Czech/Slavic identity, in a way that other vocabulary items would not. So, it would seem that these Czech words are part of the image rather than the text of the advertisement, and the language in them is used for a fetishistic effect.

Linguistic fetish can also be used when countries seek to step outside their area of cultural competence and, as was pointed out earlier, in order to gain credibility, appeal to their culturally competent neighbour. Television advertising for Irish butter *Kerrygold* on Irish national television in the late 1980s/early 1990s provides a good example of this. In one of the ads, which took place entirely in simple French without subtitles, the naïve Irish au pair arrives at the home of her French employers armed with the gift of *Kerrygold*. The lady of the house graciously accepts the gift, but assures her that they already buy *Kerrygold*. In this, as in the other ads, the French 'sponsor' seems almost surprised that *Kerrygold* is in fact Irish. Thus, *Kerrygold* achieves its cultural competence as a food product because it is not only approved of but also used by the European cooks – all of these assertions are supported by the French language and the French accents present in these advertisements, even though the advertisement takes place in an Irish rather than a French context. Such 'testimonials' are in fact similar to those given by sports stars and celebrities. However, here it is not occupation, notoriety, appearance, reputation, knowledge and so on which is being used to support the product or which is the reason for the choice of the 'sponsor'. Instead, it is factors such as nationality, language and cultural competence. The 'French' people in these ads could be substituted by any one of their compatriots.

The German linguistic fetish[2]

There is a corner that is forever Munich
(BMW billboard advertisement for UK market, mid-1990s)

This slogan, although it uses no actual German words, and the German location referred to is given in the English version (Munich rather than *München*), is nonetheless a good place to start examining the German linguistic fetish in country-of-origin-based advertising. The words appeared beside an image of the 'corner' concerned, 'the intersection of bonnet, windscreen pillar and wing', on a *BMW* automobile. *BMW* is, of course, a German carmaker; the advertisement in question was aimed at a British audience; and the slogan just happens to allude to the poem *The Soldier* by Rupert Brooke, one of the poems of the First World War, a poem that is widely known in England, and, arguably, even one of the key texts of identity in that particular country:

If I should die, think only this of me:
That there's some corner of a foreign field
That is for ever England.[3]

It is a poem that belongs in the context of Remembrance Sunday, the annual date in November when the dead of the First and Second World Wars and other conflicts are commemorated, rather than in the text of an advertisement for a German car. It conjures up metaphors of struggle and victory, particularly against the Germans in the context of the two World Wars. Its words were used, for example, to advertise England's matches on television during the 1999 Rugby World Cup. More than this, however, the words are also infused with the misery and inhumane spectacle of the First World War, something that dare not be ridiculed. However, in the body text of the ad the initiated advertisee learns about the valiant efforts of the German engineers, which involved a level of 'precision breathtaking even by German standards'. Are these efforts then to compare to the human sacrifice of British soldiers in foreign fields? Is there, instead, or as well, a message about healthy, friendly rivalry (as in sport) or something more sinister and aggressive (as in war)? Should the advertisee think of German domination, expansion into Europe, making foreign fields into Germanies through the export of *BMWs*? Is the advertisement making the point that at the end of a century of conflict, the two countries have come so far that they can now play with each other's sacred texts, or is the message perhaps that technical dominance and the omnipresent market mean nothing is sacred now, not history, folk memory or literature?

The advertisement, as mentioned above, does not contain German words; however, it does make explicit use of the country-of-origin by citing Munich, one of Germany's best-known cities, as well as the headquarters of *BMW*, and it also invokes notions about the perceived German cultural competence when it refers to a 'precision breathtaking even by German standards'. Such a statement is only possible in the context of widely held notions about German engineering competence. This particular advertisement is just one example of the many texts in the marketed discourse of Germanness that provides the context within which the German linguistic fetish operates.

Constructing them and us

There are many manifestations of this phenomenon in the advertising of German products. Such advertising may, as in the case of the *BMW* advertisement, explicitly refer to perceived German cultural competence. An instance of this was the German brand *AEG's* decision to abandon its rather mundane trading name, '*Allgemeine elektrische Geräte*' (general electrical appliances) in favour of one that would allow its products to benefit from cultural competence in the Anglophone setting: 'Advanced Engineering from Germany'. In an advertisement (from the *Observer* magazine of 1986) as in many country-of-origin-based market discourses, place is central: the place of production and the place of the notional consumer. To this end, the advertisement showed a British car (identified through localized number plates) driving down the German Autobahn (identified by the German place names on the *Autobahn* signs), the signs ahead directing the car to Berlin, Würzburg and Nürnberg-Fischbach. The slogan declares:

> As fast as we bring them from Germany, you take them back again.

From the body of the text, the advertisee discovers just why this British driver is on German roads:

> The new BMW M635Csi is the one very fast car you can enjoy driving slowly. All the same, you wouldn't be human if you didn't want to experience its full power just once.
>
> And surely you can invent an excuse to go to Germany where you can drive it close to the BMW factory at 158 mph without alarming the police.

The advertisement is making use of the difference between the UK and Germany in terms of speeding restrictions, since in Germany there is no speed limit on the motorway, so the speed proposed in the advertisement (158 miles per hour) is about twice the level permitted on British motorways. Interestingly, although the speeds are localized (given in miles rather than kilometers to accommodate to an Anglophone audience), the advertising copy uses the German term *Autobahn* rather than its English equivalent 'motorway', presumably to emphasize what is different, exciting and special about it.

This advertisement, then, uses a number of devices. First of all, there is the very definite positioning of the consumer as British (you) and the producer as German (we); there is the explicit reference to the country-of-origin, Germany, and its received cultural competence as an engineer/ carmaker, something that is assumed to be known and accepted as common-sense knowledge by the British advertisee; and there is the use of German lexical items such as Autobahn and the place names in the motorway signposting Berlin, Würzburg, Nürnberg-Fischbach. All of these devices/strategies work together in the advertisement.

A *Volkswagen* newspaper advertisement (that appeared in the British daily broadsheet, the *Guardian*, in the early 1990s) not only explicitly acknowledges German cultural competence, but also the widely held consensus about it. Beneath the graphic of the new *Golf* model, the text reads:

> One thing Europe seems to agree about.
>
> From Strasbourg to Brussels, London to Paris, Madrid to Rome, it was smiles, handshakes, pleasantries all round. The reason for this communal chumminess? Our new Golf. Fifty-nine top motoring writers from eighteen European countries had just voted it Car of the Year. A welcome win, for sure. Though, to be frank, not entirely unexpected.

In keeping with the approach at the time, the advertisement is also superior in tone (for example, 'Though, to be frank, not entirely unexpected'). The advertisement alludes, of course, to the dissent within the European Union, something which was particularly topical in the early 1990s, at the time of German unification, and in particular the wrangling about Monetary Union – referred to in the final sentence of the advertisement (see below). In its final paragraph, the text of the advertisement again refers to this notion of German competence as agreed across Europe, using the main European Union languages (English, French, German, Italian, Spanish) to highlight the cultural and linguistic diversity, and contrast this with the unity about German engineering:

> All good stuff. But what about performance?
> Any torquier? Mais oui.
> The drag factor. Any lower? Natürlich.
> The handling. Any sharper? Certo.
> And the fuel consumption. Still generous?
> What, more generous? Claro que sí.
> As many a European knows, such things are common currency with every new Volkswagen.

The advertisement contains many different styles and uses of language. On the one hand, although it is clearly an advertisement for a German product, and this is made explicit throughout, the English language used includes a number of typically or even stereotypically English colloquial items, for example, 'chumminess' and 'all good stuff' – a type of language display, in Eastman and Stein's (1993) terms and a form of condescension, taking Bourdieu's (1991) point of view. On the other hand, there is the use of expressions from other languages, and, in this, German is not actually privileged, but instead appears as just one of the many European languages. Linguistic differences, it can be argued, are one of the European Union's distinguishing features in terms of identity, and here the listing of expressions in different languages serves on the one hand to symbolize Western Europe, and on the other, to point to the greatness of *Volkswagen* and German engineering in general, in that it can overcome these differences (symbolized by the languages) and reach multivoiced agreement, where the institutions of the European Union, with their commitment to multilingualism, cannot.

The superiority approach

The superiority approach based on acknowledging and exploiting country-of-origin competence was a popular trend throughout the late 1980s and early 1990s, a time when those formulating market discourses about German products seemed determined to use stereotypes – both positive and negative – about Germany's country image to their advantage. And, given that this approach starts from an ethnocentric base, it also implies that the receiver of the discourses, the advertisee, primarily though not exclusively based in the UK, perhaps needed to position German products in this way at that particular time, linking intertextually with political and economic texts about European unity and German unification. The *Continental* tyre brand, for example, was, for many years, quite unconcerned with pointing out its 'Germanness' and it is unlikely that many uninitiated consumers were aware of its nationality. The name itself sounded as if it could be American, while the abbreviation used at the time, '*Conti*', sounded Italian. There was nothing particularly German about either. In an attempt to benefit from Germany's engineering reputation, *Continental* launched a billboard campaign in the mid-1990s using slogans such as 'Put your foot down and insist on German tyres', and, more controversially, 'Dull, grey and reliable: Just what you expect from a German'.

Some further examples include this extract from a print advertisement (in British broadsheet Sunday newspaper magazines) for the new *Audi* 100 from the early 1990s:

> German safety tests, as you'd expect, are noted for their thoroughness and efficiency.

Likewise, in another *Audi* print advertisement, from the *Sunday Times* magazine of 1992, a British registered *Audi* is pictured in pouring rain beneath a motorway flyover with an air-ambulance helicopter circling overhead. The heading reads:

> If it's a real emergency they send in the *Audi*.

The text beneath reads:

> Above, the Royal London Hospital's emergency helicopter. Below, their Audi 100 2.8E Quattro Estate. About 1.27 million cheaper and, in bad weather or really tight situations, a life-line.

Here, as in the previous examples, a distinction is made between an implicit German 'we' and a British 'they' (cf. van Dijk, 1998).

Another advertisement in the same series took a similar line. The graphic shows a red *Audi* driving up a snowy, rocky mountain. The slogan:

> Most cars couldn't drive down it. The new Audi 8- Quattro has just driven up it.

Yet another magazine advertisement for *Audi* from 1996 takes up the theme of superiority, but in a much more blatant, and potentially antagonistic way, perhaps poking fun at the British stereotype of sports-manship. In a one-page advertisement in Sunday newspapers, the title of the advertisement, beneath a graphic of an *Audi* motor racing car read:

APOLOGY
Audi and their winning driver, Frank Biela, wish to apologise to all the other drivers for having to make them go through the motions in the last few races of the RAC Auto Trader British Touring Car Championships. Frank shall endeavour to make sure this doesn't happen again next year.

Exploiting negative stereotypes

Once the boasting trend had been exhausted, advertising for German brands began thematizing and exploiting non-product-specific German stereotypes. So, *Becks* beer, which only seemed to feel the need to emphasize its origins in the mid-1990s, chose to do so through a series of humorous television advertisements poking fun at, for example, the perceived German obsession with punctuality. *Audi* also joined in this trend, exploiting the 'beach-towel wars' which took place between the British tabloid, the *Sun*, and its German equivalent, *Bildzeitung*, in the late 1980s. The impetus for this was 'tension' between Britons and Germans over the 'bagsing' of sun loungers by German holidaymakers in Spanish resorts, by placing a beach towel over them. This quickly turned into yet another stereotype about the German public and was analogized with German military action, again alluding to the Second World War, something that is all too often present, although not always as overtly as this, in media and market discourses between Britain and Germany. This is explicitly thematized in an *Audi* print advertisement from that time aimed at a British audience:

Why the Germans no longer worry about getting to the beach on time.

The slogan is positioned against a background of a couple driving in an open-top car down the winding roads of a sunny holiday island. The message of the advertisement is that the stereotypical German is in no hurry to get to the beach to reserve his/her sun-lounger, since s/he can 'cruise in open-topped comfort' in an *Audi*.[4]

Having started with the humorous approach, *Becks* went one step further with a campaign in the late 1990s, which attempted to overturn the stereotype of Germany as the European prefect, the pro-European advocate of further integration. In response to a proposal by the

European Commission that water used for brewing be standardized across Europe, *Becks* launched a campaign in the UK quality weekend press (for example the *Independent on Sunday, Sunday Times, Sunday Telegraph* and *Observer*) attacking European bureaucracy, a favourite theme of the British press, thus linking intertextually with media and political texts about European integration and regulation in the UK. The advertisements clearly identified *Becks* as a German brand and used German vocabulary items such as *'bier'* (beer) and *'Brauerei'* (brewery), and emphasized German pedantry, thoroughness and efficiency in the production of beer. However, what the campaign also tried to create was a type of affinity with Britain and with British Euro-scepticism. So, for example, typically British institutions such as cricket, the red telephone box, the Green Man pubs and so on were all cited, and the advertising copy was at pains to point out the German admiration for stereotypically British characteristics, such as 'gentlemanly conduct' and 'sense of fair play', for example, in an attempt to build commonality between the concerns of the ordinary Briton and the ordinary German. The style of the texts themselves again involved a kind of language display (Eastman and Stein, 1993), in that they are more reminiscent of editorials from the right wing, anti-European press in the UK than advertising copy in their use of the discourse and vocabulary of Euro-scepticism (Kelly-Holmes, 2000b):

> Brussels have suggested that along with its cucumber companion it's time the banana conformed. Permutations on this plucky plantain are discouraged and it should now comply to a standard size.

Nonetheless, underlying all of the advertisements is the German cultural credibility in beer-making and the need to preserve this and indeed the whole notion of cultural competence and difference, something which the standardizing bureaucrats in Brussels would, its seems, gladly sweep away making beer a standardized product across the Union.

Vorsprung durch Technik

Though the themes, scenarios and models may change, three German words have remained a constant presence in the various *Audi* advertisements cited above: *'Vorsprung durch Technik'* – arguably one of the best examples of the German language engineering fetish in advertising. From the late 1980s, this became the watermark of *Audi* advertising, appearing under the brand name in billboard, print and television advertising. The non-translated slogan has meaning independent of its utility or communicative meaning, and this symbolic value or meaning is in fact greater. If the utility/referential value or meaning had been rated more highly, then the slogan would have been translated for advertisees in non-German-speaking countries. Through the process of fetishization, the words and their origins have been mystified and obscured: they are never explained to the Anglophone advertisee, since their utility value is irrelevant and they achieve their symbolic value, thus contributing towards the success of the advertising message, on the basis of shared notions about cultural competence in the area of engineering, rather than anything they seek to explain. The advertisements are for cars, more specifically cars made by the European carmaker. It is on the basis of these intercultural perceptions and relations that the symbolic value of '*Vorsprung durch Technik*' outweighs its referential value. The phrase is identifiable as German, it sounds and looks appropriately Germanic – and by implication technical – and thus its symbolic value (indicating the cultural credibility of *Audi* as a carmaker) is communicated successfully, its utility meaning being irrelevant. The fact that this is irrelevant can be seen in the development of this phrase from advertising slogan to cultural icon, seen, for example, in its use in the song 'Parklife' by British group Blur, and in headings such as 'Vorsprung durch Shopping' (a report in the *Guardian* 'Weekend' supplement in 1996 about CentrO, Germany's first 'mega-mall' shopping centre) and 'Vorsprung durch Panik' (the heading of a report in the *Economist* from 1992 detailing how Germany, following Unification in 1990, was now less attractive to foreign investors, who were panicking and leaving for less-expensive locations (*Economist*, 1992). As stated earlier, the contextualization role is key here: the language-switch provides the context within which to interpret the advertisement, that is the realm of Anglo-German relations, the German reputation for carmaking and also reporting of German political and economic developments in the British press, and so on.

As the success of '*Vorsprung durch Technik*' shows, the German language has been fetishized with a certain engineering quality which now pervades advertising for German products in the UK. So, *Volkswagen* called 'the world's cleanest car' '*Umwelt Diesel*' in its English-language advertising – '*Umwelt*' being the German for environment. In a *Continental* television advertising campaign on British television from the mid-1990s, the text of the ad was read in German while English subtitles appeared on the screen. In this particular ad, the German language seemed to act like a carefully chosen and highly appropriate soundtrack – the perfect accompaniment to an ad about an engineering product – even though (or perhaps especially because) it would not be widely understood by the target audience.

The *Bier* fetish[5]

The following advertisement for *Löwenbräu*, which appeared in quality Sunday newspaper magazines in the late 1980s, shows the other main fetish associated with the German language in advertising, namely the '*Bier*' fetish:

HELGA, HOW MANY GERMANS DOES IT TAKE TO CHANGE A LIGHT BULB?

AH IS THIS THE ONE ABOUT the highly-trained quality control checkers at the Löwenbräu brewery here in the beautiful city of Munich where they have to carefully check that each and every stage of the bier brewing process adheres to the Reinheitsgebot ancient brewing laws laid down in 1516 which set minimum standards for the purity of the ingredients otherwise they'd be subject to extremely enormous fines so quality control is a very important job both in terms of the quality of all the Löwenbräu biers and of course the financial good health of the company from the checking of the malted barley with the hops not forgetting the pure Bavarian spring water by any chance?

WHAT WE GERMANS LACK IN HUMOUR, WE MAKE UP FOR IN OUR BIER.

Like many German brewers (for example *Becks*), *Löwenbräu* has for some years been using the German '*Bier*' and also a number of German vocabulary items in its advertising, most notably – in this case – the *Reinheitsgebot*, the ancient German brewing law.[6] This language display, as Eastman and Stein (1993) would term it, is successful, not least because of the fact that it sounds German due to the homophonous *Rein/Rhein* element, which would be instantly recognizable for Anglophone consumers. It is sufficient to leave these German lexical items unexplained. They are easily understood by the Anglophone advertisee, and, in any case, their utility value is secondary to their symbolic value. As in the case of 'affective code-switching' (see Chapter 1), the appearance of the German words acts like speech marks, quoting the composite German, the European brewer, and the effect adds authenticity and credibility to the product. The *Löwenbräu* ad is also interesting in that it takes a negative stereotype about Germany (lack of humour, seriousness), uses it to identify the nationality of the product, and then subverts it by producing a humorous advertisement.

A further interesting example of the *Bier* fetish is provided by an advertisement for *Warsteiner* beer, which appeared on the back outside cover of an issue of *Geo* magazine dealing with the return of Hong Kong to Chinese sovereignty in 1997. The graphic of the advertisement features a glass of *Warsteiner*, a ray of light shines diagonally across the bottle, highlighting the brand on the glass and the logo in German:

Eine Königin unter den Bieren [queen among beers].

The title of the advertisement, 'Miss Germany' puts an additional interpretation on this diagonal band of light. It seems to refer to the bands worn by 'Miss World' contestants, on which their nationality is stated (in this case, 'Miss Germany'). So, is *Warsteiner* the 'Miss World' of beers or, perhaps more correctly, *Biers*? There is, however, a further angle provided by the double meaning of the title. The details of where to get *Warsteiner* in Hong Kong are all provided in German (details about distributors and so on), so it is not inconceivable that the advertisement is also aimed at German nationals working and living in Hong Kong, who are missing Germany and German *Bier*. Apart from 'Miss Germany' and the addresses, all the rest of the text is in German, although *Geo* is published in English:

Das Einzig Wahre Warsteiner [The one and only Warsteiner]
Spitzen-Pilsener der Premium-Klasse [The best Pils in the premium range]
Auf höchstem Niveau auch WARSTEINER PREMIUM LIGHT und alkohol-freies WARSTEINER PREMIUM FRESH [also top quality Warsteiner Premium Light and non-alcoholic Warsteiner Premium Fresh].

It could not really be the case that these German ex-pats in Hong Kong would not be able to speak English and would need this kind of information in German; however they might like to receive it in German, in order to summon up images of home for German nationals (and Europeans in general). The use of German also works on another level, however, in that it alludes, for the non-German-speaking advertisees, to the German brewing competence.

Language as theme

As the above examples show, linguistic fetish is not always confined to lexical items. Syntax, style, accent, dialects – all of these are exploited in advertising and can stand alone as an independent source of meaning, and in the process give meaning to a particular product in terms of cultural competence. In the *Löwenbräu* ad cited above, the syntax of the sentence seems to reflect the perception that German is an unwieldy language, full of interminable sentences, which are in turn packed with unnecessary and pedantic nominalizations, as famously parodied in the writings of Mark Twain. Likewise, in a UK Sunday newspaper magazine advertisement for *Audi* from the mid-1990s, the advertisee is introduced to Dr Jörg Bensinger, an *Audi* engineer, who is being interviewed by two British car journalists. The portrayal of Dr Bensinger is of a reliable, efficient pedant. In fact, his long-winded way of speaking is almost a means of reassuring the advertisee about his *Gründlichkeit*, his German thoroughness and attention to detail. For example:

His English was impeccable. But why couldn't he just say it cornered more safely?

And, later in the text:

We [the British journalists] were ready to digest more typically German thinking.

In this particular *Audi* advertisement, the narrator of the advertisement is constructed as a part of the British 'we', unlike in many of the examples above, with the German 'they' represented by Dr Bensinger.

Another interesting example of language as theme is a 2003 advertisement for the C-Class *Mercedes*, which appeared on the back page of the *Observer* (UK Sunday newspaper magazine). The German word '*Kompressor*' is circled on the back boot of the car, and a line leads to an explanation for Anglophone advertisees:

German for supercharged.
(In case you've wondered as it disappeared into the distance.)

While it seems like an obvious strategy for an identifiably German brand to use the German language in promoting its products, the next example, which thematizes the German language, involves what is considered to be an American product. Motorists, cyclists, passengers and pedestrians negotiating Dublin's busy streets were confronted with the following billboard in 2002. Next to the image of the latest edition *Ford*

Focus car was the following slogan:

Focus: German for reliability.

The attribute used here to promote the product is not a technical feature or design innovation, but a language, the German language. This language, however, has no ostensible link with the product or with the utility of the marketing message – it is neither the language of the country-of-origin (USA), nor of the country of the target advertisees (Ireland). Its role is to give the product credibility. German here is a synonym for reliability, and, by association here, so too is *Focus* and perhaps the whole *Ford* brand. The advertisement seems to be based on the assumption that the motorists, passengers and pedestrians who encounter the message know the reputation German cars have for reliability. It also builds on their assumption that American cars have not, traditionally, been viewed as being as reliable as their German or Japanese counterparts, at least among European consumers. Thus, the message here might be that *Ford* cars have become more German, closer to the ideal, more like the cars made by the world's carmaker.

Another interesting example of this is a German-language advertisement broadcast on British television in 2004. The advertisement is entirely in German with English subtitles. A prototypical manager is talking to his team as they view a presentation on a new car. He is talking (in German) about the one thing that he does not like about the car: 'Do you know the one thing I don't like about this car?' he says, challenging the team. The viewer is led to believe that he is talking about one of the company's own cars, since he is speaking from the country of Europe's carmaker, the scene being 'illustrated' by the language. Maybe it is a *BMW*, an *Audi* or a *Mercedes*? Finally, he reveals what he does not like, namely the fact that 'It is not one of ours'. Only then does the advertisee see that the car in question is the new (Japanese) *Toyota Avensis*.[7]

Although the German linguistic fetish examples here are taken from a European context, it is interesting to look at how the German language functions commercially outside of its more 'natural' habitat. In his study of the symbolic values of foreign languages in Japan and their usage in advertising, carried out in the 1980s, Haarmann (1989) found that, although the German language was rarely used in slogans or body text, it did appear in product names and, also, the English slogan 'Made in Germany'[8] was used to invoke the positive stereotype of the German economic miracle. The Japanese view of Germany was in his opinion a positive one and he also proposed that the German language had the image of 'the language of men in the business world' (p. 25).

Anti-country-of-origin approaches

The seemingly widespread consensus about German cultural credibility is confirmed by the fact that products that do not fall within the domains of engineering and beer rarely if ever attempt to exploit a country-of-origin and linguistic fetish effect. As international branding consultant Wolff Olins points out, while

> the cold, aggressive images ... may have suited the export of German robotics, they can hardly be useful for organizations such as Nivea, a German cosmetics company with a reputation for excellence – and for being anything but German. (Olins, 1999)

In fact, in an advertising feature for *Nivea* in British women's glossy magazine, the BBC-published *Eve*, the title of the promotion '*Crème de la Crème*', invokes the French linguistic fetish and alludes to France as the country-of-origin for the product, not Germany. In another advertising text from *Nivea*, found in a UK family women's magazine in 2003, further evidence of this anti-country-of-origin and anti-German linguistic fetish approach is found. The advertisement is entirely in English, the website address given is local, with a '.co.uk' suffix, and the advertisement is also localized in the final sentence:

> Nivea is proud to work with race for life. And women of all ages can join in.

Here, *Nivea* is constructing a non-national, female identity, the 'Race for Life' breast-cancer charity being locally based in the UK. The phone numbers given, the website address and the charity registration number of 'Race for Life' are all local to the UK. The only hint at anything not British is the parent corporation name, *Beiersdorf* that appears in the top left-hand corner. The following quote from the history of the *Nivea* brand, reproduced on www.nivea.co.uk sums up the anti-country-of-origin approach:

> Sold in some 150 countries, Nivea products are trusted around the world. In fact, in many countries consumers are convinced that Nivea is a local brand! Beiersdorf regards this slight confusion as a great compliment. Through the twist [*sic*] and turns of almost a century of change, one thing has remained the same – Nivea means gentle care.

The 'twists and turns of history', is, presumably, a euphemistic way of referring to the reason why German products might have a negative image, something *Nivea* presents itself as detached from. In fact, in the chapter of its company history relating to the 1930s, it is claimed, 'the Nivea message remained free of Nazi ideology' (www. nivea.co.uk).

In his proposal for the rebranding of Germany's image, international brand consultant Wolff Olins included *Nivea* in a section of his report entitled 'surprising brands'. The objective was to show that consumers are generally surprised to learn that such brands are in fact German, since they do not market themselves as such, and they do not fall within the limits of 'acceptability', in Bourdieu's terms, for being German. In fact, it could be argued that they go further than this and try to hide their Germanness. The title attached to the pot of *Nivea* cream reproduced in the report is: 'So smooth it must be French'. And, indeed, this assumption is not surprising, given the product's use of the French term '*crème*', that has now practically assumed the status of proprietary brand name, its use invoking an expectation of a French beauty product.

Other brands included in the 'surprising brands' section are *Joop* fashion and cosmetics brand (discussed below) and SAP, the German software company that is a major world player. The title Olins uses for the SAP brand, 'Isn't all software American?', echoes a familiar reaction to the idea that one of the world's biggest software companies could actually be German, and provides yet another example of Bourdieu's statements about what is acceptable and not acceptable in this type of discourse. Another interesting case is that of *Wella*, 'Germany's largest and the world's second largest producer of hairdressing products for home and professional use' (www.wella.co.uk), which has never attempted to present itself as a German brand and thus cash in on the German linguistic fetish.

It was proposed earlier, that food products would not attempt to position themselves as German, and so avoid using the German language, because of the established fetishes of that language, namely engineering and beer. *Müller* dairy products have, for example, never tried to market themselves as German, because the idea of a German food product being superior would be unacceptable, in that it would contradict the stereotype German products exploit and the identity they have created, and thus there would be no advertising bonus from the association with Germany or the German language. In fact, in its most recent television advertising (2003/4) *Müller* is using recognizable regional UK accents to give aural illustration to its advertisements.

Further evidence is provided by the following advertising text for *Müller* that appeared in UK family women's magazines in 2003. The product is 'My first Müller corner':

> A little love for your little love.
> Introducing My First Müller Corner.
> With thick and creamy fromage frais on one side and smooth fruit puree on the other, it not only tastes great but provides all the goodness of added vitamins and calcium too.

The graphic of the advertisement contains a child's hand holding onto the finger of what is clearly his/her mother's hand. This is communicated by the fact that the hand is female and the woman is wearing a wedding band on her ring finger. The advertisement is localized or domesticated (in Venuti's terms) by the fact that the wedding band is on the ring finger of the left hand, as is the tradition in the UK, whereas in Germany – and a number of other European countries – the tradition is to wear wedding band on the right finger. Thus, the message is constructed entirely as an intra-cultural one. The advertisement also contains the *Müller* logo, 'Müller love' in white letters against the background of a red heart. The advertisement provides an interesting intersection of texts, voices and languages. The only German word to appear in the advertisement is the brand name *Müller* with its foreign *Umlaut*. The received perceptions of gentleness and femininity constructed by the image could not be further from the world of beer and cars. In this, the advertisement contains the texts that create constructions about motherhood in the society in which the advertisement is designed and in which it is expected to function. The language of science, for example 'vitamins' and 'calcium', ensures that the healthiness of the product is conveyed, while the only foreign language present in the body text is French. Here, too, the brand makes use of the French, not the German, language (*'fromage frais'*) in order to exploit associations of that particular language and lend credibility to the product.

The French linguistic fetish

To a certain extent, it can be argued that the French linguistic fetish is more established than its German counterpart. The reason for this is that in some domains, such as food and cosmetics, French words are used in the domestic lexicon of domains such as restaurants and department stores. Indeed, one of the most significant aspects of the French linguistic fetish is the fact that French terms such as *'parfum'* and *'vins de pays'* have evolved to become 'proper' product names. In many ways, this development is analogous to the evolution of what are considered to be 'ordinary', that is not proper, nouns from proprietary names or brands, for example sellotape, tippex, post-it and so on, although unlike real proprietary brands, the French words are used more by consumers when looking at labels and menus, than in everyday conversations. However, like proprietary brands, such terms have also become signifiers in generic terms. Thus, when advertising French wines, either generically or specifically, the French *'vin de pays'* is used as a brand name to ensure top quality – the use of the French language being the guarantor of this. This 'guarantee' is explicitly thematized in an advertisement in the UK women's glossy magazine, *Red*. The advertisement combines the French language, the country image of France as romantic and received notions about French cultural competence in winemaking. Against a backdrop of young lovers enjoying coffee and wine in a French café, the text reads:

> It's so easy to fall in love. And when it happens, you'll know it's for real. By the familiar French names of the famous French grapes. By the warmth of the reds, the freshness of the whites. By the three little words that signify so much. Vin de Pays.

In another example, taken this time from the *Observer* (UK Sunday newspaper) magazine, these foreign French words are accommodated syntactically into the English text, appearing as a proper name or brand name:

> Vins de Pays are some of the most enjoyable, exciting wines to come along in years … Created to appeal to the new generation of wine loves, Vins de Pays combine centuries of experience with the panache and innovation of a new wave of French wine makers.

This usage is not confined to the Anglophone world. In an advertisement from German news magazine *Der Spiegel*, however, the French and German versions are given together, and the French term is partially domesticated by being given a German article (die). The advertisement also, reassuringly, uses the French term *Départements*:

> Die Französischen Landweine; Die Vins de Pays.

The fetish, as was discussed earlier, may simply represent a decision to leave the product name in the original, whereas all other text on the product or advertisement is translated. An example here would be *Danone*'s '*crème de yaourt*' yoghurt. Or, again as was seen in the German case, the fetish may consist simply of a slogan or phrase. In its recent print advertising (2003) in the UK, French mineral water brand *Evian* uses the phrase '*L'Original*'.

As with the German examples, the French language can also be thematized in advertisements, for example in coffee brand *Carte Noire*'s advertising, the slogan used is 'French for Coffee', and the television advertising relies on French football player David Ginola's French accent to reinforce the 'Frenchness', without using any actual French words. Likewise, *Danone* in its billboard advertising in the UK and Ireland for its '*crème de yaourt*' range uses the slogan, 'French for dessert'.

French and cosmetics

Apart from its function as a signifier of food and drink, the French language has also become a social hieroglyphic for femininity, fashion and beauty in advertising communication. As in the case of the other linguistic fetish examples discussed up to now, the extent of the French language presence varies for different products in different contexts. For example, in an advertisement for a perfume from the *Guerlain* brand in the BBC-published glossy magazine, *Eve*, the graphic consists of the bottle which contains the name of the new perfume being advertised, '*L'Instant De Guerlain*', while, at the bottom of the advertisement, the text that gives the advertisee the information about the perfume is given in English: 'The new fragrance by Guerlain'. This is then followed by the omnipresent, 'Paris'.

In an advertisement for *Jean-Paul Gaultier* perfumes, the only text is '*Haute Parfumerie*', written in silver paint at the top of a picture of Jean-Paul Gaultier perfume tins. Similarly, in an advertisement in the UK edition of women's glossy magazine *Marie Claire*, the following text surrounds the image of a male and female entwined in the sea with the far horizon beckoning:

HORIZON pour homme, eau de toilette, Guy Laroche, Paris.

Because many examples such as these are encountered in the media every day, there seems nothing extraordinary about them. However, it is important to point out that these two advertisements are entirely in French in what are English-language media that are encountered and experienced in an English-language context. Yet, no further explanation is needed. The French language appears to say enough and stand on its own.

Similarly, in an advertising text for *Clyda* watches from *Hello* gossip and glamour magazine, the brand, location and French slogan appear above the graphic of the advertisement, which consists simply of pictures of the watches being advertised:

CLYDA
PARIS
L'ESPRIT DE L'ÉLÉGANCE

The content or utility message is, however, given underneath in English, although the French spelling of 'Parisian' is preferred: 'Models featured from the Parisien collection'. Again, here, in terms of font, visual presence and so on, the French words can be seen to comprise the visual rather than the textual, the latter being preserved for what is purely information.

Another strategy – also employed in the culinary domain, as discussed above – can be to simply create or deliberately use a French product name, or to decide not to translate the name into English or any other language for a particular audience. This is a tactic adopted by *L'Oréal*, with products such as '*Couleur Experte*'. The fetish is reinforced by the fact that the 'important' information about the product is given in English in these advertisements. Advertising for *Christian Dior* perfumes follows a similar tactic, with men's fragrances having the overall title of '*Dior Homme*'. Advertisements can also play with these product names. For example, in an advertisement for the *Christian Dior* perfume '*J'Adore*' – which in French means 'I love' – the name of the perfume is integrated into a half-French, half-English sentence in a print advertisement against the background of a beautiful woman. The remaining text then follows the usual formula with the brand name and the endorsement of location:

J'adore
THE ABSOLUTE FEMINITY
Christian Dior
Paris

As in the case of '*Couleur Experte*', '*J'adore*' is easily understandable by the Anglophone advertisee, and the two phrases may even be 'read' in

English rather than French: 'colour expert', 'I adore', the Frenchness simply acting as a paralinguistic device to enhance the message, just as a different font might be used.

Alongside advertising texts that simply use French product names, other advertisements will exploit a whole phrase or a greater quantity of French vocabulary, to the extent, sometimes, that this outweighs the language of the medium in or on which the advertisement appears. For example, in an advertisement for *Chanel*, from a UK women's magazine, the French statement *'rouges à lèvres'* is used for its symbolic value, calling up associations based on the French cultural competence in the area of beauty, fashion, femininity and so on.

> Rouges à Lèvres
> Chanel
> Lipsticks that protect the natural beauty of your lips

However, English is used where the utility value is greater; in other words, where there is an important message to get across and where the use of French would not guarantee accurate communication: 'Lipsticks that protect the natural beauty of your lips; the seductive brilliance of colour'. The paralanguage of the advertisement is also interesting. The brand name, *Chanel*, stands alone without any need of explanation. In terms of positioning and font size, the French slogan, *'rouges à lèvres'* is the second most important item after the brand name – in fact it is linked to it graphically by being centred above it. Thus, not only does the fetishized French statement stand alone, having independent value without need of explanation, it in fact gives meaning to the brand *Chanel*, supporting its 'Frenchness'. Likewise, in its advertising for *Trésor* perfume directed at Anglophone audiences, *Lancôme* uses the French slogan, *'le parfum des instants précieux'*.

In an advertisement for *Chantelle lingerie*, found in *Tatler and Hello* gossip/society magazines, the following slogan appears:

> Chantelle
> Paris habille les femmes du monde.

The slogan appears against a background of a beautiful woman modelling the lingerie. In the top left-hand corner, the certification *'lingerie française Paris'* appears, adding further authenticity to the brand's origin. The text of the advertisement is therefore entirely in French, and it is a French that is fairly understandable. The vocabulary chosen belongs to a field that is familiar to women who buy this kind of product and contains some key words such as *Paris*, *femmes* and *monde*. However, interestingly enough, a translation is provided in very small print on the left side of the advertisement, running vertically, in much the same way that website addresses are given on advertisements. So, although it is difficult to read, and not every advertisee will even see that this translation is given, it is available for the initiated advertisee, or the advertisee who is, perhaps, interested in language:

Paris dresses women of the world.

French fashion brand *Morgan*'s slogan '*Morgan de toi*' appears twice without a translation in a print ad for its perfumes in society magazine *Tatler*, first 'handwritten' in red in the top left-hand corner, and then printed immediately underneath the Morgan brand name. It is interesting that only a few pages after this advertisement, a fashion feature in the same magazine has the heading '*La Femme Noire*'. This example shows how linguistic fetish is often supported intertextually, not just synchronically between different advertisements for the particular brand or sector in general that are viewed and experienced at different times, but also diachronically in terms of the reading of a single magazine which contains advertisements and articles that utilize the same linguistic fetishes.

Again, here, it is necessary to keep the broadest possible definition of advertising texts in mind, as discussed in Chapter 1. In the context of the entire discourse of French cosmetics and the linguistic fetish that surrounds this, the products themselves and the packaging represent a crucial element, as for example in the following extract from the front of a bottle of foundation make-up sold in the UK:

LANCÔME
PARIS
PHOTOGÉNIC
ULTRA NATUREL
Fond de Teint Lumière Vitalité
Light-Reflecting Makeup
SPF 10

Looking at the content quantitatively, there is more French than English on the bottle, reinforcing the Frenchness of the product and linking intertextually with *Lancôme*'s other advertising texts, and indeed the entire discourse of French cosmetics and its fetishizing of the French language. Again, a bottle of foundation seems like an unlikely place to look for and find Anglophone-Francophone textual, cultural, social, economic, political and other relations enacted; however the very banality of these objects shows how normalized this linguistic fetish, and the multilingual advertising situations it produces, have become.

Something that is also striking after viewing so many of these advertising texts is the fact that for the advertisements that utilize the French linguistic fetish, both the structure and paralanguage are remarkably similar. Thus, there exists a high degree of manifest intertextuality, in Fairclough's (1992) terms, between all of these texts, something that helps to create and enhance this particular fetish even further (see Chapter 1).

Borrowing the authority of the French language

As in the case of the German linguistic fetish, it is not just French products that exploit the culinary fetish that has attached to the French language, due to the French reputation for food and cooking. For example, *Walls* ice cream in the UK (which is the same brand as *Langnese* in Germany, *HB* in Ireland) named its luxury brand '*Carte D'Or*' in order to cash in on positive associations between the French language and food, although the products have nothing to do with France. Likewise, in a rather bizarre use of the French language culinary fetish, the following text appeared in a UK family women's magazine (2003):

> Instead Of, 'Here Boy, Din Dins',
> How About, 'Bon Appetit'?

The advertisement, for *César* dog food's premier 'cuisine' brand, then introduces new 'meals' in the range, including: '*Fricassée* with Turkey and Vegetables' and 'Chicken *Provençale*'. The advertising text continues:

> You may find that César Cuisine's four delicious new recipes make quite an impression on your dog. And with ingredients like succulent slices of meat, specially selected vegetables and perfectly prepared pasta, it's easy to see why. What's more, they're all carefully cooked with the finest sauces. Magnifique.

The advertisement shows an interesting mix of voices, texts and languages. There is first of all the language of the dog-owner, with its mixture of childish and pet forms, such as 'din dins'; then there is the language of 'normal' food advertising, with its formulaic alliterated phrases, such as 'specially selected', 'succulent slices' 'perfectly prepared' and 'carefully cooked'; and, finally, there is the authoritative language of 'French' cooking, represented by *'Bon Appetit'* and *'Magnifique'*.

As mentioned earlier, there is a clear emergence of 'proprietary brands' and product names as a result of advertising fetish in the area of cosmetics. Advertising texts and products themselves (which also constitute advertising) routinely use French words such as *parfum, eau de parfum, eau de toilette, bains précieux* – and, as in the culinary fetish examples above, even brands which have nothing to do with France and do not pretend to have a French image, such as the USAmerican *Calvin Klein*, for instance, exploit these French terms. Likewise, in advertising his first perfume brand in a UK women's magazine, British fashion designer Alexander McQueen, who was awarded a CBE by the Queen for his contribution to British fashion, chose not to use the 'British' term, perfume, but instead sought the authority of its French counterpart:

ALEXANDER MCQUEEN
Kingdom
The first parfum from Alexander McQueen.

The extent of this French language cosmetic fetish is clear in an advertisement for *Joop* perfume – the product of a German designer – that appeared in German women's magazine *Brigitte*. The product is described as *'Parfum pour femme'* and there is no German text whatsoever in the advertisement, although this is, in effect, intra-cultural (like the Alexander McQueen example) rather than intercultural advertising. This example shows how the French language itself has become an intrinsic feature of the beauty product and a conduit for associations that simply cannot be expressed by the German language because of its cultural competence stereotype, even when a German brand is communicating with a German advertisee.

Créateur d' automobiles

The signature slogan *'créateur d'Automobiles'* was adopted by *Renault* in its advertising in the early 2000s, and the phrase now appears in all *Renault* advertisements aimed at audiences across Europe, just below the brand name and logo, summing up the motto of the brand, what it signifies, how it wishes to be portrayed. The phrase can be easily translated – creator of automobiles. In fact, there is probably no need to translate it. It has the advantage of being (almost) an internationalism – a word or phrase, which with minor spelling amendments is similar in a number of languages due either to a common root or origin or the fact that it is a new word that has been borrowed into a number of languages with only minor modification. It is part of what could be termed the European lexicon (cf. Trim, 2002). It therefore says something to the advertisee who speaks only English or Spanish for example. Its other advantage, however, it that it sounds and looks distinctly French. So, at one and the same time, it is entirely familiar and appropriately exotic. Looking at the actual choice of words, this phrase seems even more appropriate. Why has *Renault* decided to describe itself as a *'créateur'*, a 'creator' of cars? There are many more familiar collocations that would work and any number of alternative synonyms which would pair better with 'cars', for example, 'maker', 'manufacturer', 'engineer', 'designer' and so on. Creative work is usually the preserve of artists rather than car-makers. Creative work is done in studios in Paris, great works displayed in chic art galleries for tourists, and, one suspects, this is what *Renault* wants the advertisee to think of (as opposed to the cold, technical, mechanistic environment of the mass-production assembly line). This is not a German car, an engineered car. This is a French car, a car that has been created.

The 'creativity' motif is further enhanced by *Renault's* advertising for its 'brand ambassador', the top of the range *Vel Satis*. In a print adver-tisement, reproduced in UK quality Sunday newspaper magazines, the slogan reads:

> Most executive cars get their image from the marketing men.
> The Vel Satis' designers chose the marquetry men.
> 'Luxury' is probably the most hyped word in the executive car lexicon. But for the designers at Renault, the term is far from meaningless – as long as you are prepared to go right back to basics. Their achievement, the new Vel Satis, discards the old 3-box shape for an airy space in which the care-ful use of quality materials can make a real difference. But the Vel Satis' inte-rior goes much further than the old wood and leather cliché. The inlaid alderwood has a light matt finish; the 'grand confort' seats are finished in pale, perforated hide. 'More comfortable than a Bentley's', pronounced the Daily Telegraph. And the Vel Satis is substantially taller than the class average, allowing its passengers to ride above the crowd. And the hype.

The image in the advertisement is that of the dashboard of the car, which is a piece of marquetry, inlaid with different pieces of wood. The choice of 'marquetry' is interesting here. First of all, there is the pun (marketing versus marquetry), which enhances the model's classiness, by contrasting the smutty world of 'the marketing men' with the exclusive world of 'the marquetry men'. Then there is the word itself, which is hardly part of most people's everyday vocabulary, and seems, once again, to be an example of Eastman and Stein's 'language display' (1993). Thus, it appeals to those in the know, connoisseurs, those who are in the market, perhaps, for luxury cars. Even if they do not know what the term refers to, the elitism of the word may appeal to a desire for exclusivity. The copy actually identifies the problem facing copywriters today and points to the reason why foreign words are used, namely the fact that through hyperbole and advertising-speak, words have become meaningless. So, for those in search of greater differentiation through verbal expression, the next option is to choose a less used, less known or foreign word, hence, perhaps, the choice of 'marquetry'. This throws up another interesting aspect, the fact that the word, although used in its English form here, is etymologically French (*marqueterie, marqueter, marque*). Of course, the latter one of these is also the French word for brand, which again gives an interesting twist, since the *marque* men would, quite literally, be the advertising or marketing men too, but the French term seems to signify that they are something better than this. The term '*grand confort* seats' shows the necessary recourse to the vocabulary of the French language in order to communicate luxury in a new way. On its website, *Renault* describes the interior of the *Vel Satis* as 'a cabin truly representative of the French tradition of luxury' (www.renault.com).

The language of the advertisement also seems deliberately old-fashioned, not in a common touch approach kind of way, but in a pedantic, traditionalist way, with a concern for grammar and complete sentences, and it is no surprise that in fact, the archconservative British *Daily Telegraph* is cited as a testimonial. For example, the deliberately correct use of the apostrophe, often abandoned altogether in advertising copy, the choice of phrases like 'back to basics', 'careful use', and the final sentence, with its reference to the distasteful notion of hype. Likewise, the term 'lexicon' is not one in common usage, also adding to the exclusivity of the brand.

Language too has become a theme or topic in *Renault* advertising. For instance, in *Renault* television advertising featuring French football player Thierry Henry, the punchline involves Thierry asking his fellow session musician, in this case, Animal, a character from the USAmerican children's television show *Sesame Street*, in his French-accented English,

Hey, buddy, what's the French for va-va-voom?

The advertisement's scenario is described as follows on a *Renault* 'news and reviews' website:

> At first it appears the suave and sophisticated Frenchman is on stage playing the drums with his jazz band and entertaining the crowd with his impressive drumming skills. Just as Thierry is about to launch into a complicated drum solo, the camera pans round to reveal it's Animal who is actually responsible for the rhythmic sounds, not Thierry. As usual, the Frenchman takes it in his stride with a Gallic shrug of the shoulders.
>
> (http://www.carpages.co.uk/Renault/Renault_thierry_and_animal_
> explain_meaning_of_va_va_voom_25_10_03.asp)

The article goes on to quote Olivier Généreux, Director of Marketing at Renault UK as saying:

> Thierry Henry is the epitome of what the Clio represents – he's cool and gives the car a masculine appeal, which keeps it fresh, young and funky.
>
> (http://www.carpages.co.uk/Renault/Renault_thierry_and_animal_
> explain_meaning_of_va_va_voom_25_10_03.asp)

These comments abound with all the usual stereotypes of Frenchness, for example the inevitable collocation of 'suave and sophisticated', and the 'Gallic shrug'. The fact that the French language is also a theme in the advertisement, when Henry asks Animal, 'What's the French for va va voom?', only serves to reinforce the attribute of the product's Frenchness. In fact, it seems impossible to get away from it. In another article from the *Renault* news and reviews page, there is a feature on the England rugby team. On their victorious return from the Rugby World Cup in Australia in 2003, a number of key players on the team were presented with new *Renault* models as part of a sponsorship deal. In the reporting of this it seems that it is impossible not to mention the product's 'Frenchness' and link this in with the performance of the French team, who were beaten by their English rivals in the semi-finals:

> So even though the French team were knocked out of the semi-finals, some of the winning team are relying on French power to get them around!
>
> (http://www.carpages.co.uk/Renault/Renault_england_rugby_stars_
> score_with_Renault_07_12_03.asp)

Conclusion

Linguistic fetish, then, can manifest itself in many different ways in advertising discourse. At one end of the continuum are the texts in which only the place name or product name is left in the original, the rest of the text being translated and localized. At the other end, whole phrases, a majority of text or even the entire text is in the foreign language. In all of the cases examined, the language choices are symbolic in the sense that they are about constructing identities for the product, the producer or brand, and for the advertisee, rather than communicating facts. Furthermore, without recourse to connotation, many of these advertising slogans are meaningless. The fetishization process means that these foreign words take on a meaning and significance far greater than the merely denotational.

It also appears that in many of the cases examined, foreign words function more in terms of the form of the advertisement rather than the informational content, enhancing the visual and/or aural texture of the message, while important information is conveyed in a utility manner in the local language. As was pointed out in the opening paragraphs of this chapter, ethnocentrism, 'our' view of the 'other', is at the heart of these messages, and this becomes clear given the fact that almost all of the texts cited in this chapter were created by local agencies acting in collaboration with the foreign parent.

Of course there are many sectors of advertising in which linguistic fetish does not present at all; the banking and insurance sectors spring to mind here. Likewise, it is not found in industrial advertising, a very major contributor to the advertising economy. This is ironic, considering that this is one sector where people frequently find themselves in multilingual situations, having to find a *lingua franca* and negotiate cultural difference. I would argue that the lack of linguistic fetish in the market discourse of these various sectors strengthens the argument that this strategy is primarily one of symbolic rather than informational communication. There is no room for symbolism in the 'nuts and bolts' type of advertising found in industrial magazines, and in the worlds of finance and insurance, 'foreignness' would not seem to be an attribute that inspires trust.

Finally, it is interesting to contrast this exploitation of linguistic difference and the highlighting of the multilingual nature of the world in many advertising texts with the downplaying of this very phenomenon in the co-texts surrounding them. In the films, documentaries, even the news programmes and articles within which these texts are embedded, communication between nationals of different cultures functions seamlessly, the only concession to a multilingual reality being an accent, which mildly distorts an otherwise perfect domestic syntax, grammar and vocabulary. In such a context, it can be argued that multilingual advertising texts based on linguistic fetish achieve an even greater effect.

3
The Special Case of English

The title of this chapter rightly throws up an obvious question: Why does English deserve special treatment? For many people in the world, it is simply a foreign, other or second language, and so its contribution to multilingual advertising communication could just as easily be dealt with in a chapter like the previous one that also looks at French, German, Spanish and other languages. The main argument for having a special consideration of the English case lies in the fact that the language has meaning, use and significance, to a large extent, independent of the countries in which it is spoken, and its use in multilingual advertising is, not exclusively but very often, not motivated by a desire to allude to the perceived stereotypical characteristics of countries with which the language is associated. This makes it, on the whole, a very different case to the use of French, German, Spanish and other languages discussed so far in advertising.

It may seem naïve to argue that the use of English in advertising is not generally linked to culture-specific stereotypes. After all, is English not the language of Anglo-American cultural imperialism, disseminated by media discourses such as advertising? It would be absurd to dispute the dominance of English, or to assert in contrast to critics like Alastair Pennycook that its role is 'natural, neutral and beneficial' (1995, p. 9); or, to overlook the part it plays in 'linguistic curtailment' (ibid., p. 14), in other words the squeezing out of other languages from various spheres, in this case the media/market. However, terms like 'linguistic imperialism' (Phillipson, 1992) seem inherently problematic, particularly when they are couched in dichotomous debates about what seem to be good and bad languages – attaching values to languages is, after all, what advertisers do. This is not to say, however, that the issue of English language dominance is not at the centre of this chapter, and that the use of English in advertising globally is not something to be observed with a critical eye.

This chapter addresses the 'special case' of English in multilingual advertising by highlighting three different contexts. The first part of the chapter discusses the various fetishes of international English, using German-language advertising discourse as an example in an attempt to explore these various associations. The Internet is often seen as just one more medium in which English will push out other languages, and so the second part of the chapter looks at linguistic choices made by global brands and corporations on their various international and local websites. Finally, the issue of English in advertising discourses in Central and Eastern Europe is examined using examples from a number of countries.

The various fetishes of international English

Although English is generally used in international advertising for purposes that are not directly linked to country-of-origin competence (cf. Piller, 2001, p. 64), the language may in some cases be employed in order to exploit the cultural competence of Britain or the USA or any other English-speaking country. The associated fetishes are therefore quite complex and the various uses of English in German advertising highlight many of these aspects. One such example was British carmaker *Jaguar*'s use of an English slogan, 'Don't dream it, drive it' in its German advertising in the early 1990s. Why English is used and what it is trying to signify needs to be understood in the context of received perceptions of English culture in Germany. In this particular ad for *Jaguar*, the German title reads '*Die perfekte Balance zwischen Innovation und Tradition*' ('the perfect balance between innovation and tradition'). Interestingly, although this title is in German, it contains the English word 'balance'. The graphic also sets the scene within which the English slogan has symbolic meaning. It represents a stereotype of (upper-class) England, the country house, the beautiful garden – all symbols of tradition. Otherwise, the format of the advertisement is very 'German' – it is overloaded with technical information, and since the communicative value of this information is key, it is given to the targeted advertisees in German, the local language. In this way, the advertiser is attempting to marry two apparently contradictory notions. On the one hand, *Jaguar* does not want to lose out on Britain's cultural competence in the area of tradition; on the other hand, it must appeal to Europe's carmaker on the basis that tradition can provide the basis for innovation and also guarantee quality. The traditionalism (the symbolic aspect) is communicated by the English language, the innovative and technology aspect (the utility message), through the German (Kelly-Holmes, 2000b).

In an advertisement for *Rover*, however, directed at German advertisees, the referential/utility meaning and symbolic value seem to be equally important. The ad, from German news magazine *Der Spiegel* in the early 1990s, not only uses English words but also thematizes the English language – a tactic found in a number of French and German examples in the previous chapter. The English language slogan of the advertisement reads:

> More is often more.

Below a graphic of the model in question, the German text begins with a discussion of this English expression, a play on the more familiar adage 'less is often more', and how this relates to the *Rover 600*. The advertisement finishes with the phrase:

> You're welcome.

This phrase and the opening slogan are given visual prominence in the advertisement through increased font sizes and bold typeface. They are also set apart from the main body of text, the information part. The slogan is, most probably, easily understood by the targeted addressees; however, it is the associations called up by its comprehension that form the basis for its use in the ad, the words themselves being in effect meaningless, because of the context created by the ad. 'You're welcome' alludes to the British/English reputation for good manners; it does not indicate any communication between advertiser and advertisee, and bears no relationship to the rest of the ad's text. Thus, there is a situation where the communicative value of the message also seems to have been fetishized. It is not just the English words, but also the associations of the phrase, the actual words that carry symbolic value (Kelly-Holmes, 2000b), even though they are meaningless, in denotational terms, in the context of car advertising and in the context of the particular advertisement.

The technical display

This country-specific fetish, while still in evidence, was more a product of the 1980s–1990s. The use of English in German advertising today is, it would appear, not motivated by a desire to reproduce associations with English-speaking countries or cultures, but is instead the product of other motivations and language associations. For example, the dominance of English in many technical and scientific domains has resulted in its usage in a number of areas of advertising. This is not to say that its use here is not commercially motivated or driven by English-speaking countries, in particular the USA, but the inclusion of English words in advertisements for such products is, it could be argued, simply evidence of the technical lexicon, the *Fachsprache*, leaking through to mainstream texts such as advertisements. Another interesting point is that although the motivation may not be to allude to the perceived qualities of a particular language, as in the case of linguistic fetish discussed in Chapter 2, there may in fact be a similar, though not explicitly intended effect on perceptions about language by the advertisees who encounter the advertisement. So, for instance, in a German advertisement for *Toyota*, the following headline is used:

> Für die Konkurrenz war es ein schwarzer Freitag. Der Toyota Yaris. Sieger im Crash-Test.
> (It was a black day for the competition. The Toyota Yaris. Crash-Test Champion.)

Toyota, a Japanese brand, would not necessarily want to exploit the cultural competence of the various countries-of-origin associated with the English language. Indeed, the slogan of the advertisement is fully in German: '*Nichts ist unmöglich*', or 'Nothing is impossible'. Thus, the use of the English 'crash test' here seems to be a leakage across the boundaries of the international technical language of automotive design and testing. In this particular text, the term is almost 'domesticated', in that the correct capitalization is used to denote that it is a noun in German and it is also embedded in the correct case (dative). It could therefore be argued that it appears simply as a *technical* word rather than an *English* word in the text. However, its appearance in the advertisement may serve to enhance notions about English, about its suitability for technology and about certain qualities that the language may have, which in turn ensures the success of other advertisements using this particular term and other English technical terms, thus creating an international technical fetish for the language.

The cosmopolitan/modern fetish

The second case is where the international English fetish is used to create a cosmopolitan and modern association, as in the following examples:

METRO Group
The Spirit of Commerce

Metro is one of Germany's main retail groups. The advertisement appeared in German news magazine, *Der Spiegel*, and, in common with many such examples, it is the slogan or punch line that is in English, while the rest of the advertisement, giving details about *Metro*'s holdings and activities, is in German. Again, this points to the symbolic use of English in such advertisements: the informative part of the advertisement is generally in German; where English words do occur in this part of the text, they are part of the accepted '*Fachsprache*' or professional dialect of the particular business domain; however, in this particular case, it is in the visual part of the advertisement that English words appear, either as part of or beside the logo or brand name. This makes the usage more similar to the German and French fetishes discussed in previous chapters, where the foreign language is more part of the visual texture of the advertisement than the body of text (as in the example of the technical language). This use of English in the construction of an international image is reinforced by the *Metro* website – the address being given on the advertisement – which contains headings such as 'Meeting Metro' and 'Investor Relations'. Again, these should be seen as more graphic in nature than textual. When the individual clicks on these titles, the related text part then appears, and this is in German. In these linked information texts, English words only appear when they are part of the accepted and conventionalized language (or '*Fachsprache*') of that domain.

English-language slogans are a popular strategy adopted by German brands that want to appear international. When *British Airways* attempted to relaunch its image as a global airline rather than a British one, it chose a Maori song (cf. Bell, 1999). In the *British Airways* context, then, it would seem that the language of an indigenous people on the other side of the globe best conveyed an internationalist/cosmopolitan fetish. By not choosing English, *British Airways* was conveying an openness to the rest of the world. However, for many companies and brands that are 'native' to countries in the non-English-speaking world, it is possible to use English for just this effect, whereas for *British Airways* to use the language would have smacked of colonialism and cultural imperialism. For German national carrier *Lufthansa*, this image is attempted through the use of English, as the following slogan in an otherwise German advertisement in *Der Spiegel* illustrates:

There's no better way to fly.
Lufthansa

This 'internationalist' approach is mirrored in *Lufthansa*'s dot.com website, the address of which is given in the ad. The website opens on an English language page, even though the default 'domicile' to be entered in order to obtain details of flights and prices is Germany, and the website name is *Lufthansa Deutschland*. In order to get a German version, customers need to press on the 'German' option, given in English rather than '*Deutsch*'.

The neutrality association

In an advertisement for the Swiss watch brand, *Chopard*, also in *Der Spiegel*, the following slogan is used:

L.U.C. PRO ONE – A look that spells adventure

The German language is a *lingua franca* between the country-of-origin, Switzerland, and the target country, Germany, and so is a resource available to advertisers. Despite this, the slogan, 'A look that spells adventure', is in English. The technical details of the watch are, however, given in German, this type of information not being trusted to English, while the company brand, *Chopard Manufacture*, is French. Interestingly, the *Chopard* website offers a number of linguistic options: English, French, German and Japanese. However, on the German-language site, English headings such as 'Spirit' (a section describing among other things the history of the company) and 'Happy News' (the brand's magazine), 'Events', 'VIPs' and 'Filmclips' are used, as well as standard English-language Internet items such as 'Home', 'Sitemap', 'website' and so on. Another interesting phrase observed on the website was the following linguistic hybrid sentence:

Die brand neue L.U.C. Quattro Tourbillon.

The English adjectival qualifier 'brand' is integrated into the German construction to recreate the English 'brand new'; '*Quattro*' represents

Italian; while '*Tourbillon*' appears French. As Piller (2001) points out, advertising:

> in its multilingual practices ... shows an avant-garde like readiness to embrace postnational discourses of unsettled, hybrid identities as expressed through the use of different linguistic codes. (p. 182)

Thus, in a situation where a brand belongs to a multilingual culture, and where there is therefore no immediately accessible linguistic fetish, international English can be used (Cheshire and Moser, 1994), alongside multilingually constructed sentences. As Cheshire and Moser (1994) have also pointed out, in linguistically contested commercial situations, as in the Swiss case, English has come to acquire something of a neutral, unifying association, and its use overcomes the problem of having to choose one group's language over that of another when attempting to represent national cultural competence.

English as cool

Another English linguistic fetish utilized in multilingual/multi-voiced German ads is that of 'coolness', which is again linked to the international/cosmopolitan fetish discussed above, but also to associations with UK and USAmerican influenced popular culture. This fetish is found in an advertisement for *Volkswagen*:

> Hello Sunshine.
> Das New Beetle Cabriolet.

To put this text in its sociolinguistic context: *Volkswagen* is a German brand, it is known internationally as a German brand, and, in fact, it is probably one of the most prototypically German brands; the advertisement appeared in a German magazine, *Der Spiegel* (2003); and the target market in this context is German speakers. Thus, it would be assumed that the advertiser and advertisees comprise a community of communication and there is, therefore, no communicative or referential reason why the advertisement should not be entirely in German, and conversely no reason why any English should be used in the advertisement. The use of English here seems to target a self-selecting group, something indicated by the product itself. The *Cabriolet* is a 'trendy' car designed for 'trendy' people, and, in fact, this image/identity seems best constructed and conveyed through English, and for this ideal advertisee,

English is in this context fetishized with this quality. Part of this trendiness is the ability to use English at more than a basic level, something much of the population of Germany is already able to do.[1] Instead, this target group can understand linguistic puns and wordplays in the language. For example, the first line of the text, 'Hello Sunshine', has a number of possible meanings: in the graphic the sun is just breaking through the clouds in the aftermath of rain; the particular *Beetle Cabriolet* featured in the graphic is sunshine yellow; and the phrase alludes to knowledge of British English varieties in which 'sunshine' is a term of endearment. The use of 'new', integrated into the German phrase, is also intended in a similar vein.

In her study of multilingual practice in German advertising, Piller (2001) concluded that English is used in 'the most authoritative parts of the advertisements', and that the language is used in advertising discourse by 'people characterized as having one of the most desirable model identities available in that discourse' (p. 182). As a result, 'German–English bilingualism' is, in her opinion, 'vested with a highly valued form of linguistic capital' (p. 182). Her findings point to an important aspect of use of English in German advertising, as well as in advertising in other Western European countries: on the one hand, there may be more comprehension of the particular vocabulary items used because of the widespread teaching of English as a foreign language across the continent; however, this does not mean that its use is driven primarily by the desire to convey facts and information – in general this is still left to the local language. Although there is understanding, the English language still functions as a kind of fetish, at the level of connotation rather than denotation, creating identities – as in the case of the *Beetle* advertisement – for the advertiser, advertisee and the commodity. The only localizing German reference in the advertisement at all, apart from the definite article '*das*', is the web address: www. volkswagen.de. On the website itself there are further examples of the 'trendy' English fetish and Euro-linguistic hybrids (as was the case with *Chopard*), such as:

Der New Beetle Arte.

The difference in the marketing approaches and brand identities is underlined by the fact that the new *Volkswagen Golf* model, '*das Original*', is simply

Das neue Golf.

Here the form of phrase is the same, 'the new X model', but the difference of one small adjective – the German '*neu*' rather than the English 'new' – constructs an entirely different image for the car and the advertisee. Furthermore, the paralanguage of this phrase also supports the original, traditional image. The linguistically incongruous capitalized adjective (New), which makes the previous phrases look like linguistic hybrids, is dropped in favour of the normal, non-capitalized adjective. This looks and feels like a 'normal' German sentence, and this in turn creates a more traditional image for the Golf.

The international *lingua franca* fetish

In the cases of *VW*, *Lufthansa* and *Metro*, German brands seem to be attempting to invoke the various associations of English to construct images and identities for their products. However, this is rather different to the majority of brand names and slogans that appear in English in German advertising texts, simply as a result of the fact that the particular brand has adopted a global or international strategy or message and this, by default, is in English. For example, in an advertisement for *Honda* (from German news magazine, *Der Spiegel*), the brand name and slogan 'The Power of Dreams' appear in the top right-hand corner above the graphic. However, this is the only international element in the advertisement. *Honda* is recognized as a Japanese brand, although it has manufacturing facilities all over the world, and the *Accord* among other models is manufactured in the USA. Apart from the international slogan, the advertiser goes to great pains to localize the text for a German audience. For example, the car in the graphic has a German registration plate, and the rest of the text is in German, with a German telephone number and website given. The final punchline of the advertisement is also revealing:

> Der neue Honda Accord Tourer. Du hast freie Hand.
> (The new Honda Accord Tourer. You have a free hand.)

The brand and model name are 'domesticated' into the noun phrase. The *Tourer* is given a gender and the correct agreement of the German adjective '*neu*' means that the sentence looks more German, more local, more normal, than the *VW* examples discussed previously. The advertising slogan also makes use of a wordplay through the German phrase '*freie Hand haben*' (having a free hand), which means being free to choose, as well as literally having a hand free because of the design of the model. The fact that the advertiser attempts highly culture-specific tactics such as puns and word-plays shows a desire to be seen in a local context, rather than appealing to advertisees through the construction of a foreign or exotic identity for them or the product. The use of the familiar you ('*Du*') also displays local knowledge used to target the local market, probably a segment of younger and less formal individuals. However, this is interesting too, since in the informative section of the text, where details of how to find dealers and special offers are given, the following sentence is found:

> Ab 5. April bei Ihrem Honda Automobilhändler.
> (At your Honda dealer from 5. April.)

In this part of the text, the customer is addressed using the formal 'your' or '*Ihr*' in German. This points, it can be argued, to a symbolic use of the domestic language as well. The formal 'you' is reserved for what could be termed purely 'communicative' purposes; while the informal 'you' is used for unimportant – in terms of informative content – parts: in other words, for symbol and decoration. In this particular case, therefore, the advertisement is highly localized, although it utilizes a global brand and global English-language slogan.

A similar strategy is adopted by Swedish car manufacturer *Volvo*. In an advertisement in the same edition of *Der Spiegel*, against a graphic of the particular model, the following German slogan is found:

> INTELLIGENZ KANN MAN TESTEN. (YOU CAN TEST INTELLIGENCE.)
> ODER FAHREN. (OR YOU CAN DRIVE IT.)
> DER VOLVO V70 DIESEL JETZT FUER 220,- EURO/MONAT. (THE NEW VOLVO V70 DIESEL NOW FOR 220- EURO/MONTH.)

This is followed by a German text, giving the technical and detailed information, a localized German number plate, with K for the German city of Cologne. The English brand slogan is found in the top right-hand corner:

> Volvo
> for life

It seems very clear that these two English words in fact belong to the graphic of the advertisement, not only because of where they are placed – far apart from the textual body – but also because of their function, that stands in stark contrast to the functions of the German text in the rest of the advertisement. The two-word phrase neither gives information, as does the German text at the bottom of the advertisement, nor does it attract attention and arouse interest – as does the German headline/slogan. It is purely there as an integral part of the brand logo. It is, like the brand name, simply a reassuring presence, a mark of authenticity and credibility. It does not need to persuade, it simply needs to be present. What is interesting, however, is that so many corporations and brands choose to give this reassurance, this sign of credibility, the symbol that they are a major player and that their brand needs no explanation, through the medium of the English language.

An interesting use of English is found in an advertisement in *Der Spiegel* for the *Maserati Coupé* car. The ad contains a small amount of text of a technical nature in German, with some English domain-specific words used. The text is arranged around two photos of the *coupé*: one an interior, the other an exterior, which, significantly, has an Italian number plate. In fact, it is the registration for Modena, the Italian city where *Maserati* is based. The particular model is described as: '*Der Grand Tourismo*', and although the Italian name (*Tourismo*) is integrated into the German noun phrase through the addition of the masculine definite article '*der*', the sentence seems to be another Euro-linguistic hybrid with the English/French adjective 'grand' standing unagreed in the middle of the sentence, as if it were a noun. The final punchline of the advertisement at the very bottom of the page in red letters is:

SPORTSCARS HAVE ITALIAN NAMES.

This slogan creates a link between the Italian 'hints' in the text: the Italian family brand name, the Italian number plates and the Italian model name. In this final slogan, the advertisement also thematizes language and makes explicit something that is usually the preserve of behind the scenes marketing conversations, namely the common-sense assumptions about the interrelationship between products, countries and languages, something that is usually embedded in texts rather than being made the overt theme. It is also interesting that this statement is made in English.

The purity fetish

With all of these examples, it is easy to form the impression that the language of German advertising is a type of German–English hybrid. However, despite the wealth of English lexical items in much German advertising and marketing discourse, it is equally interesting to observe and comment upon the many advertisements that do not use English words. Significantly, a large number of them come from the domestic food sector. So, for example, in the advertising of German food brand, *Maggi*, part of Swiss multinational *Nestlé*, the following English-free text is found:

> Jetzt: Maggi Heisser Becher
> Etwas Heisses in Sekunden zubereitet. MAGGI Heisser Becher – siebenmal anders, siebenmal lecker: Tomate, Champignon, Spargel, Rindfleisch, Lauch – alle mit Crutons – und Huhn mit Nudeln sowie Kartoffelcreme mit Roestzwiebeln.
>
> (Now: Maggi Hot Cup
> Something hot ready in seconds. MAGGI hot cup – seven times different; seven times more tasty: tomato, mushroom, asparagus, beef, chive – all with croutons – and chicken with noodles, as well as crème of potato with roast onions.)

This lack of English may be coincidental, or it may perhaps have something, consciously or subconsciously, to do with the fact that *Maggi* is seen as a very German brand. According to *Nestlé*, the *Maggi* brand is its most successful in Germany, and the corporation claims that *Maggi* products are found in the cupboards of 88 per cent of German households. Therefore, it could be argued the use of English in this advertisement would contradict the image constructed for the product as wholly German.

In the previous chapter it was observed that banking, insurance and financial services in general comprise one sector in which there is very little use of French, German or other foreign words. One reason proposed for this was the fact that such advertising needs to construct a relationship of trust with the consumer, and this is best done through the domestic or local language. Interestingly, this finding also seems to hold true for the German advertising context. For example, the following advertisement for the *BKK* (the *Bundesverband der Betriebskrankenkassen*; the federal association of social health insurance schemes) from *Der Spiegel* has no English lexical items on display:

> Eine gute Krankenkasse nimmt Sie so, wie Sie sind. Ohne Wenn und Aber. Sie arbeitet effizient und bietet jedem genau die Leistungen, die zu seinem Leben passen.

(A good social health insurance scheme takes you as you are. No ifs and buts. It works efficiently and offers everyone the exact services that are suited to their lives.)

The company's slogan, in bold letters against a black and white photograph of a mother pushing a daughter in a wheelchair, reads as follows:

Wir sind hier.
(We are here.)

The use of a more standard form of German here, free of the trendy international associations that English words bring, seems to suit the content of the advertisement and the image of the advertiser: the formal you (*'Sie'*); the simple slogan (*'Wir sind hier'*; 'We are here'); the old-fashioned sentiments expressed in the advertisement, for example, that a company should take you as you are; and, finally, the appeal to traditional German values such as efficiency. The use of English here would completely contradict this image: it would then be about trying to construct the advertisee as something they are not, rather than 'taking them as they are'.

Websites and English

As many commentators have pointed out, the web is a major focus for many advertisers because of the possibilities it offers in comparison to other media, for example the fact that advertisements can be viewed in different countries, at different times, in different contexts, and in an economically efficient way (cf. Rotherburg, 1998, cited in Myers, 1999). Greg Myers lists the many different ways in which advertisers approach websites, and what they hope to achieve through using them. For example, the website may be an electronic catalogue that enables direct sales; or it may enhance the brand of the particular product; it may be used simply as a poster, similar to an outdoor billboard; it may be primarily there to provide information about local outlets and to support the activities of these; or it may be used to facilitate a type of club, to which users of the product 'belong' (cf. Myers, 1999, pp. 138–40). However, despite its possibilities, the individual who wishes to buy a car is still more likely to start by visiting his/her local garage rather than the dot.com website of a particular brand.

Another issue is the way in which individuals use the web. Most 'respectable' brands do not engage in unsolicited email or pop-up advertising. Therefore, unlike television or magazines, where viewing the advertisements is simply part of the experience of the medium as a whole, with the web the advertisee has to come to the advertiser, s/he has to visit their site. It therefore seems unlikely that web-based advertising has the same functions as more traditional forms, or that it is likely on its own to persuade someone through a commercial message. However, if the hypothetical car-buying individual, thinking over the various models viewed at the local garage, then decides to get additional information from the Internet, and one of the particular brands s/he is interested in does not have a website, then it can be argued that this will somehow undermine the credibility of that brand. This example points, I would propose, to what is probably the most important function of many websites that are not based on the direct sales model, namely the respectability factor. To be a credible brand, company, service, organization and so on, today, is to have a website. This also leads to another interesting conclusion. If websites, for many global brands, are really a place where they stake their claim to a global presence, then these sites take on the nature of 'mission statements' rather than persuasive advertising. Such sites offer the company or brand concerned the opportunity to say what they are, what they stand for, either directly or implicitly. Part of this message, this statement of identity, is, of course, language, and the language choices of brands, corporations and so on may either complement or contradict the branded image. More than this, however, these choices can also either challenge or reinforce the common-sense assumptions about languages and 'linguistic capital', in Bourdieu's terms (1991), about which languages and speakers are taken seriously by the market and which are not.

A further interesting dimension to the Internet is that its very nature means that the boundaries between commercially driven market discourses and other types of texts are being further eroded. The broadcaster has to decide, based on scheduling demands, or is dictated to by licensing and legislative curtailments about when and how to schedule advertisements. Thus there is a clear differentiation between advertising texts and content texts (although this is weaker on some channels, as will be seen in Chapter 5), and this is also true for print media. Advertisements look different and they appear in different places. However, on the Internet, these distinctions are broken down. A search using a particular term will throw up both commercial and non-commercial sites and uses, and these sites, when viewed together, do not look hugely different in format to each other. Equally, from the advertiser's point of view, when airtime or copy space is paid for, the advertiser is ensuring that his/her product or brand is viewed at the optimum time, in the optimum way, by the ideal advertisees. On the Internet, however, all such control is lost. By entering the brand name in a search engine, the Internet user – and potential advertisee – will not only be directed to the brand's website, but also to a whole host of conflicting and contradictory texts such as competitors' websites, critiques of the brand in question, news stories in which the brand features, and so forth. The multi-voiced, multi-texted chaos of the Internet removes the advertiser's control over how the advertisement is seen and used. For instance, a search on the *Google* search engine using the term 'mcdonalds' lists the corporate website of *McDonald's* first, but the McSpotlight website, which is a campaigning forum against the *McDonald's* brand, is listed second.

Another difference between web-based advertising and advertising based on more traditional media is that the former offers the possibility for more 'real', person-to-person-type communication. One consequence of technological innovation, it has been argued, may be a more dialogic form of communication (Tuominen, 2002). The monologism of the traditional media is a relatively new phenomenon, linked with the origins of print capitalism (cf. Anderson, 1983; Billig, 1995). Sampson (1993) points out that far from being a self-evident fact – the norm or default it is often presented as being – monologism was born at the turn of the nineteenth century when printing and publishing began to be industrialized and the voice of the speaker became so overwhelmingly dominant as to drown out any response. Indeed, the nature of broadcasting from its earliest years has not facilitated feedback or interaction. The only 'dialogue' possible occurred through readers' letters or complaints to independent authorities or, the ultimate feedback, when people turned off or switched the channel. These are not, however, analogous in any way to a normal conversation where feedback is given instantly in the form of dialogue. However, the Internet is one medium that makes it very difficult to communicate in a monologic way, because of the manner in which information is presented to the user and the ability to set up, relatively easily and inexpensively, one's own counterpart website (as in the case of McSpotlight). On websites, unlike feedback programmes on television or radio which were traditionally reserved for non-peak viewing time, the feedback section is generally a heading on the site, co-equal with all other headings; furthermore, discussion groups and noticeboards make it possible to read all or most messages uncensored. This is something which the founder of the World Wide Web, Tim Berners-Lee (1999) actually wanted, namely the provision of a space within which people could interact electronically and dialogically in order to generate knowledge and ideas. Thus, new technologies do seem to be changing the way in which individuals relate to media, but how this occurs through language(s) and what impact this will have on language(s) remains, to a large extent, to be seen. It is, however, important to remember that not all communication on the Internet is intended to occur dialogically. As Androutsopoulos (2004) points out, home pages are basically constituted as monologic, and this, it could be argued, is particularly true of corporate ones. Such dot.com pages set down, as argued earlier, the company or brand's identity, how it wishes to present itself to the potential consumer. Thus, it is also interesting to see how language is used in this context, and what possible effects this has on the status of particular languages, notions about multilingualism and the visibility of multilingualism on the Internet.

Practising language policy

A survey of the dot.com as well as different country- or region-specific websites of international brands and companies leads to the inevitable conclusion that these brands and companies are practising language policies and politics, however implicit this process may be. *Volvo* is an interesting case here. Although, of course, a Swedish brand, it has never really marketed this aspect of its product or exploited a Swedish linguistic fetish – in the way that, for instance, *Ikea* has (see Chapter 2) – in the promotion of its cars. This non-activation of a Swedish linguistic fetish is borne out by *Volvo*'s website language policy, with the language of the country-of-origin (Swedish) dropped in favour of English as international *lingua franca* on the dot.com website. The various *Volvo* country websites then have varying degrees of English. For example, the Mexican and Peruvian websites are almost totally in Spanish, with English appearing only in the titles of corporate campaigns such as 'Volvo Ocean Race' and the word 'showroom' which are given as links. The equivalent Brazilian site, however, has much more English, with fewer links in Portuguese. It is also interesting to see how the corporation deals with different alphabetical and orthographical systems, as exemplified in the different approaches to the corporation's Chinese and Japanese websites. For instance, apart from the graphic use of English in the 'for life' slogan, there are no other English words on the corporation's Chinese website, and the same applies to the Greek website; this is in contrast to the Japanese one in which English links, slogans and terms abound. For example, 'Volvo sporty life campaign',

'Care by Volvo', 'Welcome to Volvo cars Japan', 'New Series', and so on. However, it would be wrong to think of this as a bilingual website, since a Japanese explanation/equivalent is given for all of these terms, and once the user clicks on the link in question, they are dealing almost exclusively with Japanese. This ties in very much with Haarmann's (1989) findings about the symbolic use of English in Japanese advertising. The websites then seem to reflect the respective situation of symbolic English in the particular country, or, perhaps more accurately, the corporation's perception of this.

Corporate language policies and politics are, however, not just about the extent to which there is lexical decorating with foreign items, but about the actual language of the website itself in multilingual contexts. Invariably, the particular choices made and policies practised seem to reinforce the role and symbolic importance of English as an Internet language. For example, the South African and Hong Kong websites of the corporation are wholly in English, with no attempt to use the other main or dominant written languages in these contexts, for example Afrikaans and Chinese respectively. These choices that impose English as an international Internet language or language of compromise in multilingual marketing situations globally (for example the South African and Hong Kong websites of *Volvo*) are in stark contrast with the language-policy decisions apparent in relation to the brand's European sites. The Swiss site, for instance, is strictly multilingual in German, French and Italian (although of course the fourth official Swiss language, Romansch, is minoritized and excluded in this context). Similarly, the Belgian site is very careful in its equal use of French and Dutch, with only tokenistic use of English in brand slogans for example, in the case of both language websites. Reviewing these different websites, then, it seems impossible not to get the impression that the corporation sees certain languages as having linguistic capital and speakers of certain languages as 'worthy' advertisees, while others are deemed to be the opposite.

Furthermore, the degree of accommodation and localization also seems to be determined by these factors. For example, the different country websites vary in the degree of English used, depending on a number of factors, not all of them to do with knowledge of and competence in English on the part of the target culture. For instance, knowledge of English as a second language is fairly widespread in Western Europe; however, every different country in Western Europe gets its own fully localized website with minimal English. By making language policy choices on its websites, the corporation also gives the appearance of following a particular brand of geo-politics: the Israeli website, for instance, is entirely in Hebrew, with only tokenistic uses of English ('for life') and no Arabic link at all, despite the language's official status in that country. The Canadian site, when first called up is entirely in English, but does have a '*Français*' link, reflecting perhaps the corporation's desire not to upset a linguistic minority that is seen to have linguistic capital. This impression is further enhanced by the fact that on the Quebec website, for the first time, the brand slogan is reproduced not in English, but in French ('*pour la vie*').

Another telling example is the Canadian website of *McDonald*'s. The website is scrupulously bilingual: the viewer is presented with two equal choices, English on the left of the *McDonald's* logo, *Français* on the right – not one on top of the other, which might imply some kind of superiority. The respective versions contain the same information and offers. What is particularly fascinating, however, is the message that appears when the individual viewing the English version of the site wants to leave the Canadian site to go back to *McDonald*'s corporate pages. Upon clicking the appropriate button, what could only be described as a warning text pops up on the screen telling the viewer that they are 'about to leave the *McDonald*'s Canada website for the *McDonald*'s Worldwide Country Sites page', and that they should note that 'content on the worldwide site is not fully bilingual'. This seems worthy of comment on a number of levels. First of all, and perhaps most bizarrely, the message is in English and only appears when the viewer is leaving the English language version of the website, not the French one. This begs the question of why such a person should need this information. Secondly, the page listing the various country websites is *entirely* in English, regardless of the country being described. There are a number of links to particular countries, most of which are in the local language with varying degrees of English content. Thus, the suggestion implied by the comment 'not fully bilingual', that there is somehow a degree of bilingual content present, seems unnecessary. Thirdly, if *McDonald*'s global corporate pages were to be bilingual, what should the second language be – taking for granted that the first language is English? Finally, and perhaps most significant of all, there is the rather inexplicable fact that this 'warning' does not appear on any of the links back from the country-specific pages (in German, French, Turkish, Spanish and others) to the corporate pages. All of these factors combined with the almost apologetic tone of the message, which is normally reserved for public service organizations, give the impression that *McDonald*'s wants to recognize and be seen to recognize and respect the linguistic rights of this particular group of consumers, French Canadians. The question is: Why should this be so? Why is this particular group of consumers more worthy of this treatment? Why, if McDonald's is so interested in respecting linguistic diversity is there no Spanish contained on the US website? The answer seems to be that the corporation is more concerned with being seen to follow official language policy guidelines than respecting linguistic diversity.

Volkswagen, which was described earlier as a brand that is not only German, but recognizably so, appears to adopt a similar strategy to *Volvo* in its various country/language-specific websites. For example, the Russian website is entirely in Russian, the only English to feature being in the product names, and no German words feature at all. The Israeli site is also entirely in Hebrew, apart from the international-English-type product names such as *Beetle*. What is interesting, however, is to see the use of language in the actual animated clips for each product, made available on the Israeli website. The one for the *Polo* model, for example, finishes up with the car being parked outside what is ostensibly a hotel. The model name, *Polo*, appears in the top right-hand corner, a Hebrew translation beside (not underneath) it. The only other words in the picture are in English, and they are part of the illustration of the scene, rather than part of any information contained in it: 'Five stars hotel', 'Beach café' and an international 'stop' sign. The advertisement for the *Beetle*, a problematic marketing concept in this context since the *Beetle* was designed as the 'people's car' by a regime that was intent on annihilating the Jewish people, concentrates in its animation on 1970s hippie images, with English words such as '*Beetle* classic' and 'new *Beetle*' accompanying them. This presentation of *Volkswagen* as an international, a-national brand seems particularly targeted to the Israeli market and is in contrast to the Japanese site, where the German origin of the product and the German language are not hidden. On the Japanese site, in contrast, the greeting 'Welcome to *Volkswagen*' alternates in the top right-hand corner of the site between English, Japanese and German. This website has by far the most English of any of the other international sites, far more than any European counterpart, despite the very high levels of competence in English in many European countries. It is not just the headings and announcements that are in English ('Accessories', 'Simulation', 'Webradio for your P.C.'), but also all links ('My VW', 'News', 'Cars', 'Dealers', 'E-Shop') and basic housekeeping/legal items ('Company', 'Site map', 'Contact', 'Legal Aspects', 'Help'). When the cursor is moved onto these headings and links Japanese characters do appear; however, the first impression on looking at the website is that the site may perhaps be that of a Japanese product aimed at an English-speaking market, so minimal and tokenistic is the presence of Japanese characters on the home page.

Taking sides

The examples of the *Volvo* and *Volkswagen* Israeli websites reflect very definite decisions on the part of these two global brands with regard to language policies and politics. The absence of Arabic from the website seems to disregard the fact that Arabic is the second official language of that country, and to take sides with a particular linguistic community, namely Hebrew speakers, or, perhaps more accurately, with the Israeli State. Furthermore, it sends a message about who is being targeted, and that group can be self-selected on the basis of being able and willing to use Hebrew. So, it is not just about who is being targeted, but also about maintaining the idea that Hebrew and English are the languages of serious commerce (cf. Shohany, 2003). To put Arabic words on the website would have the effect of 'taking sides', and indicating a political stance through language choice, whereas this type of choice, itself equally political, is not seen as offensive.

It is worth contrasting this approach with that of *Toyota's* site for North America (www.toyota.com). It states on the website that this is the website of Toyota Motor Sales USA Inc, and that the 'information relates only to US vehicles'. The website is otherwise in English; however, one of the main headers is '*en español*', linking to a Spanish version. This strategy is also followed by *Nissan* on its dot.com website. By clicking on '*en español*', the viewer is taken to a completely Spanish version of the site. If any further links are not available in Spanish, '*en Inglés*' is included to inform consumers of this. Here then is a situation where *Toyota* and *Nissan* are not adhering to any official language policy that recognizes the largest linguistic minority in the USA, Spanish speakers. Instead, they are either reacting to everyday bilingualism and/or making a statement about a commitment to diversity – both of which reflect interesting decisions about how the company wants to be viewed by its consumers. Although the situation is not as politically difficult as the Israeli one, the 'English-only' debate in the USA is a hotly contested one (cf. Crawford, 2000, and Dicker, 2003) and there is no reason why companies should go out of their way to make statements about language. *Toyota* does not seem to be coming down on the 'official' side, and, unlike *Volvo* and *Volkswagen*, it does not seem upset at the prospect of annoying the linguistic majority by reminding them of the everyday bilingualism on their streets. Finally, these two Spanish words on the website indicate that the company is prepared to do business with people in their language, that they do not have to come to the majority language to be credible customers, something *Volvo* and *Volkswagen* would appear to be demanding of their Arab customers in Israel.

It is, however, important to note that even the most linguistically aware brands and companies only go so far in accommodating to linguistic minorities, usually the largest ones. The US-based car-rental group, *Hertz*, boasts on its 'History' page, that one of its 'firsts' was the launch of its multilingual website in 1999. Visitors to the dot.com site, which is in English, can choose a language option from a pull-down menu. If Spanish is chosen, the individual is asked where s/he lives, and there is an option to choose the USA, which leads to information geared towards a USAmerican market. This is one concession to USAmerican everyday multilingualism. However, if Korean or Portuguese are chosen, both of which are spoken by immigrants in the USA, the individual is immediately directed to the site of that particular country. In fact, if, for instance, an individual chooses Japanese as the language, but states that they live in the USA, the following message appears, which, in effect, tells them that their situation is not possible:

> The dialect you selected is currently not available. We believe our standard Japanese website would be best suited to your needs.
>
> (www.hertz.com)

Is English taking over?

It has been widely posited that the Internet will only help to consolidate the position of English as global *lingua franca* (cf. Crystal, 2001; Baron, 2000). However, looking at a sample of *Toyota's* country-specific websites adds some weight to the counter-argument, namely that English is not taking over corporate websites. For instance, on the French website English is noticeably absent; the only English there is, apart from some of the product names ('land cruiser', 'station wagon'), is 'showroom' which features as a link. Looking at a country that is, in theory at least, more open at an official level to English than France, such as Germany, there are certainly more English vocabulary items, 'Goodies', 'Newsletters', 'Sitemap', 'car check', 'Financial services', 'Fleet and business' and of course product names, but on a home page of approximately 140 words (apart from the product names, some of which are English, most of which are not), there are only 10 words in English, as opposed to 3 on the French site. Interestingly, there is even less multilingualism on *Toyota's* websites for much 'smaller' language communities. For example, on the Icelandic one, the site is totally localized in Icelandic, and the only English that appears is in the product names.

In the context of all of this linguistic diversity, however, the corporate image itself is presented as international and this is achieved through English. It is, for example, quite difficult to reach the Japanese language site of *Toyota*, and no attempt is made to use Japanese in a tokenistic or decorative way on the corporate English-language dot.com. website. Here, the impression is certainly given that English is the language of the company, Japanese being purely of local interest. Furthermore, it is interesting to contrast the international multilingualism evidenced by the sites discussed above, where the linguistic sensibilities of relatively small groups of speakers are catered for, with *Toyota's* Chinese site. The impression given by the home page is that English is the major language of the site, and the most visually attractive words are in English. For instance, a large moving graphic greets the visitor with 'Welcome to *Toyota*'. English language links jump out at the viewer ('AsianXtour', 'click'), and although there are some equivalents for these words given in Chinese characters, this is not always the case. In the top left-hand corner, the viewer sees the English title 'TOYOTA IN CHINA'. Roman characters and English words dominate the space on the home page visually. A link entitled in English, with no Chinese equivalent, 'Worldwide' leads the visitor to the English-language corporate site in Japan, although, as noted above, there is no sense of being in a Japanese company. How then to explain this preponderance of English on the website of a major language, the biggest first language in the world, with the conspicuous lack of English on the websites of much smaller languages, for example, Icelandic? One theory could perhaps be that the linguistic fetish phenomenon has, to a certain extent, run its course, or at least become more embedded and less obvious in the commercial texts oriented towards consumers in more developed consumer societies, whereas it still has mileage in developing consumer societies such as China. Another explanation might be that in the local inter-cultural context, it may perhaps be more acceptable for *Toyota* to present itself as international rather than as explicitly Japanese in China, and the English language helps the brand to achieve this.

The juxtapositions that the Internet as medium make possible can also subvert notions about languages. The Polish *Toyota* site gives an interesting, if perhaps possibly unintentional impression about English. The site, in common with the other local versions, is entirely in Polish, and the only English language words to appear are the product names and the international term 'club'. However, English is used in the two links listed on the home page, toyotakids.pl and toyotajuniors.pl, which are aimed at a younger generation, and offer games, downloads, competitions and so on. It is significant that this approach to the younger generation is made using English, albeit only in the headings. The most interesting effect, however, is when the reader clicks on the link 'English summary'. Here there is a rather cursory summary of information needed by non-Polish speakers. The text appears to have been written by an ESL speaker, and the reader is given a list of addresses to contact in case non-Polish speakers have questions or need assistance. The effect is to imagine the English-only speaker as a kind of pathetic lost soul in a sea of Polish speakers in need of emergency help. It is only an impression, but it is an unfamiliar one in which Polish is presented as 'stronger' than English.

The universalist approach

Corporate 'language policies', as stated earlier, can either enhance or detract from the brand image. A good example here is the website of *Benetton* (www.benetton.com). The website is fully in English, and even if the .it suffix is entered for the Italian site – Italy being the 'home' of the *Benetton* brand – the viewer is automatically connected to the dot.com website. This also happens when a number of other country-specific suffixes are used, such as .de for Germany and .fr for France – countries with 'important' languages that are used to having specific websites. This policy of directing consumers to one global website in English ties in with Benetton's 'one world' philosophy summed up in the 'United Colours of Benetton' slogan. In this context, the English language becomes a signifier of the 'commercial internationalism' or even 'commercial cosmopolitanism' that has become *Benetton's* trademark. The language choice complements and extends other statements on the website, for example, the foregrounding of *Benetton's* international status:

> Today the Benetton Group is present in 120 countries around the world;
> A global brand, and one of the best known in the world, United Colours of Benetton has an international style;
> … a gipsy, multi-ethnic look. (www.benetton.com)

Later the viewer is told that *Benetton* is 'a group with a strong Italian character whose style, design expertise and passion are clearly seen' (www.benetton.com). These are stereotypical qualities to collocate with

'Italian', particularly passion, and they sum up perhaps Italy's image as a country of origin (cf. Chapter 2). This is reinforced to a certain extent by *Benetton's* tokenistic use of Italian in its branding, for example, in the use of the Italian '*Mama*' for its maternity collection and '*Uomo*' for its men's wear. However, this limited 'display' (Eastman and Stein, 1993) never threatens to overshadow the international English that is the medium for the brand's commercial cosmopolitanism. This 'international English' image is further enhanced by the type of language chosen on the website, which is free of normal corporate jargon. For example, instead of standardized Internet terms, such as 'corporate history' and so on, the options are 'Who we are', 'What we make', 'What we say'.

Another aspect to this commercial internationalism is a downplaying of the issue of language, something that has been a feature of *Benetton's* often controversial billboard advertising, in which image is king. So, for example, the following statement is found on the website in relation to the '*Colors*' magazine published by *Benetton*:

> Pictures are, above all else, Colors's expressive medium: a method that is universal and reaches the greatest number of people with a strong, immediate impact. Using this visual language, Colors themes alternate between serious, challenging topics, such as war, ecological issues, the fight against AIDS, and the frankly frivolous such as shopping, fashion and toys, but each is seen from an unconventional, irreverent perspective.   (www.benetton.com)

One issue of the *Benetton* '*Colors*' magazine contained no words at all. The intention was to provide '... a pictorial conversation', a series of 'visual essays' that would enable the 'reader' to view a range of topics from all possible points of view (www.benetton.com). Here is evidence of the problematizing of language: language forces the individual reader or writer to take a particular point of view, words are partisan, as are linguistic choices, and without them, images, it seems, are not.

This problematizing of language is one feature of the 'universalist' approach, and it is a fairly logical one. After all, if a corporation has not only recognized and decided to respect the linguistic diversity of the world, to the extent that it becomes part of the brand identity, where does it go from there? The task of always speaking to everyone in his/her own language without any compromise is an impossible one. So, it is necessary to create a 'universal language' that can transcend all of these problems. And, it also becomes necessary, however subtle the approach, to make language part of the problem, yet another barrier to human coexistence, like religion. In such a context, then, the use of English is excused, because its use is driven by higher aims. This is, then, another application of the neutrality fetish to English, as seen above in the case of Switzerland. It is important to distinguish this approach, best described, as stated above, as 'commercial cosmopolitanism' or 'commercial universalism' from a globalization strategy as practised, for instance, by a brand or corporation that is either unaware of or unbothered by linguistic diversity, and for this reason imposes English on website users who are speakers of other languages. Although the end effect may be the same, the motivation is certainly different. The universalist approach is seeking to create common ground, to find universals while preserving diversity; the global strategy approach is seeking to ignore and even eradicate difference. The former is multi, the later mono. However, both are examples of language choice (the latter perhaps more of a non-choice) that are driven by market motivations and that become part of a brand's 'identity' and part of people's experience of languages in the market.

English and market discourses in Central and Eastern Europe

The functioning of the various texts discussed so far in this book has been predicated on the notion of socialization into the language and rituals of the market society and its predominant discourse, advertising, something which in turn is posited on a particular type of economic ideology and system, namely that of the 'free' market or capitalism. Up to the late 1980s and early 1990s, there had of course been an alternative system in operation in Central and Eastern Europe, namely that of the planned economy. In this context, there was very little need for market discourses such as advertising – although there was a large degree of state and political advertising – since production was, in general, decided and controlled centrally, rather than being dictated, in theory at least, by the interaction of demand and supply as in the capitalist model.

One of the most striking aspects for those travelling from Western to Eastern Europe at that time was how the lack of advertising and other market discourses impacted on the streetscape, the mediascape, and the 'linguistic landscape'. This lack of advertising was celebrated by some as allowing 'areas to retain a certain majesty or at the very least quiet beauty' (Glenny, 1990, p. 20); while for others the region beyond the

Iron Curtain was 'far from the colourful variety of western advertising' (Schlosser, 1990, p. 76). Whatever one's point of view, it is very clear that the type of consumer socialization that appears to take place so seamlessly in market societies and cultures was absent in such societies and was replaced instead by a very different type of socialization. Commercial discourses were present, but they were very different to the type to which consumers in the West are accustomed. Advertising, in a planned economy based on Marxist-Leninist thinking, was seen as '… truthful. Its task is to spread the data on commodities, create and foster new wants and tastes in the population, make propaganda for and introduce new commodities' (from the *Large Soviet Encyclopaedia* in Harris and Seldon, 1962, p. 190). Although this might not seem vastly different from the Western notion of advertising, the practice, role, functions and status of advertising, as well as the ideological context within which it took place, were profoundly different (McNair, 1991). Furthermore, as the principal discourse of the market and medium of capitalist ideology, Western advertising was seen as a hostile discourse and 'an enemy of the people' (Harris and Seldon, 1962, p. 190). The lack of advertising was therefore both an inevitable consequence of the economic system and the result of a deliberate policy and worldview (cf. McNair, 1991, and Schlosser, 1990). However, as with all ideologies, theory and practice do not always converge. It would be wrong to think that there was no advertising or sense of consumerism in the countries of Central and Eastern Europe. As Kosztolanyi (1999) points out, while the state denounced consumerism, ordinary society was 'consumer-oriented', and state-sponsored consumer advertisements on television encouraged individuals to buy whatever goods were in surplus. His conclusion is that Hungary, for one, is best described at the time communism collapsed, as 'a hybrid, a semi-consumer society', with a rather schizophrenic relationship to the market. Likewise, individuals from the Yugoslav Federation were free to travel and shop in Italy where they were able to experience Western consumption and its discourses firsthand (cf. Sredl, 2003). The 'transition to a market economy' as the process is generally known, has involved not just learning and experiencing this new economic system, but also learning its language and the conventions of its primary discourse, advertising. For example, in Eastern Germany (the former German Democratic Republic), West German banking corporation *Dresdner Bank* ran a series of television programmes in the early 1990s presenting and explaining the language of Western banking practices to their new consumers in the East (Kelly-Holmes, 1995, 1999a).

Increasing linguistic diversity?

The region now referred to as Central and Eastern Europe represents a hugely varied area, culturally, linguistically, socially and economically. However, there is a sense that, far from increasing linguistic diversity, the expansion of 'Europe' as a market to include the previously disregarded economies and consumers of Central and Eastern Europe may actually have the opposite effect and instead result in greater homogenization and a consolidation of the position of English as the language of the market. The enlargement of the European Union with the accession of 10 new member states in 2004 has sparked a discussion among linguists and minority language activists about this particular topic. Given that English, French and German, the big-three languages, tend to dominate now, despite the Union's commitment to multilingualism, how will it be possible to accommodate in a fair way so many additional languages from Central and Eastern Europe? This problematizing of the linguistic situation in the region is a common topic in business publications, the following being just one example:

> Eastern Europe is a fragmented market, and Western applications have to be customized for the customers. Not only does the software have to be translated into more than 20 local languages, but some of them even use a different alphabet (Cyrillic – Russia, Belarus, Ukraine, Bulgaria, Serbia ...) ... it can be pretty intimidating to contemplate investing in a foreign market whose languages you don't understand, and which had been labeled for decades as an off-limits-for-most-Westerners region – the dreaded 'behind the Iron Curtain' world.
>
> (http://djurdjevic.com/ Bulletins/emerging/96-32.htm)

The fear of the unknown in the form of linguistic and cultural complexity is allayed in such publications by invoking the globalization argument:

> Most American business people would be amazed how 'American' these countries have become, while managing to maintain their own cultural uniqueness. And not just by the presence of the symbols of the American retail culture – Coke, Pepsi, McDonald's, Pizza Hut ... Or by having Cindy Crawford smile at you from hundreds of billboards.
>
> (http://djurdjevic.com/ Bulletins/emerging/96-32.htm)

The assumption behind such statements is that a kind of 'normalization' has taken place.[2] The evidence of this 'normalization' is found in global brands, global media 'personalities', the presence of the texts of capitalism that create a familiar landscape for the Western visitor, and the medium of this normalization, the English language. This downplaying of linguistic and cultural difference in an attempt to make these economies more attractive for investment is not just a feature of the discourse of Western companies and organizations. The following quote is taken from a Romanian website in English designed to give business information to potential investors and business travellers:

> The official language is Romanian, a language of Latin origin having much in common with the Italian and Spanish. It uses a Latin alphabet. One fact worth mentioning is that Romanian is the only Latin language in Eastern Europe.
>
> (http://romania.gopages.net/directory/index.htm)

The text is, in effect, advertising for investment in and business links with the country, and the message seems to be that Romania is less different than Slavic countries, it will irritate less, fit in more, that it is more globally and less locally focused, by virtue of the origin of its language.

Added to this, there is also a trend towards the non-thematizing of language by marketing and advertising professionals – MMD a public-relations consultancy that has offices across the CEE region, and claims to be the dominant company in a number of these, issued a statement entitled: 'EU Accession – an unprecedented PA opportunity', in which language and more specifically the English language are never mentioned. Instead it is 'communication' that is thematized, being specifically mentioned five times:

> Communications is at the heart of EU accession policy for the EU institutions themselves. Some €28m is being spent by the EU on enlargement communication to CEE audiences (between now and 2006). So the communications landscape is certainly not barren: PA professionals will need to dovetail their messaging with that coming from EU institutions themselves. The number of people communicating and receiving communications is expanding at an unprecedented rate – so now is the time to build relationships and influence.
>
> (http://www.mmdcee.com/ index.php?c=&page=14&l=1n/)

The linguistic diversity of 'CEE audiences' is completely ignored, as is the fact that a large portion of the budget for 'communication' will have to be allocated to translation. It is statements like these, which divorce communication from language in what is undeniably a multilingual situation, that give rise to the fears that English will increasingly take over in a market context. The conclusion is that English will, more and more, become dominant, squeezing out not only national languages, but also the other big-two of German and French, since English has quickly established itself as the main foreign language in the CEE countries, which up to the late 1980s/early 1990s had generally been Russian in many cases, and this tends to become a self-perpetuating truth in the business and market discourse about the region:

> 'In the three capital cities – Budapest, Prague and Warsaw – we are seeing an increase in call center activity, as English has become the dominant business language and companies are even more aware of the highly educated workforces', says John Verpeleti, DTZ's managing director for Central and Eastern Europe.
> (http://www.bizsites.com/2004/ January/article.asp?id=543)

The free-market fetish

More than this, however, knowledge of English and the ability to use the language seem to have become equated with success, as in the following example where the collocation of 'excellent English' with positive market buzzwords such as 'energetic', 'young' and 'go-getter' reinforces notions about English as the language needed for economic success:

> The country [Hungary] sales manager for IBM, an energetic young executive who speaks excellent English and epitomizes the 'go-getter' attitudes of the new Eastern European breed of business people.
> (http://djurdjevic.com/Bulletins/emerging/96-32.htm)

This fetishizing of English with associations of success in such texts echoes Piller's (2001) findings about the use of English in German advertising. Here, too, the language is used to summon up associations of the future and success. Her conclusions were that the English speakers being alluded to in these texts are not actually native speakers from Britain or the USA, rather they comprise a 'young, cosmopolitan business elite' in Germany (p. 180), and the same seems to apply in Central and Eastern European countries as well.

English has the added advantage in the context of consumerization in Central and Eastern Europe of being a language fetishized with associations of freedom, democracy and consumption, and both Western and local marketers have been quick to exploit this freedom fetish. One such example is cigarette advertising, which is heavily regulated in most Western European countries – and practically banned in some. Cigarette adverts in the CEE reform economies, however, not only 'portray a successful Western lifestyle', but also use brand names such as '*West Brand*', which are backed up by country-of-origin tactics such as 'American blend'. In terms of content, the advertisements frequently thematize 'freedom, thus capturing the spirit of new-found democracy in society'. Finally, the English language, in the form of advertising copy, appears alongside local informational copy, to complete the image (http://web.idrc.ca/en/ev-28838-201-1-DO_TOPIC.html). As Sredl points out in her ethnographic study of advertising and the development of consumer society in Croatia, 'fundamentally, consuming as Westerners is at the heart of Western lifestyle. And this is probably what most consumers are searching for' (2003, p. 3).

English is also a commodity in the reform economies of Central and Eastern Europe, which have become the new growth market for the English as a foreign language (EFL) product. Advertisements, like the following one, where assumptions about language values act as both form and content reinforce the inevitable association between English and the market economy, thus strengthening the market fetish of English in Central and Eastern Europe. English is presented as both an inevitable consequence of the marketization of such economies, and, at the same time, almost one of the driving forces behind the transition to a market economy. Such assumptions create the context within which both the English as a foreign language commodity and the free market/democracy fetish can function at the level of consumer advertising:

The transition to a market economy in many parts of Central and Eastern Europe has resulted in a huge demand for English language teachers, particularly in the business sector. (www.esljobfind.com)

English and websites in CEE countries

There is also an extent to which English is becoming the '*Fachsprache*' or professional dialect of advertising and marketing in CEE countries, even for agencies that are locally based. Increasingly, for example, English is required in order to work in advertising and marketing, as for example by this web-based advertising agency, located in Varna, Bulgaria:

> All candidates [for positions in the company] should be able to communicate in English, verbally and in writing. (www.design.bg)

The websites of advertising agencies in Romania, the Czech Republic, Hungary and other countries in Central and Eastern Europe all reinforce this association between English and market discourses, underwriting the position of English as the language of serious business. For instance, on the website of Romanian-based advertising agency, IMO Advertising, the information about the company and its services is given bilingually in Romanian and English – the Romanian version being placed visually above the English, and so taking precedence in terms of communication, and suggesting that the company is talking to its fellow compatriots rather than simply international businesses. However, the name of the company is in English only (IMO Advertising), as is the slogan that appears beneath the company name ('Perception is everything'), as well as the advertising message of the company that runs in tickertape format across the top of the website ('Our specialists create smart solutions for you and your company'). None of these are translated into Romanian, despite the otherwise bilingual nature of the website. It would seem that the English language functions here as a highly effective graphic. It was argued earlier in the chapter that having a website bestows authenticity and credibility on a brand; it would seem that for companies operating in the reform economies of Central and Eastern Europe, particularly those working in the sectors of advertising and marketing, in other words those involved in formulating market discourses, it is also necessary to have English words on that website in order to be credible. The primacy given to English over other foreign languages in the advertising world has two effects. On the one hand it strengthens the English free-market fetish, while on the other it means that in practical terms there is more English in the content of the advertising discourses that are experienced in everyday life.

On the Internet, English tends to become present in a number of ways and to varying degrees. To a great extent, the particular sector plays a large role in this, and the utilization of the English linguistic fetish does seem to be somewhat product-related. For instance, on a Romanian language website of a producer of 'traditional earthenware products', there are no English words used at all. Similarly, websites for insurance and financial services use few English words apart from standardized

Internet items, something that has been found in the other two case studies looked at so far in this chapter and the previous one. Where the topic is the Internet, however, and the company is offering services in this area, far more English words appear in the content, such as 'e-business, e-health, e-learning, e-government, e-business solutions' (www.siveco.ro), as well as in the form of Internet vocabulary such as 'contact', 'feedback' and so on. It is worth noting that localized equivalents exist for all of these terms, and there are many websites in all of these countries that choose not to use English, so the appearance of none, some or all housekeeping items in English is evidence of a language policy decision at some level by the designer of the website. On a website for a Romanian-based company selling yachts, the site is entirely in English and there is no Romanian language option. Sometimes, as in this case, the use of English seems designed to attract Western clients, but more often it appears to be an exploitation of the Western market fetish that has attached to the language in many of these countries in advertising, branding, signage, promotional material, labelling and packaging aimed at a domestic audience. So, for instance, a shopping centre in Bucharest is branded as 'Unirea Shopping Center', and on its website the children's attractions are labelled 'Kids Land'. Similarly, a company selling industrial cleaning equipment uses the name 'comintelshop', and the English slogan, 'comfort's intelligence', but its promotional materials and website are otherwise in Romanian. Likewise, a furniture company is named 'Froesen by design', but apart from choosing these English words as part of the title, the site communicates with the consumer in Romanian. Here the words seem very much part of the linguistic decoration and are primarily symbolic in character, although, again, it is interesting to note that English is chosen in all cases to provide this decoration, since, particularly in the case of furniture, there would be other contenders; for instance, geographically, linguistically and culturally, Italian would seem a more likely candidate.

When reviewing some websites, the language policy is so doggedly monolingual in favour of English that the user has to check to see whether the country-of-origin is correct or not. The Bucharest-based website design company, www.archi-web.com is one such example. The home page tells the viewer that the company is 'headquartered in Bucharest, Romania' and also has offices in the United States. Thus, the country-of-origin is not hidden, and Romania rather than the United States is placed at the centre. Likewise, in another part of the website the company reassures the client that 'we always remember where our roots are'. However, there is no Romanian version of the site offered at all, and the language does not appear on any part of the site, except when the user views some of the websites that the company has designed. There is no mention of language, although the choice of language must be an issue for the company and its clients, and some sort of decision about a linguistic strategy must also be part of the design and development process. However, companies operating in this sector in these countries either prefer to ignore or downplay this aspect in their advertising, or else it is so much a part of the advertising process that it is almost impossible to see it and describe it as a separate problem. This is a very different situation to that of agencies working with minority allochthonous and autochthonous languages, as shall be discussed in the next chapter, where language seems to be omnipresent in their descriptions of their work and promotional materials.

This phenomenon of ignoring the language issue is also present on the global chemical corporation *Unilever*'s Romanian website. Again, as with the archi-web site, there is no attempt to disguise country-of-origin, since the site tells visitors that *Unilever* is 'one of the top international investors in Romania', having acquired the local brand *Dero* in 1995, and having built a factory in Ploiesti (http://www.archi-web.com/unileverromania/rom.htm). Under 'products', local brands are also listed separately to international brands. However, there is no option to choose a Romanian language version of the site. Furthermore, under 'job offers' the only criteria listed are that applicants have a good honours degree, are under 27 and are 'dynamic' 'fresh graduates'. Nowhere is there an English-language requirement. This would perhaps lead the viewer to think that these offers were aimed at applicants outside the country. However, the potential applicant is told elsewhere in the advertisement that:

> Unilever presentations are held at all major Romanian universities where you will be provided with an application form.
> (http://www.archi-web.com/unileverromania/rom.htm)

So, the recruitment advertisement *is* aimed at Romanian applicants, but the information is given entirely in English. It is not provided in a Romanian version, and there is no explicit requirement for the applicant to have an English-language qualification or to display competence in the language. Thus, in this example too, it seems to have become so taken for granted and such a part of common-sense knowledge of the habitus that any serious contender for such a position who fulfils all of these other criteria (young, fresh, educated, dynamic) would have English, that the requirement is not even worth mentioning.

English may of course also be used for creative expression, as just another advertising device along with graphics, flash applications and so forth on websites. An example of this is the website of a Romanian based fish import–export business, www.gti.ro. The company's name, although in English, is reminiscent of a communally or state-owned enterprise of the previous era, General Trade and Invest Ltd, and has none of the snappiness of more recent brand and company names. The website is available trilingually in Romanian, English and Spanish. However, the core language of the website is English. For example, the day and date are in English, as well as housekeeping items such as 'contact', 'about us' and so on. In addition, English is also used for linguistic decoration on the graphic: the word 'love' appears on a sign held up by a frightened fish faced with a hungry shark. The market fetish of English is complemented by the fact that fish are constantly turning into euros and dollars in the graphic.

Even where a website has adopted a basically monolingual strategy, with the exception perhaps of a few housekeeping items in English, it is hard to maintain this monolingualism in the CEE context because of sponsors and advertising pop-ups and links that bring English to the site. So, for instance, on an insurance website that is basically in Romanian, apart from housekeeping, an advertisement for Mastercard introduces English and French token items in the following rotating sequence:

No cash. No card is more accepted: Bon Appetit; Bon Voyage; North South East West; Mastercard.

Since these items are constantly moving, the eye is inevitably drawn to them, thus leaving the viewer with the impression of having seen quite a bit of English on the site, even though this is not actually the case in terms of the real content.

English and print advertising

As with websites, English has come to be present in print advertising in Central and Eastern European countries in a number of ways which are, in general, detached from any country-specific fetish, while at the same time being very attached to a 'Western' fetish. The first minimal presence strategy simply involves the transfer of brand names, logos and slogans. For example, in an advertisement for the Finnish-based *Nokia* mobile-phone company in the Czech news magazine *Reflex*, the international slogan 'Connecting people' appears underneath the brand name in an otherwise Czech-language text; similarly, in an advertisement for Epson copiers, also in *Reflex*, the slogan 'colour your life' is printed alongside the brand name, the other words in the text being Czech, apart from 'hotline'. Even if the quantity of English words is as small as this, their presence still introduces more English into a situation than there was previously, and thus changes the sociolinguistic context, the habitus and common-sense assumptions about language and languages. If English names or words are present, then names or words in other languages are not. Similarly, if English is experienced in everyday consumption discourses, then not only does knowledge of the language and about the language increase, but the association between English and the market becomes strengthened, and advertisers will exploit this fetish further. For example, Grey Worldwide Russia's billboard campaign for *Kitekat* cat food keeps the original name in the Latin alphabet (*Kitekat*), while giving product information in Russian. A similar approach is taken in its advertising for *Lenor* fabric conditioner (one of *Procter and Gamble's* brands). The English language in this context is therefore very much part of the visual of the advertising and labelling. In the Russian-language version of the website, the name of the agency itself, Grey Worldwide Russia, is left in the original English, taking on the features of a logo or a type of language graphic rather than communicating any information. In the case of Russian, these examples are even more acute, since the Western words stand out against the Cyrillic script.

Other examples include an advertisement for the *Ford Fiesta* car in the Czech women's family magazine *Žena a život*, which contains the slogan '*Ford Fiesta* Family'; an advertisement for *DHL* couriers in gossip magazine *Instinkt*, where the slogan 'We move the world' appears, without a Czech explanation, beside the brand name in an otherwise Czech-language text; and, further on in the same magazine, the slogan 'you can' is printed above the *Canon* brand in an advertisement for photocopiers. However, the same patterns of usage of English words appear to be present in the Czech advertising market as in its German equivalent. So, for instance, advertisements for banks, insurance and financial services in general are one of the few adscapes in which English language words do not appear, particularly where the advertiser is native. Furthermore, as in the case of German food and drink products, the English language appears also to be absent from native Czech food and drink advertisements. An example here is an advertisement for *Budweiser Budvar*. This brand was forced by legal action on the part of the USAmerican *Budweiser* corporation to call itself *Budweiser Budvar*, even though it is the original beer from the eponymous region. In an advertisement for the beer in *Reflex* news magazine, only Czech words are used, and, it can be argued, that it would be a wholly inappropriate advertising strategy to use English to advertise this product to Czech consumers; in fact, one could even go so far as to say that it would undermine the brand's credibility. Similarly, as in the case of English usage in German advertisements, or the use of French, German and other languages in English-language advertisements, the quantity varies between publications. So, for instance, a news magazine or a local edition of an international women's glossy magazine will have far more foreign language words than a family women's magazine or a local television guide. This has to do with the target advertisees and the nature of the products advertised in these particular media, both of which are of course interlinked. For example, in the Czech edition of international women's glossy magazine *Elle*, the English fetish moves up a gear, with a far greater quantity of the language in advertisements and even greater prominence afforded it. In an advertisement for *Maurice Lacroix* watches, which are Swiss in origin, there is no attempt to utilize the French linguistic fetish; instead, English dominates the advertisement. Beneath the brand name, the country-of-origin is explicitly referred to in English ('Switzerland'), and the slogan 'Tomorrow's Classics' appears, while the dominant text in the advertisement is also in English without any Czech explanation:

ATTRACTIVE AND RELIABLE. YES, THIS SORT OF COMPANION DOES STILL EXIST.

The technical information about the particular model featured and about where to buy it, which is in Czech, is relegated to the top right-hand corner of the advertisement, away from the main eye-catching graphic and English text, and it is reproduced in a smaller font. An advertisement for *Marc O'Polo* fragrances on the next page contains no Czech words at all, while on the following page an advertisement for the Prague Biennial Festival contains no foreign words. The next advertisement, for *Nokia* mobile phones, has a Czech slogan in the graphic and contains only the brand's global slogan in English below the brand name ('connecting people'). This is followed by an advertisement for *Nivea* which utilizes an association not known in Western Europe. In Chapter 2, it was established that *Nivea* has never attempted to market itself as German, and seems to adopt an anti country-of-origin tactic, with only the French linguistic fetish being used. However, in a Czech advertisement for *Nivea*, the graphic containing the products shows the product names in German, with the products explained in Czech in the text part of the advertisement. An advertisement on the next page for *Skoda Finance* (*SkoFIN*) is in Czech only, and a page on from this an advertisement for a food court in a local shopping centre uses a combination of French (the name of the court is *'Rendez vous'*), English (the name of the shopping centre is 'Millennium Plaza Shopping Mall' and the products listed in large print are 'fresh shakes', 'music', 'salads' and Italian and French food items, as well as a large, though not visually prominent body of text in an old-fashioned, utilitarian font, in Czech, giving information about the shopping mall. So, within the space of a few pages in a magazine, different types of multilingual text possibilities are offered and encountered.

From this constellation of advertisements, a pattern emerges about the use and non-use of English and other foreign languages in Czech advertising. English may simply be present as part of a global slogan or brand name used internationally. As such, it functions more as part of the brand's graphic identity, but nonetheless it still represents a presence of English language in media where it would not have been present before, and in fact in media – in some cases – that would not have been present until the last decade of the twentieth century. The next step involves the decision to give products English names or French names (particularly in the case of cosmetics), and to present information about them in Czech. Further on from this again, there may be no attempt to localize an advertisement at all – it simply appears in English. Finally, there will be a deliberate use of only Czech, similar to the 'purity fetish' described in the German case, in advertisements for brands that have a strong country-of-origin association – and in particular one that is known internationally, as in the case of *Budweiser Budwar* and *Skoda*, and in advertisements for products where information is seen as paramount, such as banking, baby food and so on, or where the product is a cultural or government-sponsored one.

It is interesting too to see how both new and established fetishes are present in the advertising discourses of CEE countries. For example, in an advertisement for a Czech brand of perfume/cosmetics, *Vivace*, owned by the Czech company *Salvete*, that appeared in the Czech family women's magazine, *Žena a život*, there are a number of fetishes at work. First of all there is the choice of name for the brand, the Italian for lively (*Vivace*); then there is the informative text given in Czech; and finally there are the graphics of the products, which contain words such as 'Body lotion', 'Shower Gel' and the French *'Eau de Toilette'*. On *Salvete*'s website, the visitor is reassured that the new perfumes have been developed with the help of French perfume-makers. Interestingly, the product names are given in Czech at the bottom of the advertisement, away from the graphic, for *Eau de Toilette* too. Thus, there is a clear differentiation between language as decoration (English, French and Italian) and language as information (Czech). Similarly, in advertising for *Clinique* products in the Czech edition of international women's glossy magazine *Elle*, English and French product names appear on the bottles shown in the graphic, while the information about these products is given in Czech in what is clearly differentiated as the text part of the advertisement. These advertisements are just a few examples of a very typical approach to advertising products from this domain in CE Europe.

In his 2003 book *Ignorance*, Czech author Milan Kundera writes about the unprecedented speed at which Prague has forgotten the Russian language, which Czech citizens had been forced to learn for a number of decades. In its place, the Czech capital, 'eager for applause on the world's proscenium, displayed to the visitors its new attire of English-language sites and labels' (p. 95). Kundera describes the office of a fictional business in the city,

> where Czech was no more than an impersonal murmur, a background of sound against which only Anglo-American phonemes stood forth as human words. (2003, p. 95)

Kundera's depiction is, of course, fictional and exaggerated, but a small survey of Czech advertising does leave one with a similar impression. Many of the advertisements are almost a visual representation of Kundera's observation of the backgrounding of the Czech language by English in business contexts, a practice that will only serve to enhance the fetishizing of English as the 'serious' language of business, even if this happens, in the main, symbolically.

Conclusion

Internationally, then, English seems fetishized with a number of associations such as modernity, internationalism or cosmopolitanism, trendiness, success and, in the context of CE Europe, the market and democracy. Having said that country-of-origin issues are not paramount in the use of English in advertising internationally, it is important to highlight a point made by Ger and Belk (1996) in their work on 'globalization of local consumptionscapes'. They argue that the country-of-origin effect can be strong for USAmerican products, not because of any association with cultural competence but because the country of origin of the brand or product is seen to have a strong consumption ethic. This is particularly the case, in their opinion, in developing consumer societies, and so this would seem to be a strong factor in the use of English in advertising in Central and Eastern Europe.

In terms of global and local websites, companies and brands seem to follow different policies. Some simply adopt a policy of commercial monolingualism, whereby English is the language of all Internet sites, however these are not the majority. Commercial multilingualism is much more in evidence on the Internet sites of global multinationals, which seem at first glance keen to accommodate to local linguistic differences. The extent of this policy seems to reflect a particular political or apolitical stance, with certain language minority groups seen as credible consumers worthy of a differentiated linguistic strategy, while others are not. A further important point, however, is that even for companies pursuing a strategy of commercial multilingualism, their dot.com website, the site that stakes their claim to global credibility and authority, is almost always in English regardless of the country of origin. In addition, there is also the policy of cosmopolitan monolingualism, which at first glance appears to be the same as commercial monolingualism in that one language is used. However, in such a strategy language is downplayed to the extent that it is presented as insignificant in an advertisement, as a barrier to international communication, just one more problem in the world.

A final important point to remember when discussing the use of English language as a fetish in advertising is to remember that such fetishes and associations (freedom, internationalism, Westernism, Americanism and so on) are also gross, commercially driven generalizations. Certainly, 'the United States remains the principal producer and consumer of advertising' (Russell and Lane, 2002, p. 61), and so the English language does seem to have the role of a medium of American cultural expansion. However, no one would really suggest that watching *Audi* and *Renault* advertisements gives people a lived experience of Germany and France respectively. So, how can people really know what USAmerican culture is if they only experience a commoditized version of it through global media? As many commentators have pointed out, culture in the USA is just as much a victim of this commodotizing promoted by corporate institutions (cf. Klein, 2001; Schlosser, 2002; McAllister, 1996). The voice of American culture mediated via television screens across the world has little to do with the reality of ordinary lives, languages or economics in the USA. And, while sociolinguists and those who argue against English language imperialism are very careful in describing 'peripheral' cultures in respectful detail, the complexity that is 'American culture' is dismissed and reduced to a marketed version of the world according to advertising agencies. Likewise in the British context, it is very hard to sum up British culture – it is incredibly diverse and this linguistic, economic, political, social, educational diversity is rarely reproduced in marketed discourses that use English. Just as the marketed and mediated images of Germany, France, Spain and other countries discussed in previous chapters rely on reductivism, so too does the use of English. A further issue is that this type of terminology personalizes the power relations at issue; instead of being about economics, corporations and what market-driven discourses do with and to languages, it becomes about people who by accident of birth speak English and/or live in the USA. It is almost as if people in the 'Centre' have the power to influence and steer what are largely anational corporations; that these individuals are not somehow subject to inequalities and power relations, but instead subscribe wholeheartedly to the mediated images that are presented to and of them. Finally, many of these criticisms of 'American' commercial culture are in fact based on what are sometimes superficial analyses, and it is important as analysts of advertising discourse not to fall into the country-of-origin traps laid out. For instance, *Coca-Cola* and its advertising is considered by many to be the incarnation of the voice of American capitalism, as expressed through English. However, the Publicis advertising agency, based in Paris, the spiritual heart of *Francophonie* and cultural bastion against American popular and commercial culture, has for some time handled the advertising for this brand in 44 countries worldwide (Lorin, 2001, p. 94).

4

Minority Languages, Accents and Dialects in Advertising

Le chéile arís?

So, you've fancied getting back together with the Irish language … . why wait to make a date?

Ná fág ar an méar fhada é – dean coinne leis an teanga inniu!

Caith seal leis an teanga spend some time with the language

Extract from advertisement for *Foras na Gaeilge*, the Irish Language Agency, from *Phoenix* magazine

Advertising today is expected to speak to people 'in their own language'. Despite the very high degree of planning and design that goes into the advertising message, it is doubtful whether many people would regard the genre as a formal or serious type of communication. This is in stark contrast to the origins of advertising, when a very formal register was used, both traditionally in print advertising, and later when the first audio and later audio-visual advertisements were created. In the context of the 'information era', advertising texts, like many other texts, have become informalized, or perhaps more accurately they have taken on the characteristics of informal communication. This reflects a general trend in institutional and mass communication whereby an attempt is being made to present such messages as being more like spontaneous or one-to-own communication, and to shake off their institutional context. Probably the worst thing that could be said about an advertisement today is that it is old-fashioned, that it uses formal registers, that it is overly polite and respectful, and that it does not treat the advertisee as an equal, but rather as inferior or superior. This informalization is of course more superficial than real and refers only to the appearance of the advertising text, not to the way in which the text is put together or to how the communication takes place. Advertising is still institutionally created and disseminated discourse.

One result of speaking to people 'in their own language' has been the growing degree of 'multi-voicedness', in Bakhtin's terms, in advertising, something that is reflected in the greater diversity of accents and dialects now used in advertising compared to a few decades ago. Parallel to this has been a move towards some recognition of minority language rights in education and other spheres, and advertisers, too, have come to learn the pragmatic value of speaking the languages of minority groups. This trend has been both pioneered and enhanced by the emergence of 'ethnic' advertising agencies. Yet another factor in this equation is increasing regionalization and the revitalization of regional languages that has characterized Western Europe in particular. These movements have utilized the technology and strategies of what are seen primarily as globalizing forces such as satellite, cable and digital television and the Internet.[1] In this way, more media outlets and opportunities for language diversity and multilingual media experiences are created.

This chapter attempts to give an overview of these many and varied developments and their implications. First of all, the issue of languages and 'ethno-market' advertising is dealt with briefly in general terms. The remainder of the chapter is then devoted to a case study of the Irish context, which highlights many of the issues of concern here, namely the uses and abuses to which accent, dialect and indigenous minority languages are put in advertising.

Languages and ethno-marketing

The key difference between the use of languages to target ethnic and linguistic minority groups through advertising as opposed to the use of foreign languages, as discussed in Chapter 2, is that the context, motivation and target audience are entirely different in both cases. In many of the examples discussed up to now, a foreign language, which is associated in the mind of the domestic advertisee with another country, is used to advertise to that domestic, mainly monolingual advertisee as part of a marketing strategy that uses this language as a product attribute alluding to this foreignness. In cases where ethnic minority languages are used in advertising, an everyday multilingual context is assumed, and the objective is to target a minority language group constituted by recent or relatively recent immigration, with the objective of advertising the product in 'their' language to them. Thus, the former objective is primarily symbolic, whereas the latter is primarily communicative. This is not to say that there is not a large symbolic element to this type of advertising as well, since the 'community' in question will consist of a diverse constellation of individuals and their relationship with the language or languages in question will range on a continuum from the language of everyday use to a language with which they have only a symbolic or heritage relationship. So, the decision by a company to use the particular language may be motivated, on the one hand, by the desire to mark the product as associated with an ethnicity and conjure up for the targeted public notions of a homeland and an identity, and, on the other, by the desire to communicate most effectively and easily with individuals in that language group. In the case of the former motivation, the objectives of such advertisers are very close to those advertisers who use minoritized indigenous languages, dialects and accents in order to create a feeling of community and to associate this with a particular product, as will be explained below.

Language in ethnic marketing

Although the USA is one of the largest English-speaking countries in the world, and, more than this, its cultural and commercial products and their discourses have, as explored in the previous chapter, played a large part in consolidating the position currently enjoyed by the English language, in practice the country is a multilingual one. In the 2000 Census, almost 18 per cent of the population reported speaking a language other than English at home (http://www.census.gov/prod/2003pubs/c2kbr-29.pdf). Spanish is the main second language in the USA, with 28 million individuals reporting it as their home language in the 2002 Census.[2] These data led to what some advertising commentators called 'a Census 2000-driven boom in all things Hispanic', and a growth in the Spanish-language media market in the USA that outstrips the general media market (Wentz and Schnuer, 2001). Industry journal *Advertising Age* has been hosting an annual 'Hispanic Creative Advertising Awards' event since 1999. Often these Spanish-language advertising strategies are regionally created and based in the main centres of significant Hispanic population, for instance Miami, Los Angeles and other cities in California, New York, Chicago, San Francisco, Houston and Dallas (Zbar, 1998). Since the early 1990s, both global and national brands – for example *McDonald's*, *Kentucky Fried Chicken*, *Taco Bell*, *Burger King*, *Budweiser* and so on – have been targeting Spanish speakers with

Spanish-language advertising campaigns, which not only use Spanish, but also claim to adapt to the particularities of Spanish-speaking cultures (Hamstra, 1995).

The *McDonald*'s language policy is certainly an interesting one, and worthy of comment here in the light of what was said in the previous chapter. On the one hand, as stated above, the brand promotes its product to Spanish speakers living in the USA through Spanish-language marketing; on the other, its USA dot.com website, as pointed out in Chapter 3, does not have any Spanish-language option. So, it would seem that while the corporation is pragmatic enough to realize the benefits of ethnic language marketing, when it comes to making 'official' statements about what the brand stands for, corporate marketing discourse is not prepared to be bilingual or to recognize the multilingual reality of everyday life in many parts of the USA, and instead it appears to opt for towing the line.

The Internet market for Spanish sites in the USA also indicates an interesting trend. The demand for sites in the language is growing rapidly, as is Spanish-language usage of the Internet among Hispanic Americans. One reason for this increase, according to a study carried out by the Roslow Research Group in 2000, is more widespread usage of the Internet among older generations, whose language use is 'more Spanish-dominant' (in Wentz and Schnuer, 2001). Up to now, users had been younger and more proficient in English, and so the demand for Spanish-language sites in the USA had not been as great. This ties in with the findings of a UNESCO-sponsored study of multilingual Internet usage in a number of countries internationally that would seem to suggest that as Internet usage becomes more general and less exclusive, linguistic diversity increases on the Internet. So, while a small elite group that has access to the Internet is happy to use English sources, once use spreads to a wider population, national and in particular 'big' international languages (such as Spanish in this case) may push out English (Kelly-Holmes, 2004).

There are many examples of Spanish being used to target the Hispanic community in the USA. For example, in the Miami market where there is a strong Hispanic presence comprising individuals of Cuban origin, in particular, a Spanish-language commercial is used by a grill and bar restaurant to try to convince Hispanics to abandon more traditional dishes in favour of 'baby back ribs', which is considered to be 'a non-traditional Hispanic product' (MacArthur, 2000). *Nissan* created its first Spanish-language advertising campaign for the USA in 1996. The campaign, which ran on the Spanish-language network Univision and on

Spanish-language radio, featured well-known Hispanic celebrities from the spheres of soap opera, film and television (*Automotive News*, 1996). *Heineken*, a Dutch beer, uses Spanish-language advertising to target what is seen to be a lucrative minority language market in the USA (Lang, 2000). It is worth noting that although this is the most developed ethnic market, Spanish-speaking Americans are not the only ones to be targeted by national and global brands in the USA. For example, in 2002 the *Chrysler* Group launched a Chinese-language campaign in California.

While this advertising may have started out being regionally based, as stated above, a number of brands are now targeting Spanish speakers through national media. The reasoning behind these changes is that the Hispanic population now has significance beyond the traditional centres mentioned earlier. In the words of one media account director: 'It used to be that if you advertised in 17 markets, you reached 85 per cent of the Hispanic population. What you find now is that the Hispanic population is growing in every state' (Kaplan, 2002). Such a move, from the regional or local to the national in terms of strategies and campaigns, will alter the linguistic media landscape of the USA, creating multilingual media experiences for individuals who would otherwise live monolingual lives. The multilingualism of the country will become even harder for policy-makers and individuals to ignore when it becomes present in media on a national scale. There are of course two crude scenarios in terms of what the result of such a trend could be. In the first, the effect would be greater awareness of the situation and a gradual 'normalizing' of multilingualism. In the second, this mediatized and marketized evidence of diversity might reinforce the drive towards an English-only policy, spearheaded by bodies such as 'US English'.[3]

Attempting bilingual market discourse

The problems that have arisen in Spanish language or bilingual Spanish–English publications in the USA throw up some of the issues concerned with this type of advertising. Pharmaceutical companies advertising over-the-counter or direct-to-consumer products for conditions such as diabetes have run into criticism for running bilingual advertisements. In such advertisements, the advertising copy, slogan, message and so on are in Spanish, but the directions for use, or prescription information, and contra-indications are written in English. The publisher of one of the magazines concerned, which received complaints, saw no problem with this procedure, saying, 'Our circulation goes to a dual-language audience'. However, another publisher claimed that translation of prescription and contra-indication advice 'is a difficult and time-consuming process many companies "don't want to bother with" ' (West, 1999). In addition, a spokesperson for pharmaceuticals group *Merck* claimed in the same article that the US Food and Drug Agency (FDA) requires that this type of information be printed in English. These three lines of argument or explanation highlight the many complex issues, contexts and motivations that are at play in this type of advertising.

First of all, there is the fact that most, although not exclusively all, minority language speakers are to a greater or lesser extent bilinguals. In the 2000 Census, for instance, a majority of Spanish speakers reported that they spoke English very well (http://www.census.gov/prod/ 2003pubs/ c2kbr-29.pdf). Their everyday lives are in general lived bilingually and therefore such bilingual texts could then be seen as an attempt to embrace this bilingual existence and not categorize individuals as speakers of this, and only this language; as a member of this, and only this group. This is the approach taken in 'cross-over advertising' that targets 'Hispanics who speak Spanish and English', and who 'have the best of both worlds' (Zbar, 1998).

This point has also been made about Turkish-language media aimed at the Turkish 'community'[4] in Germany. Through satellite channel, TRT-INT, the Turkish state broadcaster reaches the Turkish diaspora in Germany and other European countries. The main daily Turkish language newspaper, *Hürriyet*, was originally imported into Germany every day. Today, a European edition of the paper is printed in Germany, although the German editorial team is still ultimately managed by the Turkish headquarters (Hibbeler, 2002). It is estimated that the combined circulation of the Turkish language daily press in Germany is about 250,000, while a survey conducted by the Centre for Turkish Studies in Essen estimates that 92 per cent of Turkish-origin Germans watch television programmes from Turkey via cable and satellite; however, 88 per cent of these also watch German channels (Bundesministerium des Innern, 2001). These Turkey-based media have often been criticized for not representing accurately the reality of the lived bilingual, bicultural Turkish–German experience, particularly among the second and third generations. An example of this was the coverage in some of these media of the European Union's decision not to allow Turkey to join with the first round of applicant states from Central and Eastern Europe in 2004. Papers such as *Milliyet* and *Sabah*, that are distributed and read in Germany but printed in Turkey, were particularly critical of German politicians in this regard, Germany having traditionally been seen as an ally of Turkey. Where are third-generation Turkish-Germans to position themselves in such a debate and in relation to such media (Özdemir, 2002)? A study carried out by the *Bundespresseamt*, the Federal Press and Information Office, in 2001 showed that 57 per cent of Turkish-Germans questioned wanted bilingual media (Hibbeler, 2002). However, the problems experienced by the fledgling bilingual weekly newspaper *Persembe*, which went out of business after only six months, do not bode well for such media. At the very basic level, one problem was where the newspaper would be displayed in shops: in the Turkish or in the German section?

This, again, is a very concrete example of the desire on the part of the market to segment and categorize in the easiest possible way, rather than confronting the 'messy' business of bilingual reality. As Cem Özdemir, the first member of the Turkish community to be elected to the German parliament, puts it, many of the younger generation read the leading German daily, the *Süddeutsche Zeitung*, as well as *Hürriyet*, and watch the German public broadcaster, ARD, as well as TRT. Turkish media are, in this scheme, complementary (Özdemir, 2002), and the media offered the need to understand the complexity of having a German home – Özdemir uses *Zuhause* rather than *Heimat* – but Turkish roots. Özdemir has called for a German–Turkish version of Arte, the Franco-German-Swiss bilingual arts channel to encourage integration and understanding between the (main/second/minor) culture of over two million individuals of Turkish origin in Germany and the dominant linguistic culture. However, Özdemir's choice of Arte as an example is telling, since the channel is not a market enterprise, but is instead a cross-cultural, publically funded initiative. This again highlights the perception that market- driven media do not favour multilingualism and that it is up to the state sector to provide bilingual media services.

The second aspect thrown up by the example of the pharmaceutical advertisements shows this type of advertising in a more negative light. Rather than responding to the lived experience of bilingualism, the advertisements can be seen as examples of linguistic fetish or display. The non-important part of the ad, in other words the part of the text with symbolic functions, is in Spanish, whereas the most important, informative part is in English. Such a strategy demonstrates the use of the non-majority language for mainly tokenistic purposes; the Spanish words in such a scheme are simply a marketing tool, like a slogan, rather than a real attempt to communicate information. In addition, the approach also shows a lack of genuine commitment to bilingualism or linguistic diversity. It reinforces notions about the status and functions of the non-majority language: it is suitable for 'feel-good' type messages and snappy slogans, but it is not suitable for the serious, legal part of the message.

Although the context is a very different one, the in-flight magazine of Canadian national carrier, *Air Canada*, highlights this particular point about minority languages and advertising. The French language of course does have official status in Canada, and as the national carrier, *Air Canada* would be expected to respect this bilingual situation. The title of the magazine, *'enRoute'* is 'ambilingual' in the sense that it works in both languages, in the original French and as a term that, having been originally borrowed into English, is now no longer really seen as a foreign term, except when it is explicitly associated with things French. The magazine itself, like the product delivered in the airplane, is strenuously bilingual. All titles and articles and every bit of information is given in English and French. This is the state or official aspect, the national carrier fulfilling its national duty. However, when the market, which has no such commitment or obligation, becomes involved, in the form of advertising, this is not the case.

A brief survey of the advertisements reveals how this strictly bilingual relationship between the languages breaks down, quite dramatically. A typical issue (July 2003) contains 23 advertisements in English only. Two of these, one for *Air Canada* and one for *Hertz* rental cars, have a counterpart in French that appears in another part of the magazine. Apart from this, there is only one advertisement in French alone, from the Canadian Air Transport Security Authority, and this has no English counterpart. In contrast to the bilingual co-text of features, profiles, articles and information, there are only four actual bilingual advertising texts. Two are for 'public-sector' organizations/companies: the Montreal Museum of Fine Arts and Air Canada, while one is an anti-drink-driving advertisement sponsored by the international drinks group, *Diageo*. The final one, for a national rental car company, is perhaps the only truly *commercial* bilingual advertisement in the magazine. Interestingly, while the text of the advertisement is entirely bilingual (for example, low rates: *bas prix*), the company brand, 'rent-a-wreck', and its slogan, 'Drive a good bargain', are in English and are not translated into French. This appears to be in line with the policy in the *Diageo*-sponsored anti-drink-driving advertisement as well, in which the punch line/slogan 'PLEASE ENJOY RESPONSIBLY' is in English only.

Finally, coming back to the partially bilingual advertisement for drugs, there is the third issue of the official sphere, or perhaps most importantly *notions* about the official sphere and the part these play in the context. Although the spokesperson for *Merck* claimed to have thought there was a requirement for the part of the text containing prescribing information to be in English, it was only his understanding, and the FDA did not wish to comment on this aspect (West, 1999). Here, then, there emerges the context of a country without an official language policy, but where there are widely held notions about a hypothetical official language policy, and where in practice there is a multilingual context. In such a situation, the decisions made by advertisers are products of their own and the prevailing notions and prejudices about language, about speakers of non-majority languages and about linguistic capital.

Language and the ethnic advertising sector

The targeting of minority language consumers through advertising tends to be largely the preserve of 'minority' or 'ethnic' agencies. Although the car company *DaimlerChrysler* began Turkish-language advertising directed at the Turkish community in Germany in 1994 (Ebrahimi, 2002), 'ethno-marketing' is a relatively new phenomenon in Germany – the new 'in-word' in management circles (Schreiber, 2000) – and is not at all as developed or established as in the USA, accounting for only about 1–2 per cent of the total advertising industry. Gradually, other players in the automobile industry, as well as consumer goods manufacturers and more recently the financial services sector have followed suit (Schreiber, 2000). In fact, according to Ozan Sinan of Berlin-based media agency Lab One, Turkish-Germans have a greater affinity with advertising and are more likely to react to it, since they are not used to being appealed to directly to any great extent (Ebrahimi, 2002). These market discourses are not of course confined to traditional advertising domains, but can include, for example, Turkish-speaking agents dealing with Turkish-German clients, particularly older generations, and the provision of information leaflets and translations of complex contracts in Turkish, for example (Schreiber, 2000), anything, I would argue, where in fact a language policy is part of a commercial policy. Other groups to be targeted with market discourses in their own languages include those of Greek origin and the growing Russian-speaking population in Germany (Ebrahimi, 2002).

The heading used by Tulay-Kollegen, an 'ethno-marketing' consultancy in Germany specializing in the Turkish, Greek and Russian-speaking markets, is *'Kaufkraft mit besonderen Akzenten'* – 'Purchasing power with particular accents'. The pun on the word 'accent' refers on the one hand to the exotic difference between the immigrant groups and the Germans, and it also refers to the different language, part of that exotic difference. What is interesting here is that language is paramount for these ethnic agencies in Germany, the USA and elsewhere. Unlike their monolingual counterparts, who never seem to discuss or acknowledge explicitly a multilingual world, for these ethnic agencies it is all about language. So, for instance, the potential client is invariably assured about the ethnic and linguistic authenticity of the agency's creative team: 'The agency has 43 bilingual, bicultural members of staff' (http://www.adamericas.com/welcome.html), and 'Our staff is fully bilingual, bicultural, and immersed in the dynamics of the Hispanic market' (http://www.acento.com). It is almost impossible to imagine statements like 'Our team is 100% US American/British, and all of them speak English as a first language' on the homepage of a leading American or UK agency. And, therein lies the core of the issue: in the 'normal' state of English language monolingual affairs, language is not even worth commenting on, since it is part of the common sense, taken-for-granted assumptions. Only when the state of affairs deviates from this norm does language suddenly become central and need to be remarked upon. Even more, language is a central part of that 'deviation'. And, this, it could be argued, is the other side of the coin to monolingual business thinking that ensures that 'funny' foreign words can be used to advertise foreign products or create humorous effects.

Irish English and advertising

The Irish context presents an interesting case study within which to examine the two further issues of concern in this chapter: firstly the informalization trend whereby advertising texts seek to imitate normal everyday communication, including accent and dialect; secondly, the role of a minoritized indigenous language in advertising. The Irish situation, like most linguistic situations, is not, however, a straightforward case in which there is a dominant code and a dominated one. There is an official language policy, established in the Constitution, which states that Irish is the first official language, while English is recognized also as an official language for a variety of purposes. Up until the nineteenth century, Irish, an Indo-European Celtic language, closely related to Scots Gaelic, was the language of the majority in the country. However, a variety of conditions conspired to reverse that situation over the last two hundred years. One of the main factors was the famine of the late 1840s which resulted first of all in the deaths of large numbers of Irish speakers, and secondly in widespread and long-term emigration by

Irish speakers. Since these individuals were emigrating and their destinations were English-speaking ones, parents began to change the language of their children in the hope of economic prosperity through emigration. Another factor was of course the English government's policy in relation to the language, which was one of imposing English on the population. This meant that the language was largely unknown by many individuals prior to political independence, apart from those living in certain areas where the language had been maintained and those who had consciously made the decision to learn the language as part of their political convictions.

Following independence from the UK in 1921, efforts were made to reinstate Irish as the normal language of communication in all domains, the main starting point being education, and Irish is still taught in school from the first year (age 4–5) to the final year of obligatory schooling (age 16), and for many, in reality, until 18. However, for everyday communication English is the dominant language, with Irish being reserved for certain domains and functions such as education, official, public and civil-service matters, government and so on.[5] According to data from the 2002 Census, 1.57 million people in Ireland report themselves able to speak Irish (out of a population of approximately 3.9 million), and 21.6 per cent of these report speaking it on a daily basis – although almost 78 per cent of these were of school-going age (CSO, 2002). However, it is still significant that such a great proportion of the population claim to be able to use the language, and it is a resource that advertisers could use. In terms of the *Gaeltacht*, the officially designated Irish-speaking areas,[6] these comprise a total population of about 86,000 (http://gaeltacht.local.ie). It should be pointed out that these areas are in reality bilingual, and the 2002 Census reported that over one-quarter of the residents of these areas claimed to use the language less frequently than weekly (CSO, 2002).

So, the Irish context contains three elements in effect, all of which could be exploited by advertisers: the Irish language as the first official language of the country with largely symbolic meaning and value for a majority (Edwards, 1985); the Irish language as an indigenous, regional minority language in a largely English-speaking context; and, thirdly, English with an Irish accent/dialect. While the written English in Ireland is 'more or less indistinguishable from that of standard British English' (Harris, 1997, p. 39), there is much greater variety in the spoken form, and it is this oral variation that is seen by many as its distinguishing form, in terms of lexical and grammatical differences.[7] Through the 'writing down' of Irish-English speech, firstly in literature, and more recently through informalization (see below), it can be argued that an Irish-English written variety has evolved. As John Harris (1997) has pointed out, 'there is no such thing as a set of codified norms defining a standard Irish English accent' (p. 39), and despite the existence of notional external norms, which would also apply to English speakers in Britain, 'total assimilation to such norms is extremely rare, even in the most formal of settings' (*ibid.*). The part played by advertising in this complex sociolinguistic situation is what is of concern for the remainder of this chapter.

Informalization

As pointed out in Chapter 1, multi-voicedness, in Bakhtin's terms, does not just refer to different **lang**uages, but also to the appearance of different accents, dialects and varieties in a text. The extension of this multi-voicedness into the sphere of the media can be seen to be part of the informalization trend referred to earlier in the chapter. Norman Fairclough (1992), for example, uses this term to describe the phenomenon whereby the traditional barriers between different speech domains have been blurred and weakened and informal speech and dialect are found on what have traditionally been considered formal media. Fairclough (1992) and others (Goodman, 1996) see this development as the result of changes in social structures, and the motivation behind such informalization is generally a desire to build solidarity with the listener, viewer, reader, consumer and to construct the speaker, writer, actor, brand, company as 'one of us' rather than 'one of them'. Fairclough argues that encounters with such texts are not insignificant in constructions of identities in a mediatized, fragmented society, and this would certainly appear to be part of the motivation behind the use of such language in advertisements.

At its most basic level, this informalization can involve the writing down of spoken language, something that is increasingly seen in what was traditionally a medium of standard language, namely print advertising. The term 'print' advertising seems anachronistic now and in fact a new term is needed to differentiate between advertisements in which language is spoken and those in which language is written (for example, newspaper, magazine, billboard, shop window, signage, Internet sites, television screen, and so on). In such written advertisements, as noted earlier, the advertiser was traditionally seen as the authoritative voice – in Bourdieu's terms – and part of this image of authority was certainly conveyed by using either a standardized or prestige variety in spoken and even more prominently in written advertising. However, today,

in this written advertising language there are in fact numerous examples
of spoken language, an indication of a trend towards Fairclough's notion
of informalization. As with the foreign linguistic fetish discussed in
Chapter 2, the informalization may seem only minimal, as for example
in the following slogan in which the contracted 'it's' and 'don't' are used
in preference to the formal written standard 'it is' and 'do not':

> It's the Volkswagen that does what other Volkswagens don't.
>
> (www.vw.com)

In this German example, from international Swedish furniture brand,
Ikea, the informal '*du*' generally confined to communications between
close friends or family members, is used to create an informal situation:

> Wohnst du noch oder lebst du schon?   (www.ikea.de)
> (Are you actually living yet?).

Advertising on the British *Ikea* website uses the informal/colloquial
'stuff' to create the same effect:

> With endless possibilities for endless amounts of stuff, our PAX wardrobe
> range is the perfect accomplice.   (www.ikea.co.uk)

It could be argued that these are examples of what might be termed
'standardized informalizations'. In other words, it is informal spoken
language that is widely accepted by a larger and not specifically local
group of speakers of a language. The use of such informalizations in
'normal' everyday speech interactions between individuals is generally
viewed as being the result of spontaneous talk. However, where a company or brand produces an advertising slogan that is the result of a conscious effort, rather than a spontaneous utterance, and spends money
printing it or putting it in the market domain in which the writing
down of words involves considerable expense, then, I would argue that
a powerful message is sent about what is acceptable and unacceptable.
The use of informalizations in advertising thus contributes to their
becoming part of the acceptable, even authoritative language, as
Bourdieu would term it, of public communication in a culture.

Informalization can also be used in written advertising language to a
greater degree as part of a strategy designed to localize a text for a
particular audience. This could involve the inclusion of dialect items or
the writing down of an accented pronunciation, as, for example, on the

Volkswagen site for North America, the italicized words being typically –
or perhaps stereotypically – USAmerican:

> *Buckle up*
> See what VW *has cooking*
> Just means it might be time for *folks* to get some more detailed maps
> A *sassy* sedan at heart
> The *swanky* sedan   (www.vw.com)

Likewise in an advertisement for Scottish mineral water, the slogan ('see
for yourself how pure it is') is written in a way designed to represent a
Scottish accent:

> Seefur yersel how pure itis
>
> How do we protect the area of land that filters Highland Spring? With a
> vengeance. Because if nothing gets on our land, naturally nothing will
> get into our water.
>
> IT COULDN'T BE
> CLEARER

The product being advertised here, mineral water, is one that sits well
with notional Scottish cultural competence, and the linguistic decoration provided by the accent perfectly complements the message
contained in the text body, for example 'our land ... our water'.

Informalization and the Irish context

In terms of informalization in the Irish context, advertisers have two
possibilities. They can add colour by choosing to use an accent that is
specific to a particular part of the country, or they may choose to include
dialect items that identify the language as specifically Irish-English.
Accents associated with particular counties have not appeared in advertising to any great extent. Instead, what is widely considered a 'neutral'
Irish media voice tends to be used. Neutral is used here in inverted commas to indicate that this accent is far from having no connotations: to
the Irish ear it sounds like an educated, urbane (Dublin) voice. This is
an interesting point since accents associated with particular counties are
not absent from other realms of public discourse and are widely used by
elites in Irish society. It is also fair to say that rural accents are not seen
as class-specific, whereas urban ones tend to be associated with class

divisions. However, despite the fact that accents are heard on radio and television in interviews with politicians and other elite groups, advertisers have been wary of using accents as part of their strategy. As Harrison (2002) points out: 'It is a frequent complaint that Irish radio advertising is dominated by middle class Dublin accents that are so bland they blend into each other after a while.' The reason for this may well be that when local accents are used in advertisements, they can lead to controversy. For example, when *eircom.net*, an Irish Internet service provider and telecommunications company, used a Cork accent[8] in a recent campaign, so many complaints were received – generally from Cork people – that the ad was withdrawn and rerecorded using a 'neutral' Irish radio voice (Harrison, 2002). The reason may very well have been the fact that the Cork-accented new employee in the advertisement was making lecherous comments about the daughter of his new employer. Therein lies the heart of the problem with choosing and using accents in commercial discourses such as advertising. They tend to be used in preference to a 'neutral' voice to add colour and character to an advertisement, sometimes positive, sometime negative, and the latter can cause offence. For instance, a television campaign by the National Lottery in Ireland subverted its normal slogan, 'It could be you', to 'It could be him/her/them', in an attempt to remind people to keep playing the lottery in case someone else, someone objectionable, won instead. The construction of these individuals as objectionable is largely done through accent. For instance, one advertisement featured a man with a strong Cavan accent, often associated in Ireland with meanness, while another featured a hyperbolized upper-class English accent, a guaranteed irritant in an Irish context since it is readily associated with the colonial past.

Telecom Phonewatch, a monitored burglar alarm service, chose to portray deviant criminal behaviour using an urban 'uneducated', in this case Dublin, accent in a radio advertisement. The advertisement was aired during the Christmas season and it featured a man in a Dublin accent saying, 'Just what I always wanted', when he comes across a house that is not monitored by *Phonewatch*.

Although largely the preserve of radio and television advertisements, the use of accent and dialect is not of course confined to spoken texts, but can also be written down, as was the case in the Scottish mineral water advertisement cited earlier. The next example, from a Dublin Bus poster campaign, provokes a more positive reaction to this urban, unsophisticated dialect, presenting it as something cool, rather like a scene from the screen version of Dublin writer Roddy Doyle's novel

The Commitments. The visual features a man, holding a pint glass of beer, being kissed by a woman, and slogan is as follows:

  At the end of the night, it's a guaranteed ride.

The bottom part of the text gives information about the Nitelink bus service offered by Dublin Bus, and the logo of the company. The slogan is successful through its use of the word 'ride', which has a double meaning in this context: the standard meaning of ride, that is the drive home provided by the bus, and the colloquial, Dublin dialect term 'ride', namely sex, offered by the female. In this particular situation, speaking the dialect is presented as something positive, unlike the burglar alarm advertisement.

It is important to point out, then, that the positive connotation tends always to be a fetishized one, in that it is associated with a particular product or service from that particular area: for example in the Dublin case, it is Dublin Bus. However, when it appears in the middle of other more neutral accents, and is not linked directly with some positive product, characteristic, service or location, specifically associated with the accent or dialect, then it is often negative, as in the case of the burglary alarm advertisement. It is also important to question whether the 'positive' fetish would be deemed suitable for all goods and services, for example a brand of car as opposed to a bus service. So, what appears to be a positive portrayal of an accent can in fact reinforce perceptions about dialects and accents and their speakers.

Adding colour[9]

Brennan's Bread is the dominant brand of bread on the Irish market, and its radio advertisements have been ongoing for about twenty years (McSweeney, 2003). The advertisements follow a well-established format, which is very familiar to Irish radio listeners, in which the trusted employee recounts a dialogue between himself and his boss, Mr Brennan, who is famous for his pronouncements on current affairs, family matters, almost everything in fact. In the advertisement transcribed below, Mr Brennan shows his cynicism with regard to new technology, and throws out his deputy's suggestion that he buy a computer game for the neighbour's child ('snapper' or 'whippersnapper' in Dublin dialect) as a birthday present. Mr Brennan's thinking is that his *Whippersnapper* bread is already giving the boy everything he needs and everything Irish mothers ('mas' in Dublin English) could want for their sons:

1. 'Eh, leavin' early?' says I t'ol' Misther Brennan.[10]
2. 'Customer care' says he. >'Birthday party for the neighbour's whippersnapper'[11]<
3. 'Did you geh' him somehin' good?' says I. 'One o' them (.) compu:ther games.'
4. 'Comput her games (h)?' says he. 'Sure don't I give him everythin' he wants everyday?'
5. 'How d'yeh mean?' says I.
6. >'Whippersnapper bread' says he<
7. 'Whipper wha'?' says I.
8. 'Whippersnapper bread (h)', says he. 'Sure it's wha' the mas[12] were cryin' out for.'
9. IFRV: Brennan's Whippersnapper. A soft white bread enriched with the calcium, vitamins and iron that growing children need.
10. 'Tha's wha' they asked for (h)', says he. 'An' sure tha's wha' they got (h)'.
11. IFRV: Brennan's Whippersnapper: Today's best bread for today's growing children.

The narrator of the advertisements, Mr Brennan's employee, has a strong Dublin accent and uses dialect items that are associated with Dublin. This ties in perfectly with the brand image, since 'Dublin represent the bakery's origins, heritage and location' (McSweeney, 2003). However, far from being 'authentic' Dublin discourse, the speech seems contrived, and stereotypical features of Irish-English are found almost everywhere. For example, the use of the particle 'sure' as a discourse marker; the alveolar (for example cryin' etc.) rather than the nasal velar (crying) and the characteristic vowel sounds and diphthongs (computer = compu:ter) to mention but a few. Furthermore, there is no attempt made to rephrase the conversation as reported or indirect speech, something that highlights the informality of the approach.

Coming as it does in the middle of advertisements featuring neutralized Irish radio voices, the hyper-accented Dublin dialect seems old-fashioned and out of place. The anachronistic nature of the language is highlighted by the Irish female radio voice (IFRV). This voice, although identifiably Irish, is not coloured by any regional flavour, and is best described as an Irish radio voice, as discussed above. The handover to this more neutral voice at the end of the advertisement highlights the display or fetishized nature of the 'Dublin speech' used up to that point.

The use of the term 'neutral' here is perhaps misleading, as mentioned earlier, although this is probably how it would be described in the particular sociolinguistic context in which it is used. Far from being without connotation or association, the accent represents the authoritative voice, the voice of education and sophistication. It is the voice that has linguistic capital in the sense that it is to be taken seriously, and it is needed in order to give credibility to Mr Brennan's 'colourful' speech. In such a context, Bourdieu's observations about the patronising nature of talking to someone 'in their own language', referred to in Chapter 1, ring very true.

In the advertisement just examined, everything said by the narrator up to the point where the Irish female radio voice intervenes could be categorized as 'redundant' or 'given' (cf. Chapter 1) in terms of the information-giving objectives of the advertisement. On the other hand, 'entropic' or 'new' (cf. Chapter 1) information relies on greater input on the part of the advertisee in order for the information to be communicated, or it requires a change of strategy on the part of the advertiser in order to ensure the message gets across. Therefore, the neutralized female radio voice can be seen to signal the pronouncement of new, important information, a process Sperber and Wilson (1986) term ostension, and to help with the processing of that information. The Dublin speech is clearly perceived as not suitable for such a purpose. This reinforces the point made earlier about the bilingual Spanish–English drug advertisements in the USA.

A similar approach is taken in an Irish television advertisement for *Jacob's* 'Thai' crackers, although there is a third association at work in this particular text. A couple are shown eating the crackers while being rowed down a river in what appears to be Thailand. The narrator (who has an Irish male media voice) tells the advertisee that strange things happen when eating the crackers. All of a sudden, the couple are addressed by the Thais selling produce from river boats, but in the accent and idiom of Dublin market-stall dealers. The punchline of the advertisements reads, 'Thai with an Irish accent'. The intervention of the Irish media voice in the form of the narrator has the effect of interpreting the interplay of the accents for the listener/viewer, in order to ensure understanding, in much the same way as this type of 'neutral' voice is used in the *Brennan's Bread* advertisement.

Leakage and multi-voicedness

There has always been 'leakage' of British advertisements into Ireland through the multi-channel environment;[13] however, the BBC and ITV channels are geared to a regional audience, namely Northern Ireland (BBC Northern Ireland and Ulster Television or UTV), so there is some sense of targeting. Thus, the Southern Irish viewer is used to seeing advertisements for chains and brands that are neither known nor encountered on a daily basis. However, it is clear from location and other cases that these are part of the Northern Irish shopping context, that is both something regional and something part of a larger UK market context.

The decision to buy radio space on Irish terrestrial television or radio is, however, something different, and given the costs involved it is unlikely that advertisers give the question of adaptation no thought at all. In certain cases an Irish accent is dubbed onto an advertisement aimed at a British audience, whereas in other cases the British accent is retained. Furthermore, such choices do not always follow a standard pattern. For example, while advertisements for international detergent products such as *Bold* and *Daz* have for many years been dubbed into an Irish accent, advertisements for *Lenor* fabric conditioner feature a north of England accent and advertisements for *Persil* feature a couple with an Essex-style accent. Incidentally, this is the same pitch as used on British advertisements, and in both contexts, it would seem, the accent is intended to add to the characterization of the voices, although the regional associations are specific to the UK and would not be known extensively in Ireland. A different approach is taken in an advertisement for *Beechams 4 Flu* medication. Here, the voices are dubbed into an Irish accent, albeit a standard Irish media voice. A schizophrenic situation arises, however, from the fact that the British version of the advertisement can also be seen on the British/Northern Irish channels broadcast in Southern Ireland, while the dubbed Irish accent version can be seen on the Southern Irish terrestrial channels. This situation then opens up the possibility of a type of condescension effect (as discussed in Chapter 1), in that the Irish viewer may feel patronized by this dual-language approach.

So, there are a number of different scenarios regarding accent choice, each of which may have different effects on the listener/viewer, intended or not: first of all, there is no change simply as an oversight or because the advertiser has not considered it to be an issue, something that is in and of itself interesting, reflecting perhaps an ethnocentric view of the world and/or a lack of knowledge about different accents or sensitivities to them; secondly, there may be no change, but as the result of a deliberate tactic. Here the accent chosen for the British audience may be deemed suitable/acceptable for the Irish audience, or the associations (positive or negative), which the accent is supposed to summon up may be deemed by the advertiser to be common to both audiences, largely as a result of the media context and consequent inter-textual sphere that is partially shared. Thirdly, there may be leakage of advertisements aimed at a British audience through multi-channel broadcasting in Ireland. Fourthly, there may be a change of accent, the result of the advertiser wishing to adopt a 'host-culture primacy' approach (cf. Jain, 1990), as in the case of the *Beecham's 4 Flu*, but this may backfire, as in this case due to circumstances over which the advertiser has no control, or due to an underestimation of the complexity of the media audience on the part of the advertiser.

The Northern Irish accent

The choice not to use an accent when advertising a particular product, location and so on that has a strong accent associated with it in the context in question is equally significant. The Northern Irish accent is a problematic one in Irish market and media texts, a point well-illustrated by the next example. In an advertisement on Irish radio for investment in Northern Ireland, the two voices, one male, one female, are both prototypical Irish radio voices, as discussed above, with no hint of a Northern accent. The decision not to use an identifiably Northern accent is noteworthy here for a number of reasons. The product being sold is investment opportunities and the pitch is the fact that there are creative people in Northern Ireland, 'a hop across the border', who could benefit businesses in the Republic. Thus, one could speculate that the choice of a Southern media voice here seems an attempt at neutrality, designed to de-emphasize differences between North and South, to transgress or even obliterate the political and economic border between these two places. A further objective may well be to move away from the received association of a Northern accent and its 'map of meaning', to use Stuart Hall *et al.*'s (1978) notion, in Southern Ireland, namely its connotation, in a media context at least, of the 'Troubles'. The Northern accents most frequently heard on Southern Irish media are those of politicians posturing, or of entrenched 'community leaders' – none of which connote well with creativity and investment. So, in this context, the associations of the accent are not exploited for commercial purposes, rather they are in fact downplayed. This confirms what Raymond Hickey (1986 cited in Harris, 1997) has pointed out, namely that 'in neither of the states of Ireland is it considered desirable to emulate the phonological norm of the other' (p. 46).

A further interesting observation about this particular piece of advertising is its lexical choice of 'the North'. A whole volume could be written on this topic, but basically the vocabulary choice between 'the North' and 'Northern Ireland' indicates membership of the 'nationalist community' or Southern Irish nationality in the case of the former ('the North') versus membership of the 'unionist community' or perhaps British nationality or a desire to show sensitivity towards these 'groups' in the case of the latter ('Northern Ireland'). Thus, by using 'the North', the advertiser is going even further in an attempt to identify with 'the South'. This lexical choice would certainly not figure in a UK-wide advertisement, which would most likely use 'Northern Ireland'. Through the linguistic choices made in the advertisement, both in terms of accent and lexis, the advertiser is placing the advertisement firmly within the cultural context of Southern Ireland.

The Irish language and advertising

In the English-dominated context of Irish media and market communication, what role can Irish play as a language within market discourses? Two main functions were proposed earlier: firstly, a symbolic function that can be activated to exploit a sense of Irishness for the population in general; secondly, a medium for communicating with Irish speakers.

The Internet is perhaps one place where minority languages can find a space for themselves, given the relatively cheap way in which information can be presented in different ways and languages. The leading Internet search engine, www.google.com offers an Irish-language version on its local www.google.ie site. On the site, visitors see the following message: 'Google.ie offered in *Gaeilge*' – the Irish name for the language – and are then directed to a fully Irish version of the familiar google.com page. The Irish language *Google* home page is fully in Irish, and in format is more or less identical to the English version. The effect of seeing Irish being presented in an equal way to English, in a technologically advanced medium and in a forum that is both global and part of everyday working and leisure life, should not be underestimated. This presence adds greatly to the credibility of Irish as a contemporary language, something Nancy Dorian (1991) has commented on in relation to the presence of minority languages in modern media in general.

Furthermore, the fact that when a search term is entered in Irish, the Irish language results are prioritized, and only once these have been listed do English-language sites featuring the particular word appear, also sends a powerful message about the status and importance of the language. However, these effects are somewhat undermined by the fact that two links are missing in the Irish-language home page, namely 'Advertising solutions' and 'Business solutions'. The one link that does remain, '*An tEolas ar fad faoi Google*' ('All about *Google*'), leads to an English site which then contains the advertising and business solutions links in English. These omissions, although seemingly minor, are rather telling. From the user's point of view they tend to reinforce notions about the 'acceptability' in Bourdieu's (1991) terms (cf. Chapter 1) of Irish as a language of the market and confirm the idea that English is the language for doing serious business.

There is a wide variety of Irish-language resources on the Internet, some commercially based, most not. The Irish language Internet magazine, *Beo* (literally meaning 'alive'), has advertising and sponsorship on almost every page. Some of the advertising is wholly in Irish and links to Irish-only or fully bilingual sites; while other advertisements are in Irish, but then link to wholly English-language sites; and, still more advertisements are in English and link to English-language-only sites. In terms of commercial links, there are a number of interesting advertising texts worth commenting on, for instance, an Irish-language advertisement for a bilingual 'Friends reunited'-type website, www. cairdeschoilecaillte.ie/www.lostschoolfriends.ie. It is significant that this website, based on a number of models in other countries, which seeks to reunite old schoolfriends, should choose to present itself bilingually. The period of compulsory education is the time in which the most Irish is spoken, heard, seen and written for the majority of the population, and this tapers off dramatically once people leave school. Furthermore, a certain percentage of the population will have had their schooling, either primary or secondary, or sometimes both, through Irish. Thus, the language has a strong association with 'school days' for many individuals. And, even if the individual does not use the Irish version of the site, the presence of the language does, I would argue, help to enhance the image of the 'product'.

An all-Irish ad for *Gaelsaoire*, Irish-language holidays in the Galway *Gaeltacht*, links to a bilingual site in which the Irish and English options are placed, significantly, side by side (rather than one being placed in a superior position). There, is, however, no standard practice with regard to use of the Irish language, even within the same sector. For example, an ad for www.litriocht.com links to an Irish-language bookshop. The site is bilingual, but the housekeeping and standard Internet terms are in English. On the other hand, an advertisement for www.coislife.ie, also an Irish-language publisher, links to a website that gives a choice of a number of languages, Irish being listed first, before English, French, Dutch and others. In the non-Irish messages, visitors are 'warned' that all publications are in Irish. When the visitor selects the Irish option they are linked to a fully Irish site in which housekeeping matters, standard Internet items and so on are all in Irish. The multilingual policy is followed through in the other language versions of the website as well. It could be argued that this policy is, to a certain extent, motivated by the same objectives as those that drive linguistic fetish. For example, it is clearly seen as important for the image of a minority language publisher to pursue a genuine policy of commercial multilingualism, and, in such a context, to treat English as just another language. Thus, it would, arguably, contradict the publisher's image to have English language items on a non-English website. This is the opposite to the policy of using English to create an international image for websites, as discussed in the previous chapter. However, the motivation, using languages and notions about languages to sell products, is not dissimilar.

Another advertisement for www.smaointe.com, literally 'thoughts', links to an online Irish-language card shop. The site is basically bilingual, but uses English for housekeeping and standard Internet items. The dot.com suffix here is an interesting one, and worth commenting on. The company is actually based in Northern Ireland, and it would appear that there is a trend for Irish-language websites based in Northern Ireland to opt for this type of non-country-specific suffix, rather than the more usual dot.co.uk one that would immediately give away the company's identity and single it out as 'British' rather than 'authentically Irish'. Likewise, the website address of *Lá*, the Irish-language newspaper based in Belfast, is www.nuacht.com, literally 'news'.

Another advertisement on the '*Beo*' website is for the 'Milwaukee Irish Fest'. Folk music and heritage festivals are, it can be argued, a standard commercial domain within which the Irish-language features. However, when the link leads the viewer to the actual site of the Fest, s/he finds only tokenistic use of Irish-language vocabulary items with a fair number of what the expert or even the fairly competent user of the language would recognize as mistakes. A further example of the commercial use of Irish for purely tokenistic purposes is found in another link from the website featuring the Irish traditional music group Clannad. There is, in fact, very little Irish on the website; however, in the list of names of the band members, the 'Gaelic' (*sic*) is given, along with the phonetic pronunciation. So, there is the bizarre situation – rather reminiscent of many school situations where Irish versions of names were assigned to pupils – whereby someone who is called in everyday life by an English name has it translated into Irish for what, in this context, can only be described as commercial decoration. This conclusion is supported by the fact that the translations are missing necessary accents and misspellings are common. The overall impression, then, is that these aspects are not important since this particular version of Irish is not really for Irish speakers and does not have a strictly referential purpose. This is enhanced by the use of 'Gaelic', rather than 'Irish' or *'Gaeilge'*, to describe the language, a term rarely (if ever) used by individuals who know the language, but one often used by those who only know of it.

The language ideology approach to marketing

Another link from *Beo* leads to the site of the *Europus* translation agency, based in the Galway *Gaeltacht*. Its clients include the public and civil service and it provides the teletext service for the Irish language channel TG4 (http://indigo.ie/~europus/europus.html). The site is fully bilingual, the introductory sequence requiring a choice of language at the beginning. It would be unthinkable for such a site to be fully in English, or even to allow the use of English for Internet housekeeping purposes, since to do so would not only undermine, it would actually negate the necessity for the product being offered, namely translation into and out of Irish. So, here is an example of the language-as-product type of approach to minority-language advertising. More than this, however, a type of minority-language ideology advertising strategy seems to be operating here. As the following extract shows, a chauvinistic discourse of superiority of the Irish language is present in the advertising language used:

> Why not express yourself in the most professional and correct way in the most learned and versatile of languages. Use that which is more authentically Irish than any other aspect of our most ancient but vibrant culture – OUR LANGUAGE.   (http://indigo.ie/~europus/)

Two further examples serve to highlight this 'language ideology' advertising strategy. As in the case of *Europus*, they both come from the domain of the communications industry, which is not surprising since for such companies the Irish language is the product being sold. The first, www.fiosfeasa.com, is a producer of 'Irish interactive media'. The introductory page requires the visitor to opt for *Gaeilge* or English, both placed side by side, and once this choice is made the *Gaeilge* version is fully in that language, although the slogan 'Irish-interactive media' does remain present. The sales pitch for the product, Irish-language interactive media, is made using the following text (the English language version is quoted here):

> It has been the spoken language of Ireland for over two thousand years, and has an extensive literature stretching back to the seventh century. While Irish speakers are very much a minority in the Ireland of today, they have an importance to the cultural life of the nation far out of proportion to their numbers. (www.fiosfeasa.com)

The second example, www.webbery.ie, a web-design service, follows a similar design to fiosfeasa.com in terms of its bilingual format. The company is attempting to persuade individuals and other companies to have a website that is in Irish, or at least bilingual:

> On each page your customers will be able to choose between English and Irish. Alternatively you may choose to have a site in English only or Irish only. We encourage the use of the Irish Language. You will find that the use of Irish will attract users to your site as it adds to the unique flavour of an Irish business. (www.webbery.ie)

In the webbery.ie example, the advertiser is admitting not only to a language-ideology-driven business strategy, but also to the inherently fetishistic rather than referential function the language has in a market context, in that 'it adds to the unique flavour of an Irish business'. Examining the taken-for-granted common sense being promoted by these texts leads to the following conclusions: the Irish language is minoritized, but inherently superior; it is very old; those who speak Irish are somehow culturally superior; to be authentically Irish is to use Irish; linguistic decoration in Irish adds to the Irishness of the product or message; the Irish language is 'our language'. It was asserted earlier in relation to Spanish-language advertising agencies in the USA that the statements made about language and the prominence given to language in the promotional material of these agencies would not feature in comparable material of English-language agencies operating in the USA, who are, in effect, operating in the default language. However, the tone and nature of the statements made to promote the products and services being sold by the three Irish-language consultancies cited above could never feature in relation to statements about the English language in Ireland. In such a context, the language-ideology approach to advertising is permitted for the minority language, but not for the majority one. The final point about these communications products is that none of the promotional texts puts forward a communicative/informative argument for using the language on websites, in multimedia or in other business documents. All of the advantages of using Irish in a commercial context or reasons for doing so have to do with symbolism.

Irish language advertising and the public sector

One of the main domains where Irish language advertising is found – although always in a bilingual version – is in the public and civil sector. This has to do with the status of Irish, as discussed above, which means that government and legal documents have to be produced in Irish and English versions. In addition, many positions within the public and civil service have to be advertised bilingually, and information coming from government agencies often has to be provided bilingually. For example, leaflets from the Department of Health advertising the flu vaccine are produced in Irish as well as English, and *Iarnród Éireann*, the state-owned Irish railway company, provides a certain level of bilingual signposting in stations and on trains and publishes Irish language advertisements and information for customers in the *Gaeltacht*.

Aer Lingus is the Irish national carrier, and as such has traditionally been seen as having a duty to represent the nation and its symbols, and one of these is, of course, the Irish language. Consequently, air stewards have always said the '*cúpla focal'* – literally a few words, used by people to indicate that they will make an effort and say something small and tokenistic in Irish before moving onto the important information (in English) – to welcome the assembled passengers onto the airplane. So, there is an element of tokenistic code-switching involved: the few words in Irish make the group feel cohesive; it makes them feel good about being Irish; and, it emphasizes the product's difference for tourists and visitors. However, the safety demonstration that follows the '*cúpla focal'* would never be given in Irish, nor would it be given bilingually. So, the effect of this linguistic decoration is, once again, to reinforce the symbolism at the heart of using Irish in many domains in Irish society.

What is interesting to note in this discussion is the notable absence of Irish from some rather obvious domains in this 'public' sector. The best example of this is the website and promotional materials of Tourism Ireland. Tourism Ireland was set up following the Good Friday Agreement[14] – one objective of which was to institute more North–South, cross-border cooperation at an institutional level – and is dedicated to 'promoting the Island of Ireland overseas' (www.tourismireland.com), in other words, Northern Ireland and the Republic. This agency has taken over the role and functions of *Bord Fáilte*, literally 'welcome agency', the tourism agency in the Republic of Ireland which, in its name at least, used tokenistic Irish to differentiate the product being offered. However, Irish does not appear at all on the Tourism Ireland home webpage, nor on the many country-specific versions that are basically translations of the home site. The only linguistic fetish used on these French, Dutch, Danish, Finnish and other. versions is English, in the form of phrases and brands such as 'Ireland Welcome Offers'. Also noteworthy in this context is the respect given to Belgium's official bilingualism. The Belgian site offers the option to view the site in French or Dutch, but no such option is available on the Ireland site.

Irish and food

There are also cases where a commercial venture operating in the 'public' sphere will opt to use Irish. So, for example, the local dairy in Limerick writes a bilingual 'letter' to parents of school-going children to encourage them to subscribe to the school milk scheme. The milk packaging the children receive is also bilingual, with the Irish *'bainne úr'* on one side and 'fresh milk' on the other. This type of display/fetish/ association makes sense for a product like milk that is so bound up on the one hand with children – Irish, as stated earlier, being a language primarily associated, for most people, with school and childhood – and, on the other, with agriculture, an important facet of both country image and country identity in the Irish context. In fact, food advertising in general is one place where Irish is found, either on product labelling or in supermarket aisles.

Superquinn, a highly successful, upmarket domestic retailer has always used bilingual Irish–English signposting in its supermarkets. What is interesting about this approach is that at the time *Superquinn* began doing this, there were no major British chains operating in Ireland. The main competitors were the domestic chains, *Dunnes Stores* and *Quinnsworth*. In the previous context, the use of Irish could be seen to be part of *Superquinn*'s policy of differentiating itself from both of these entities. *Quinnsworth* was owned by a Canadian retailer who, although domiciled in Ireland, was not the 'real thing', as the very visible head of *Superquinn*, Feargal Quinn, was. *Dunnes Stores* is an Irish legend, founded by the famous patriarch Ben Dunne, a brand 'interwoven as it is into the very fabric of Irish society' (www.dunnesstores.ie). However, *Dunnes Stores'* approach to Irishness can be seen to be analogous to that of *Ryanair*. It is a utilitarian one, not a symbolic one, and so there is no room in this type of image for the Irish language. *Superquinn's* stores were at that time mostly located in the better-off suburbs of Dublin, they stocked unusual and high-quality foods and they knew that people who visited their stores, on the whole the middle-classes, valued the language and the notion that it made them different, particularly from British people. Today, the main competition remains *Dunnes Stores* and the British-owned *Tesco Ireland*, which bought out *Quinnsworth*. In this new context, the strategy of commercial bilingualism adopted by *Superquinn* can be seen as differentiating itself on the one hand from *Dunnes Stores*, which although it has moved upmarket has retained its image of being about a type of down-to-earth Irishness, rather than any romantic image of the country, and on the other hand *Tesco Ireland*, which, everyone knows, is really a British company. Being sensitive to these issues, *Tesco* then also decided to adopt this policy of bilingual signposting in its supermarkets, perhaps to make it look more Irish, or perhaps to show goodwill and an openness to the local culture. Irish is, however, absent from the *Tesco Ireland* website, while on the *Superquinn* site it only appears in the tokenistic 'Fáilte from Feargal Quinn' (welcome from Fergal Quinn), but nowhere else on the website.

In the *Superquinn* shops, apart from the aisle signposting, Irish signage is reserved for the most natural of products only: bread, meat, fish and cheese. Again, this ties in with the perceived commercial domain of the language, something that is exploited by other companies, such as the Cork-based *Alternative Bread Company*. The Irish version of the brand '*Ár nArán diffiriúil*' appears underneath the English one, and again, as stated earlier, bread as a natural product is one that seems to be perceived to 'suit' the Irish language in commercial terms. However, the slogan is also a pun, and one that speaks very specifically to the domestic community. The slogan alludes to the line from the Christian prayer, the 'Our Father' or 'Lord's Prayer', 'Give us this day our daily bread', which in Irish reads as follows: '*Ár n-arán leathúil, tabhair dúinn inniu*'. 'Our daily bread' (*Ár n-arán leathúil*) rhymes with 'our alternative bread' (*Ár nArán diffiriúil*), and the brand slogan therefore seems to allude to the prayer learned in Irish by many people during their school years. Therefore, it also conjures up memories of childhood nostalgia – all images that add to the product's believability. So, in this context, the Irish language chosen for the slogan seems to have two different but complementary functions. The first is to reinforce the fact that this is a natural, staple, simple product. The second is that it is a domestic product.

Folláin, a jam-making business based in the Cork *Gaeltacht*, has an Irish name, the English explanation for which, 'the Irish for wholesome', is printed as part of the label. The company name and address are in Irish on the homepage of its website, and this introductory page also includes an Irish proverb, '*Saolfada agus Croí Folláin*' with an English translation, 'Health and a Long Life'. However, once the visitor moves past this page, the links and other pages are all in English and the address for ordering is also in English. This can be seen to reinforce the symbolism of the Irish on the introductory page, since when it is important that potential customers know the correct address so that they can place an order, the address is given in English to avoid confusion, frustration and so on, but also perhaps to place the business within the mainstream, while the Irish fetish is used to reinforce the naturalness of the product.

Advertising on Irish-language television

Advertising on TG4, the Irish-language television station, provides another interesting insight into the functioning of Irish as a language of the market. The public broadcaster in Ireland, RTÉ, does have a remit to promote the Irish language through a quota of programmes in the language. On the commercial side it is possible to advertise in Irish on public-service television, and companies/brands that do this have traditionally been entitled to a discount on the cost of advertising. However, despite this incentive, only a tiny minority have ever availed of this. The most notable has been *Homestead*, an Irish-based grocery brand, while *Erin Foods* has also produced an advertisement in which a song is sung in Irish. Again, significantly, both of these are from the food domain. The case of TG4, discussed below, throws some light on why so few take up this opportunity.

The all-Irish television station was launched in 1996 as *Teilifís na Gaeilge* or *TnaG* for short. Although TG4 is in effect a public service, receiving a subsidy from the main national broadcaster, RTÉ, like all of the public channels in Ireland it also has a commercial aspect to it and can make money through selling advertising. At the time of the launch there was, according to Anna Barry responsible for selling advertising time on the channel, great energy and enthusiasm for advertising in the Irish language to complement the new station. So, not just native brands such as *Bank of Ireland*, *Brennan's Bread*, *Homestead*, *Irish Biscuits* and *Telecom* produced advertising in Irish for the launch of the station, but also global brands such as *Kellogg's* and *Toyota* to name a few (Barry, 2003). Since there are no monolingual speakers of Irish, there was no strictly 'practical' or 'communicative' need for the former group, the native brands, to translate their current campaigns into Irish, and their motivation can be seen mainly in terms of creating goodwill through advertising, showing that they cared enough about the language to take the trouble to have the advertisements created specially in the language. It could also be argued that in doing so they were constructing themselves as 'particularly Irish' in an attempt to appeal to patriot consumers (cf. Chapter 1). For the latter group, the desire was to differentiate themselves from other global competitors and make themselves appear more accommodating to local culture (Barry, 2003). The station, however, got off to a poor start. Viewing figures were low, and in many cases it took a very long time for advertisements to achieve the airtime – in terms of potential viewers – that they had been sold. This relatively unsuccessful launch seems to have taken the momentum out of this desire to use Irish language advertising (Barry, 2003).

The station was relaunched as *Teilifís na Gaeilge 4* or TG4, in 1999. The renaming was part of a strategy to reposition the channel as the fourth national, terrestrial channel, after RTÉ1, Network 2, and the more recent addition of TV3, owned by British-based entertainment group Granada. In this scheme, TG4 became for advertisers just another channel, and this change in attitude also affected the policy and practice with regard to advertising. Before the arrival of TV3, Irish advertisers were used to reaching a huge percentage of the audience through just two main stations, and were not really interested in buying advertising on smaller stations such as TG4. However, the success of the popular TV3 changed this attitude and made advertisers more willing to use smaller stations, regardless of size, and to put together campaigns that would work across the growing number of stations in Ireland in order to achieve a synergistic effect, rather than attempting to reach their entire target audiences through one station (Barry, 2003).

This practical change in the television landscape also led to a change in thinking among advertisers, who no longer addressed the nation as group, but instead began to address groups within the nation individually. The result of this, of course, is that the advertising on TG4 is seen as nothing different, just part of a package, and so, rather inevitably, it is not in Irish. The main reason for buying advertising time on the channel is not the fact that it is in Irish, but the fact that if can offer a cost-effective way to reach about 3–4 per cent of the TV audience in Ireland. In addition, because of the shaky start which TG4 had, the main objective on the part of the station when selling advertising is simply to do just that in order to survive, and so the Irish-language factor has been downplayed. If the brand or company wants to create synergy and impact by repetition of the message, this means using the same visuals and the same voiceovers on a number of different channels, all of which, apart from TG4, are predominantly in English. If the particular individual who does the voiceover for a particular advertisement is not able to speak Irish well or at all, then this interferes with the effectiveness of the overall campaign (Barry, 2003).

A good example would be a global brand like *Procter & Gamble*, which is one of TG4's main advertising customers. The copy in these advertisements changes every month, and so the issue of translating them into Irish is seen to be too problematic since it will inevitably lead to delays. In fact, the cost of creating new copy in Irish may actually exceed the cost of airtime (Barry, 2003). So, with survival the main consideration, the station is not going to force advertisers to put their copy into Irish, although they would gain between 10 per cent and 20 per cent extra airtime if they did. There is, Barry believes, no lack of goodwill towards the language among national and international brands, and many would be willing to broadcast copy in Irish. However, the time and cost factors preclude them from doing so. One suggestion has been that TG4 provide free Irish copy for these advertisers, but this is not viable within the resource constraints under which it operates.

There are, however, some positive things to report from this case study. The first is that the most expensive time to advertise (an indication of the size of the audience and the demand for advertising space) is in the evenings, between 18.00 and 23.00, and this is when the Irish-language programmes for adults are aired.[15] Secondly, except for the English-language films shown on the channel, the next most sought after advertising slots also revolve around Irish-language programmes. These are the Irish-language travel show hosted by national celebrity 'Hector', sporting features such as Ladies Gaelic football and *Rugbaí Beo* (Live Rugby), which have commentary in Irish, and, the very popular Irish soap opera, *Ros na Rún*. Thirdly, the children's programmes on TG4 in the afternoons, aired under the title *Cúla*, have proved so popular that the station has been able to attract global children's brands, although these brands advertise in English. However, their presence is seen as important in that they make the channel look more like its main competitors, Nickleodeon and Network 2 (Barry, 2003). The significance of this is that children who are not living bilingually can be attracted and retained because of the presence of these national and international brands and their advertising texts, something that makes the station seem more 'normal', more mainstream. And, it is then incidental to them that they are watching programmes in Irish. It also changes the associations the language has, namely with school, by viewing it and hearing it in what are 'normal' commercial contexts and in the middle of 'normal' market discourses that are not trying to sell holidays in the *Gaeltacht*, but are trying to persuade children to pester their parents to buy the latest *Playstation* game. So, although Irish may not be the vehicle for commercial messages on the station, it is still the reason why the channel is able to sell its ratings, since the prime-time viewing takes place during the Irish-language programme times. Like Spanish speakers in the USA, Irish speakers thus have the commercial power to attract advertisers; however, unlike the former group, who are also bilingual in the main to a greater or lesser extent, there is no feeling among advertisers, or even among the representatives of the station, that the issue of language is so primary that it is necessary in order to communicate with the target audience.

Today, the main advertisers in Irish on the channel comprise the 'usual suspects': Irish-language newspapers *Foinnse* and *Lá*; Irish-language radio *Raidió na Life*; and, the education sector advertising courses that take place through the medium of Irish. Of 400 campaigns running in any month, only about five will be in Irish (Barry, 2003). Where an advertisement does not fall into the category of Irish publishing, media, education and so on, and is instead from the outside world of national or international brands that are not associated with the language, or even with *language* in general, it certainly stands out if it is aired in Irish. A recent example was an advertisement for the British optician chain *Specsavers*, aired during the afternoon children's television schedule. According to Anna Barry, who is responsible for selling airtime on TG4, the decision by *Specsavers* to have its copy in Irish rather than in English was to do with a desire to overcome an image of being British. Through such a goodwill gesture, the company can show that it is keen to be part of the domestic landscape and that it has set up branches in Ireland to fit in rather than to conquer. Here, then, are the two cases where Irish is currently found in an advertising context on TG4: first, there is the ideologically-driven variety, advertising funded by people who believe in the language and want to maintain it, and so use it to advertise; secondly, there is the tokenistic use, driven by a desire to construct a brand in a particular way as symbolizing something with which the target community can sympathize.

Conclusion

As stated at the beginning of this book, the language choices of advertisers are, it can be argued, never purely arbitrary, and this statement applies even more to the language choices of those advertising in minority languages or in the context of minority-language media, as the examples above highlight.

In the whole area of minority language and ethnic marketing, one cause for concern is the categorizing of many diverse individuals into groups and a consequent reduction of the complexity that is a bilingual existence in a majority-language culture. While this tendency to group individuals is standard practice in marketing, the implications here are slightly more concerning. For instance, it is one thing to be assigned to a 'golfers' or 'gardeners' group, but quite another to be assigned to a 'Turkish' group, when the individual concerned might speak only German and have no contact with Turkey or an imagined Turkish homeland, other than a Turkish name.

Despite growing diversity in the use of minority languages, accents and dialects, there is evidence that these are often used primarily for display or fetish purposes, with the serious business of advertising information being left to the dominant language. Such practices in turn create associations and fetishes for those languages, accents and dialects that are then recycled into future advertising and media messages, and which, in time, come to be part of common-sense assumptions about authoritative versus non-authoritative language. In other words, can the potentially positive effect of multi-voicedness overcome the potentially negative effect in terms of status and prestige, and in terms of what purposes certain languages are deemed 'suitable' for and what purposes they are not suitable for?

There is also an interesting situation whereby official policy is often being undermined, or even contradicted by practice. For example, while governments are often willing to support and nurture autochthonous minority languages, for example Irish in the case of Ireland, or Welsh in Wales,[16] they are correspondingly less willing to lend the same degree of support to the maintenance of allochthonous languages and linguistic communities constituted by immigration. However, it is the latter group that seems to be demanding and getting some kind of response from the 'market' in the form of media and advertising in their language, which is commercially-driven and profitable, and which reflects a 'real' supply-and-demand situation.

This contrasts sharply with the presence of autochthonous languages in the commercial sphere. From the study of the Irish context, it seems clear that this particular minority indigenous language tends to be used in commercially-driven discourse, first of all, for tokenistic purposes in order to create a sense of being at one with the community of the language, or showing goodwill to those who feel they belong to that community. The use may also be driven primarily by fetishistic reasons, and this becomes clear when the range of advertising domains using minority languages is examined. The language becomes associated with particular spheres – in the case of Irish it seems to be primarily food, publishing, music and so on – and its use in advertising then becomes confined to products from those sectors wishing to exploit these associations. This point is made very clearly in the advertisement featured at the beginning of this chapter. The mainly bilingual advertisement, with the heading *'Le chéile arís?'* or 'Back together again?' is an advertisement for the all-Ireland body responsible for promoting the Irish language, *Foras na Gaeilge*. It appeared in the Irish weekly magazine, *Phoenix*, an English-language publication that is a curious mix between business news and satirical political commentary. On the positive side, what is interesting about it is that it is not strictly bilingual, and assumes that the individual can understand more of some aspects of Irish (for example the heading), but less of others. On the negative side, however, it is not an advertisement for clothes, records, commercial services, or other products, but an advertisement for language.

Language choice in commercially-driven discourses may also be the product of a language-ideology-based marketing approach, in which the language is either a core part of the product, and so it must be used in order to add to the credibility of the product – as in the case of the translation agency discussed above – or because the business concerned is headed by individuals who are language-rights activists or involved in language maintenance, or see their customer base as comprising individuals with these convictions. This is particularly the case where the language in question is a language in the process of revitalization or revival, or where there are very few or even no monolingual speakers of the language.

A final important point to make about this particular case study is that all the influences talked about in previous chapters are also at work in this context as well. Linguistic fetishes from other languages are present in the advertisements of global brands, and these are as much a part of the linguistic adscape as ads in Irish-English and the Irish language. This point is brought home when an advertisement on Irish radio for a web-based skiing holiday company is considered. The advertisement opens with a man speaking in English with an 'Austrian' accent and using some German tokens. The speaker is conducting interviews with skiers on the slopes in Austria, trying in vain to find a 'real' Austrian on holiday. The first person he talks to has a strong Irish accent, while the second person answers him in the Irish language. The slogan of the ad is that because of *Ski Direct*, there will be 'more of us over there'. In the advertisement, three different uses of language/accent create three different effects: the fake, hyper-accented German accent constructs the Austrian, the person 'over there'; the strong Irish accent creates the ingroup of Irish people on holidays in Austria; and the Irish speaker represents the most Irish person of all, overwhelming proof of a strong Irish presence on the Austrian ski slopes.

This example illustrates how important it is to remember that the complexities of language use in advertising are not confined to the obvious facts about the sociolinguistic situation of a particular country or region, that instead what is involved is the interplay of the more global with the more local. Likewise, the fluidity of this sociolinguistic situation and its interaction with market discourses also needs to be considered. Data from the Irish census in 2002 put the percentage of 'non-nationals' (as these individuals are termed by the Irish authorities) living in the country at nearly 6 per cent of the population (CSO, 2002). This may not seem large by international comparisons, but it represents a rapid and fairly dramatic change for the Irish context. Already, speakers of other languages are heard on Irish streets, and while 'ethnic marketing' is unlikely to take off to the same extent that it has done in the USA, in many of the larger centres of population, Russian and Arabic signs now appear on streetscapes, giving commercial expression to this new multilingual context.

5
Multilingual Advertising in a Pan-National Media Context

> **want to speak to 46 million young europeans?**
> **we speak their language**

From www.eurosport.com

In previous chapters, the role of multilingualism or 'heteroglossia' in advertisements was examined using what could be termed established or traditional paradigms; in other words, in familiar ways. The notion that people within a geographic, linguistic, economic, political, group will have a common identity and that this identity will be somehow different to those in other geographic, linguistic, economic or political groups is a more familiar one. The self and the other provide a well-established, comfortable and tangible framework or 'habitus' within which the advertisements described in previous chapters can function. This chapter attempts to go beyond this framework to examine the functioning of multilingual or heteroglossic advertising within new paradigms. Many certainties disappear at this point, foremost among them the certainty of the border – be it linguistic, cultural, economic or political – and the assumptions it allows. The media and cultural-communicative contexts presented here are not only new in themselves; the ways in which they are constructed are also new, and that is perhaps the most interesting aspect. There are numerous examples, both within and outside Europe, of countries where language policy requires that languages other than the dominant one(s) be given appropriate broadcasting space. However, pan-national channels such as Eurosport and Euronews are, by virtue of operating transnationally, not subject to these restrictions. Therefore the decision to operate multilingually is driven by some other motivation.

In this chapter, the new media paradigms that make pan-national advertising possible are first examined in an attempt to define what pan-European media and markets actually mean in cultural and linguistic terms, before going on to look in detail at Eurosport, a pan-European television channel, to see the functioning of a multilingual market and media context.

New media paradigms and communicative contexts

To a certain extent, the development of 'Europeanization' and European media can be seen as part of the same trend as globalization and the increasing growth of global media. Globalizing processes have occurred to a certain extent in most industries, and the media and communications industries are no exceptions; in fact, they can be seen to play a pivotal role since the increased flow of information is both a driving force and a major consequence of globalization. However, these flows – economic, financial, production, information – are not equal or multidirectional, and the process of globalization is seen to have consequences beyond the economic sphere, for instance in terms of cultural domination and phenomena like 'McDonaldization' (cf. Ritzer, 1996, 1998).[1] Advertising agencies, the creators of national and international advertising texts, are also part of this globalization process, and the advertising industry is becoming increasingly internationalized while at the same time becoming more concentrated (Leslie, 1995). As Leslie points out, 'Globalization is at once a theoretical premise in advertising, a structural dynamic in the industry, and an emerging market phenomenon' (1995, p. 1).

Like globalization of the media, Europeanization, too, 'has the potential of creating its own public sphere, outside and, potentially, against the domain of the nation-state' (Price, 1995, p. 37). The categorization of media in terms of traditional descriptors such as public and private is, it is argued by Price (1995), less significant today than paradigms such as global, regional (that is supranational rather than internal) and local (more localized than previously). So, as Smith (1998) points out, it is no longer possible to rely on media to provide, 'the concentrated essence of a nationally authorised culture', something Michael Billig (1995), Benedikt Anderson (1983) and others have described in detail. Furthermore, Meinhof and Richardson (1999) predict that in the age of digital broadcasting, 'TV viewing as an expression of national solidarity is likely to become a thing of the past' (p. 23). They argue that television viewing in the second age of broadcasting (that is pre-satellite) was a nationally shared experience, giving rise to 'Did you see?' conversations among members of the national communicative culture, which ultimately 'ratify and deepen the common culture' (p. 24), something that will not happen when 50 individuals who live on the same street or work in the same company watch 50 different channels rather than the one national broadcaster. This points to another potential element of the fall-out from the multi-channel age of broadcasting, a transition from a 'mass society' to a more 'fragmented society', one 'in which people are seeking more personalised services and products tailored to their needs' (EBU Digital Strategy Group, 2000, p. 10).

Thus, geopolitical boundaries will, it is argued, become less important in defining a media community, their significance being usurped by 'symbolic boundaries of language and culture – the spaces of transmission defined by satellite footprints or radio signals' (Morley and Robbins, 1995, p. 10). These, it is proposed, will form the 'crucial and permeable boundaries of our age' (*ibid.*). This could, of course, be something that is liberating and gives the individual member of the audience greater choice and freedom from the earlier age of broadcasting in which a monologic broadcaster conceived and generated the voice of the nation – manifestly and constitutively in Fairclough's (1992) terms, in that it not only determined content, but also prescribed a certain accent and register.

Alongside the trend towards greater globalization and transnationalization, a push/pull towards increased localization and regionalization is also predicted by forecasters. Interestingly, unlike in the first half of the twentieth century, when modern communications 'were part of a tendency towards centralization and an emphasis of national over regional' (Price, 1995, p. 5), modern communications in the new millennium are the key 'weapon' in many regionalisms and non-state-based nationalisms. For example, for the stateless Kurds, a radio station broadcasting not from any Kurdish part of Turkey or Iraq, but from an international location (London) could be seen as a key symbol of their identity as a nation in the 1990s. Given the significance of the media, it is clear that the introduction of – or simply the opening of access to – channels which are 'acultural', 'anational' and which seek the widest possible audience from a variety of distinct national cultures means that 'the domestic public sphere is necessarily adversely affected' (*ibid.*, p. 38).

Europe as a pan-national mediascape

The European Union's policy of 'Europe without Frontiers' was intended to promote a fledgling 'post-national audiovisual territory' (Morley and

Robbins, 1995, p. 3). This was based on the idea that the way in which individuals relate to such pan-European and global media may also be different, and the ability to participate in these new media may, in and of itself, constitute an identity. Thus, not surprisingly from the European Union's point of view, these moves should primarily be driven by cultural rather than commercial motivations – and this was the reasoning behind the funding of the MEDIA projects among other initiatives (cf. Shore, 1997). However, what is a particularly interesting – and in fact defining – feature of new global and pan-European media is not only their commercial *raison d'être*, which applies even to those that operate within a public service culture, but also their predication on consumption and their unquestioned interweaving of entertainment with advertising discourse. The level of advertising on terrestrial television is a theme that is constantly under review and which viewers are quick to scrutinize. For example, a key component of the BBC's identity in the UK as a media product is the fact that it does not show advertising.[2] Likewise, advertising practices on terrestrial national broadcasters in other European countries are limited to a greater or lesser extent. However, in the world of satellite and cable broadcasting, where the broadcaster is not concerned with being the voice of a nation, commercialism is assumed, accepted and barely commented on.

As Smith (1998, p. 1) points out, 'television is becoming at its roots, international, prolific, regulated lightly if at all'. It could in fact be argued that broadcasters began to operate internationally purely in order to escape the rigours of national regulation in advertising and other spheres rather than to become truly international or to broadcast to international audiences in an international way. As early as 1992, Richard Collins passed judgement on satellite television in Western Europe, claiming that it had failed to deliver on its promises of more choice, greater competition and internationalization of audiences (p. 93). More than a decade on in temporal terms – and exponentially further still in technological terms – from this conclusion, the findings are perhaps more valid than ever.

What pan-national media may offer is the possibility to participate in what the European Broadcasting Union terms 'a global, hybridised culture'. As Price (1995, p. 55) puts it: 'Global television produces a vocabulary and syntax of consumer imagery which becomes a language of non-loyalties, inherently subversive of existing orders.' These media and their predication on the market 'suggest a power to shape existence that does not depend on the state', but rather on consumption and economic status. Thus, it is not the case that such channels are unconcerned with securing viewer loyalty – in fact, as Richardson (1997, p. 200) points out, satellite channels in common with their terrestrial equivalents, 'seek to establish and maintain communicative relations with their audiences' – but it is not national loyalty that is their objective. In common with many of the global networks, European channels also tend to be themed or subject-specific. Thus, the targeted audience is differentiated not by national group, but by interest group (Eurosport; MTV) or age group (Nickleodeon) or some other non-national factor. The result of such fracturing and specializing is a strengthening and internationalization of 'particularism', as Price (1995, p. 55) puts it. These 'particularities' in turn form the foundations of new, tentative, transnational identities and ways of communicating.

Another interesting effect of national and pan-national satellite and cable broadcasting on the collective psyche is, according to Richardson (1997, p. 202), that both temporal and spatial textual anchoring may be disturbed, lost even, and 'one hour is very much like another' (Meinhof and Richardson, 1999, p. 24). For example, re-runs and repeats (the mainstay of many such channels) interfere with a sort of national timeline. Thus, in a sense, the 'national' media memory becomes dislocated and ceases to have meaning. Equally, the origin of the broadcast is rarely identified; even the telephone numbers given are often regionally nonspecific. Price (1995), too, also points to the issue of 'locationlessness' in the effects of satellite and cable broadcasting on identity. In the past, one of the key features of radio and television broadcasting was 'their rootedness in a single place and their exclusive relation to that place' (Price, 1995, p. 12). Now, as he points out, 'the plethora of changing signals, floating, then raining from space, poses impressive problems of belonging, identification, nationalism and community' (1995, p. 4). Unlike their national, terrestrial counterparts, such channels create their own new continuities, which in turn create different anchorings for different groups. As Richardson comments in her study of the shopping channel QVC, 'continuity from item to item, block to block, day to day, is important to QVC and is part of a more general concern for program identity and, through that, for viewer loyalty' (1997, p. 206), again, such loyalty being a constituent part of an embryonic identity, that is the identity of those who watch QVC, the in-group, as opposed to the outgroup which never watches it. The former group of individuals, even where they never meet or never communicate directly, still have access to a range of symbols, rituals and vocabulary, which to them is instantly recognizable and understandable.

As Morley and Robbins (1995) point out, while Europe without frontiers may be an exciting concept on the one hand, it may, on the other, 'actually work to create anxieties and a sense of cultural disorientation' (p. 3). The European Broadcasting Union (EBU) has also described the new mediascape of digital broadcasting as a 'confusing landscape' (EBU Digital Strategy Group, 2000, p. 7), and sees the role of broadcasters as one of providing strong media and channel brands to help the viewer navigate. Furthermore, if individuals within a particular 'national' group are not only exposed to the messages of the national station, but also to those of a range of 'anational' satellite and cable channels, then the ability of the state to socialize its citizens and create a sense of national identity through the media becomes inherently weaker. Likewise, for advertisers, the consumerization and socialization discussed in Chapter 1 becomes necessarily more fragmented and specialized. This argument has also been used in the attempt by European Union countries, notably France, to limit USAmerican programmes on European channels.[3]

The paternalistic role of the state is also undermined by the removal, through easy-access satellite, and digital cable broadcasting, of a 'nation-based gatekeeper' (Price, 1995, p. 14). News, for example, loses its national character when it is not filtered through the BBC or some other such medium, but is instead viewed through CNN, SkyNews, NBC, Bloombergs, Euronews and so on. On the one hand, individual viewers may simply exchange one type of ethnocentrism for another (that is the British or German viewpoint for the USAmerican); on the other, there may be a real departure from the ethnocentric standpoint and an attempt to create genuinely 'pan-national' or even 'European' news.[4] In their study of Euronews, Richardson and Meinhof (1999) attempted to answer the questions of who Europe is, who the 'we' being addressed by the broadcaster is, who is included, and who is excluded in this pan-European news station. Interestingly, they found that Euronews was at its best – in terms of entertainment and information – when it recognized and transmitted the diversity that is Europe, particularly in terms of political opinions and reporting, giving people a range that they do not normally encounter in the ethnocentric news they receive on national channels. An important point to make here is, of course, the fact that even where such channels perceive themselves or appear to be 'anational' or 'pan-cultural', and where they are the source of 'global narratives' (Price, 1995, p. 18) they still, generally, betray some cultural heritage or have perhaps even adopted one – in many cases an Anglo-American one. As Price states: 'To say that programming is global does not mean that it comes from nowhere or has no cultural impact' (*ibid.*). It is also important to realize that in tandem with the fragmentation of audiences is an increasing concentration in ownership (EBU Digital Strategy Group, 2000, p. 7).

Europe as an advertising market

The notion and definition of Europe as a broadcasting space (for example through the European Broadcasting Union) implies some sense of shared identity within that space. Thus, many of the newer pan-European channels assume such a bond, no matter how tenuous, between the countries to which they broadcast. However, to what extent can they take 'common knowledge' for granted – the kind of knowledge acquired through media and market as well as other types of socialization, and based on intertextual and linguistic foundations? In the themed channels, which are seen as the easiest and most successful option for pan-European broadcasting, domain knowledge is of course an important element. In other words, the broadcaster can assume that the viewer of Eurosport in Germany has much the same knowledge of and interest in football as the viewer in France, Spain, the Czech Republic and other countries. Another interesting aspect which constitutes common knowledge in a pan-European context, is mutual perception. As Hugh O'Donnell points out in his study of sports reporting throughout Europe, not only do all broadcasters – regardless of their 'country-of-origin' – engage in 'insistent stereotyping' of national characters, but such stereotypes also display 'astonishing uniformity both within and across national boundaries' (1994, p. 354). He goes on to purport that the 'expanded in-group is the advanced industrialized countries as a whole'. Thus, such stereotypes constitute an element of 'common knowledge' and not only create a context within which pan-European messages will be interpretable (disregarding for the moment the issue of language), but also contribute to a European identity. Equally, the exploitation of languages for market-driven purposes using techniques such as linguistic fetish is a phenomenon found not only at an intercultural, but also at a pan-European level.

Multilingual media across Europe may be the result of language policy or language ideology, or they may be the result of the suppliers responding to demands from consumers. This is well-illustrated by the case of two pan-European channels. Part of Western Europe's image and identity is that of a linguistically varied continent, and the European Union aspires to maintain this linguistic diversity – although this may become more difficult as the Union expands eastwards. At times, however, the aspiration to create a unified European community is at odds with this goal of linguistic diversity. Eurosport, at the time it was founded by EBU members, opted to approach European linguistic diversity with one voice, namely an English one. However, this policy has gradually been eroded to the point where Eurosport is now available in 15 different languages. On the other hand Euronews, another EBU-associated initiative, opted for a 'big-languages' policy, broadcasting in German, English, French, Spanish and Italian. Micklethwait, writing in 1990 when the Euro-consumer was seen by commentators and practitioners as a much more plausible creation than s/he is today, cautioned against too much faith in the convergence creed: 'Pan-European English speaking television failed because most Europeans want programmes in their local language.' And in the same year the World Conference on Business Communication considered language 'the ultimate non-tariff barrier to international trade' (1990, p. 142, cited in Forrester and Feely, 2000).

Likewise, the notion of cluster-based market segmentation and advertising in Europe tends to ignore that fact that marketers would have to use more than one language to reach many of these clusters (McLauchlin, 1993). As a way of overcoming this problem, while still enjoying the advantages of cluster-based commonalities, McLauchlin (1993) instead proposes a dual approach to deal with the language question, whereby 'a broad-based message' is transmitted across the continent, perhaps using English 'as a link language' alongside country-specific messages in country-specific languages. It would appear that marketers and advertisers, having embraced the homogeneous Euro-consumer idea at the beginning of the 1990s, are now realizing that 'language and cultural differences do matter, and that insight is having a radical impact on TV networks as international brands' (Koranteng, 1999). Indeed, rather than reinforcing the homogenized *lingua franca* approach to international broadcasting, it can be argued that the digital age makes a move towards more heterogeneous and linguistically diverse provision possible. The European Broadcasting Union sees the role of public service broadcasters in a digital age as, 'providing content in local and minority languages' (EBU Digital Strategy Group, 2000, p. 3), while commercial broadcasters, too, are realizing that there is a demand for linguistic diversity. For example, CNN International launched a local Spanish-language version in 2000, 'its first branded local-language version' (Koranteng, 1999), and TV-Breizh, a subscription station offering programming in the Breton language, was also launched in Brittany in 2000, two of its investors being Silvio Berlusconi and Rupert Murdoch (Moal, 2001). Thus, consumer demands can now take on a linguistic dimension and this can be satisfied to some extent by the new technology, so long as this is 'viable' in market terms. In fact, the Eurosport website urges viewers to contact their local cable operator to demand provision of a soundtrack in their local language.

The language question

So, how does a pan-European broadcaster cope with 'the language question'? MTV-Europe provides an interesting case study for any would-be single-language pan-European broadcaster. English was, originally, the main language of the channel across Europe for a number of reasons, but mainly because there was a perception that a certain knowledge of English as a foreign language (EFL) could be relied upon and also because, 'language was regarded as of secondary importance compared to the universal language of music' (Roe and de Meyer, 2000, p. 148). The crisis came for the channel when the audience began to grow weary of endless videos and demanded more talk-based programmes. The problem here, of course, was that while EFL knowledge was sufficient for the soundbites of the old format, the policy of English only for interviews and so on did not prove satisfactory for a large number of viewers. MTV-Europe's 'One Planet, One Music', and apparently 'One Language', slogan was seriously challenged by the successful launch of rival German channel Viva, which not only broadcast in German but also played 40 per cent German music. MTV-Europe subsequently split into four programming and language zones (Central – German-speaking; Southern – Italian-speaking; UK and Ireland – English-speaking; Northern – also English-speaking). Significantly, in their study of MTV-Europe, Roe and de Meyer concluded that it was language rather than musical tastes that 'proved to be the main obstacle to the success of MTV-Europe' (2000, p. 155).

Euronews, which describes itself as the 'only multilingual pan-European news channel', is distributed in different ways in different countries. For example it is a subscription channel in some areas, whereas in others it is shown late at night or early in the morning on terrestrial channels. Euronews was conceived in a very different way to MTV-Europe and has always had a public service culture, albeit in a pan-European context, and a multilingual policy. In their study of Euronews, Meinhof and Richardson (1999) point out that this multilingual policy results in practice in the use of the 'big-five' languages (English, French, German, Spanish and Italian).[5] Although Meinhof and Richardson concede that this is a compromise, they argue, legitimately, that it is a start. The reasoning behind this compromise is given by Euronews as the fact that 27 per cent of the 'upmarket population' do not speak any foreign language and only 38 per cent speak only one foreign language, and that in this 'fragmented' situation, English, German, French, Italian and Spanish are the top-five languages used for business on the continent (results of EMS TV 2002 survey cited in www.euronews.net). Interestingly, language on screen, for example for titles, may either be in all five languages or may in the form of 'Euro-Interlanguage' (Meinhof and Richardson, 1999), drawing on the viewers' metalinguistic ability to interpret based on Latin, Greek or Anglo-Germanic roots (Meinhof and Richardson, 1999). For example, *Economica* is used for business news, *Sante* for health news, and so on. An important point they make – and this comes up again in the discussion of Eurosport below – is that the channel makes it impossible for the viewer to have a truly monolingual viewing experience: s/he is forced to recognize and deal with the linguistic diversity of Europe, even if it is only the fact that place names are given in their original (*Firenze*, not Florence), as in the case of the advertisements featured in Chapter 2. 'Europe is not normalized as a pseudo-monolingual space, in spite of the facility for selecting a preferred language of exposition' (Meinhof and Richardson, 1999, p. 21).

The future cultural-communicative context of pan-European market discourses may in fact consist not of a giant homogenized market, but of regional Euro-clusters[6] within which advertisees will share 'similar economic demographic and/or lifestyle characteristics which cut across cultural and national boundaries' (Vandermewe, 1993, cited in Schmidt and Pioch, 1996, p. 16). Pan-European television advertising Research or PETAR sees thematic channels such as MTV and Eurosport as the future of Euro-advertising. However, as Koranteng (1999) points out, expenditure on advertising on pan-regional and pan-national television across Europe still constitutes only a fraction of spending on national channels. Hollingsworth (2000) predicts that marketers will 'think Europe, but act local', keeping in mind, as he points out, that local 'may cover a larger area and may describe demographic groups more clearly than geographic groups' (p. 40). The question is, of course, how this impacts on and is impacted on by language and media. MTV-Europe's website provides an interesting insight into the feasibility of advertisers' and marketers' desire to segment in pan-national ways, for example based on regional clustering or on lifestyles that are non-nationally determined. The main website is in English and is intended to direct people to more local sites. The necessary information is presented visually, by a map of Europe, and textually by a number of options listed at the side under the heading 'click and check you regional site'. The options give a country or region in English and a language. So, for instance, 'UK and Ireland: English' and 'Germany: Deutsch'. The individual can either move across the map and this will highlight an option on the list, or can move to an option and this will highlight the appropriate area on the map.

Here, too, there is evidence of a phenomenon that came up many times in the examination of the use of English on websites, discussed in Chapter 3, namely that certain groups are treated with sensitivity as regards linguistic and cultural differences, whereas others are not. So, for example, no one would really have a problem with 'UK and Ireland' being a region – in fact the website has consciously not used the UK to refer to the two countries, a generic terms sometimes used in such situations, albeit incorrectly. This would seem to indicate a certain sensitivity to these issues. However, when the website user moves over the 'Germany: Deutsch' option, a pan-Germanic language cluster is highlighted on the map (Germany, Austria and half of Switzerland), without any acknowledgement that national borders have been crossed and that this is not in fact a 'Germany' cluster. A similar effect is created by the 'France: Français' option, which results in France, Luxembourg, half of Switzerland and half of Belgium being highlighted. A 'Poland: Polski' option is available that leads to a fully Polish website, but the rest of Central and Eastern Europe – apart from the Baltic States that are designated as part of the 'Nordic: English' cluster – is contained in a mass cluster entitled 'European: localized'. However, the localized sites were at the time of writing not yet ready to be viewed, and simply lead to an English-language site. The 'Nordic: English' site covers a range of countries and languages (Norway, Sweden, Denmark, Finland, Latvia, Lithuania and Estonia) just using the English language.

So, here are a number of solutions – or non-solutions – to the pan-European language 'problem'. The first is to cluster on the basis of language, where the language is seen to be 'important' or 'major', or perhaps more accurately its speakers are seen to be important. This is the case for English, Italian, Polish, Spanish, French, German and Dutch. These linguistic groupings do not always acknowledge national borders, and the users of the website may have to overcome or set aside some degree of national identity/pride in order to assume membership of a linguistic group. The other type of regional cluster seems purely based on geography and is made up of groups that are either able or willing or forced to operate in another language, and are seen as not meriting their own specific language site. Whatever the motivation, the choices listed on such pan-European websites give powerful messages about which languages and speakers are seen as important and powerful and which are not.

Speaking the language of 46 million Europeans: the case of Eurosport

> Sport is the single most powerful advertising property.
>
> (www. eurosport.com)

Eurosport, originally an initiative of the European Broadcasting Union (EBU),[7] is at the time of writing is owned 100 per cent by French channel TF1, part of the French public broadcasting group ORF, and Paris is 'home to the pan-European network' (Fox, 2002). Along with MTV-Europe, the channel is the largest pan-European broadcasting network (Stock, 2001), with an average reach in audience terms of 226 million annually and availability in almost 100 million homes across Europe (www.eurosport.com). The station has been profitable since 1996 (*Multichannel News*, 2000), and proof of its success was attested to by the fact that *McDonald*'s decided to sponsor Eurosport's coverage of the 1998 Football World Cup – the fast-food brand's 'first pan-European campaign' (*Advertising Age International*, 1998). As part of the campaign, tray-liners in seven European countries invited customers to tune into Eurosport to watch the World Cup (*ibid.*). A sector that Eurosport has been quite successful in targeting is the youth market, and the weekly extreme sports show YOZ (youth only zone) has an estimated audience of 250,000 over 54 countries. According to Michael Lams of Eurosport, the youth only zone 'is very important in nurturing young viewers and brings in advertisers we wouldn't otherwise get' (cited in Grimshaw, 2002).

European teenagers are viewed by many marketing and advertising analysts as having the greatest potential to become the first Euro-consumers, and in fact they do already make up a significant pan-European market with not insignificant spending power. For instance, MTV-Europe, which is watched predominantly by young people, gets much of its advertising revenue from pan-European ads which are broadcast uniformly and without any cultural adjustment to households throughout Europe. It could therefore be argued that a generation growing up in the different countries of Europe share a not insubstantial part of their socialization, symbols and worldview with each other, one which their parents and other people living in the same country do not share. Whether or not this is something specifically European is questionable, since as Solomon *et al.* comment, 'images of Western consumption bombarding teenagers around the world are rapidly creating a global youth culture' (1999, p. 362).

Viewers of Eurosport also make up a pan-European consumer group which, it can be argued, shares a certain communicative culture due mainly to an interest in sport. This is the cosmopolitan approach discussed in Chapter 3. As the *MasterCard* slogan for the 1996 European Cup stated, 'Football speaks every language'. The audience is defined as males between 25 and 35, and it is estimated that Eurosport takes at least 2 per cent of all TV viewing time of 16+ males across Europe. Audience ratings have been increasing, however, and one reason is Eurosport's anational sporting coverage. So, for instance, when covering the Olympics, the World Cup, the Africa Cup or the European Championships, as many games and events as possible are shown, not just those that are of interest to a particular nation or region. So, for example, a Pole living in Ireland can watch his/her fellow Pole win a medal in the walking race on Eurosport at 2.00 in the morning – when the Irish national broadcaster has long since given up caring what is happening at the Olympics. Eurosport believes that this is the reason why the 2000 Games in Sydney attracted 'the highest audience ratings since Eurosport's creation' (EBU, 2000), and as Eurosport points out, despite the fact that platform operators (that is, local cable, satellite and digital providers) have a wide variety of channels available to them they 'insist on including Eurosport in their offer to subscribers' (www.eurosport.com).

An example that illustrates the neutrality – in terms of older nation state divisions – of this shared culture, was the choice of the 'Euro 96' anthem for the European Football Championships in 1996. In the UK, the BBC, as the voice of the nation, chose the suitably patriotic hymn *Jerusalem*; commercial broadcaster ITV opted for Beethoven's *Ode to Joy*, which is also the anthem of the European Union, a choice which was criticized by many including the then UK Minister of Culture, Virginia Bottomley, for lacking patriotism; Eurosport chose a song by international (Canadian) rock star, Bryan Adams, who appears as anational, but is in fact part of the shared culture of Eurosport's audience. The sponsors for the event also coexisted happily in the anational culture of Eurosport: the Euro brand *Carlsberg* and global giants *Coca-Cola*, *General Motors* and *JVC*.

Eurosport claims to offer advertisers access, via one advertisement, to pan-European TV audiences with the attractive association of sport and sporting values (www. Eurosport.com) together with 'desirable audience profiles'; and research, it is claimed, shows that the audience is getting younger and more affluent. As a themed channel it claims to be in a better position than general-interest channels to deliver a target-market group to an advertiser and to 'target key demographics'.

Language policies

Although conceived as a European project, Eurosport, like MTV-Europe, originally opted for the *lingua franca* approach and began broadcasting in English only. However, this model[8] has had to give way gradually to the point where Eurosport now broadcasts in 18 languages and the channel claims that '95 per cent of viewers can enjoy these events in their first language' (www.eurosport.com). Eurosport News, branded the 'CNN of sport' (Bernie Eccleston, cited in Speer, 2000), was launched in 2000 and broadcasts in five different languages. Eurosport itself has six main websites, five localized in English, French, Spanish, German, Italian and Swedish (at the time of writing) and the dot.com website, which is in English. Interaction is also possible with Eurosport; viewers with the appropriate technology can click on hyperlinks on broadband to get further content in English or in the local language (Fox, 2002). Dutch, French, German and English signals are transmitted from Paris, with local language versions being mixed at local centres in various European countries. What is interesting is that the journalists working in Paris select and edit the programme content, preparing an international script in English. Significantly, the English script is the default for local soundtrack mixers and it provides the preferred guide for them, as they 'emphasize the interests of their language groups' (Fisher, 2000).

The play list for programmes and commercials is mostly the same across Europe, with the local language soundtrack added, except for Eurosport France and British Eurosport, which have more substantial differences in their programming. The establishment of British Eurosport was seen by many to be further evidence of the impossibility of appealing to a pan-European audience with a single linguistic and media product, and 'to contradict Eurosport's strategy of beaming into as many TV homes across Europe as possible to get a maximum exposure for its regional advertisers' (*Advertising Age International*, 1999). At the time, a Eurosport spokesman denied this was the case, claiming that there would be no alteration of the 'pan-European ad sales strategy'; however, the subscription-based British channel, intended to compete with Rupert Murdoch's SkySports network, has gone its own way since then. British Eurosport was also a response to the fact that Eurosport reached only 29 per cent of TV homes in the UK, compared with 86 per cent in Germany. Apart from competition from the Murdoch network, the other reason for the poor reach was that the content was for many Britons a turn-off, with too much emphasis on European winter sports such as skiing (*Advertising Age International*, 1999). Despite this concession to British tastes, the channel claimed to be 'determined to keep promoting the network as a pan-European brand' (*ibid.*), although the website currently offers advertisers both pan-European and local rate cards.

In pan-European advertising, a number of relationships are at work. First of all, a product may still be defined primarily in terms of its country of origin and the perceived culture of that country, but this is not done simply in terms of its relationship with one other country. Instead, there is a group that is 'Europe', made up of a moveable collection of European countries which comprise a composite 'other'. The relationships are thus more general, less culture-specific, since they rely on a wider consensus and mutual perception. What is interesting is that the channel is presented as a way to communicate with Europeans – as a single, homogeneous group: 'Millions of Europeans choose Eurosport to watch the best in sport' (www.eurosport.com). Advertising on Eurosport then increasingly forms the European part of a global advertising campaign, and for many multinationals differences in European cultures are deemed irrelevant, particularly when advertising on a pan-European medium. As Moriarty and Duncan (1990, in Leslie, 1995, p. 19) point out, a 'global' campaign can be located anywhere on a continuum between a fully standardized, identical advertisement viewed in all countries, to totally localized strategies and executions based on the same global concept.

However, the homogeneity approach is undermined by language, since the station also claims to 'talk to audiences in their own language' (www.eurosport.com) because of the availability of language soundtracks. In its own advertising to potential advertisers and sponsors, Eurosport actually emphasizes the language issue, rather than trying to downplay or even ignore it. So, even though Eurosport might at first seem to have the same cosmopolitan strategy as *Benetton*, its approach is actually very different to the 'one world, one language approach' discussed in Chapter 3. A good example is the channel's 'Everyone's Eurosport' campaign (launched in 2000). Beneath an image of a young girl's head shaved into a football is the slogan: 'want to talk to 46 million young Europeans? we speak their language'. Likewise, the issue of language is highlighted in the FAQ (Frequently Asked Questions) section of the website. Out of a total of nine questions and answers given, two refer to language: 'Why can't I receive the website in my own language?'

and 'What languages is Eurosport available in?' In response to the former, the following answer is provided:

> We recognize that there are many languages out there, equally important, but we must take the time to develop properly. If your language version doesn't yet exist, we hope that you are able to use another ... and once we add more versions, we'll be sure to let you know.
>
> (www.eurosport.com)

The idea of 'Everyone's Europe' is an interesting counterpart to debates about democracy within the European Union and questions such as 'Whose Europe?',[9] which allude to the supposed lack of democracy and accountability in the EU and, above all, the separation of the EU institutions from ordinary, everyday life for Europeans. This is something Eurosport is keen not to be associated with, despite the fact that its own logo is based on the European Union flag. Instead, it seems to want to provide a place where Europeans can come together and enjoy commonalities. 'Everyone's Europe' also hints at another advantage Eurosport has over Euronews, namely its reach and popularity in Central and Eastern Europe. Reasons for this are probably the universality of sport and the channel's anational coverage. However, a key factor is certainly language, with the provision of soundtracks in a variety of major Eastern European languages (for example Russian, Polish, Czech, Hungarian, Romanian). This is in contrast to Euronews, which for many is simply seen as being news about Western Europe and the European Union, Eastern news being confined to its own special programme rather than being part of the mainstream news on the channel.[10] However, Euronews seems to be responding to this multilingual challenge, by, for example, adding a Russian soundtrack in 2001 in an attempt to move the orientation from Western Europe and to provide greater coverage of Eastern European issues (and, of course, attract a bigger audience in that region).

Advertising texts on Eurosport

It is almost impossible to talk about the advertising on Eurosport without talking about the channel as a whole. Even though there are advertising breaks, each programme is in fact a collage of advertising. On screen, the Eurosport logo is almost omnipresent in the top right-hand corner – advertising the channel itself. In any sporting event, sponsorship turns the screen into an advertising landscape. For example, in coverage of motor racing, each car, each driver, each mechanic is an advertisement.[11] Before looking in more detail at this interweaving of programme and advertising content and form, it is important to reiterate the fact that the whole context of Eurosport is very different to nationally-based television or broadcasting that is coming from a more ethnocentric base. In earlier chapters the point was made that alongside the heightening of linguistic and communicative difference in advertising discourse, there is a downplaying of this difference in the various media on which these advertisements appear – to the extent that international communication happens seamlessly. However, communication on Eurosport could never be described as 'seamless': it is instead patchy, uncertain, jerky, and it has an almost amateurish quality. The viewer is very aware that s/he is dealing with different communicative cultures, different time zones and different languages. Athletes and players tend to speak their own language and are interpreted in parallel, and announcers and commentators take pains to pronounce 'foreign' names, locations and so on correctly. There is much more of a sense of operating in a multi-voiced, multilingual world and of the complexities involved in that. It is a space where compromise, in terms of vocabulary simplification, restating of questions, translation and attention to international idioms of English, has to happen in order to communicate with the rest of the world. Although English is the default and the *lingua franca*, the context assumes and, even more significantly, does not allow the viewer to forget that this is a multilingual world and this is what the viewers are entering when they watch Eurosport.

A large proportion of the advertising on the channel is actually sponsoring, a form of advertising whereby the advertiser or sponsor gives financial support to an event, in this case a sporting one, or a programme, and in return the sponsor's brand, logo or advertising message is displayed 'on-site' at the particular event (O'Gunn *et al.*, 2000, p. 521). Sponsorship of international sporting events, which are then broadcast on a television channel, is seen as ideal for 'increasing or improving global brand awareness' (de Mooij, 1994, p. 354). Sponsorship advertising can be seen as a response to the need to overcome advertising saturation and to make the particular message or brand stand out (cf. de Mooij, 1994, p. 353; O'Gunn *et al.*, 2000, p. 508ff). It would appear to provide the perfect vehicle for the pan-European advertiser, particularly since the effectiveness of 'traditional broadcast media' has been called into question in the light of an ever-increasing fragmentation of the audience and the difficulties of overcoming the distractions posed by multi-channel land and new media (O'Gunn *et al.*, 2000, p. 519). Breaks in the programme are immediately preceded by the image of the sponsoring product(s) or the brand name(s). In addition, the brand name or logo is a constant symbol in the corner of the screen during the programme.

By simply placing a brand name or logo on the screen for the duration of the sports programme, the format of which is deliberately non-specific to the culture of any particular country, advertisers save themselves the time and money usually spent on attempting to solve the problems of cross-cultural, multilingual advertising. Sponsoring also has the added bonus of being easier to process and to comprehend for mass-communication purposes and the exposure is of course much greater than with the conventional and costly ad-break. In fact, advertising practitioners recommend a limit of six words for this type of copy, which is received by a captive audience whether they are present at the sporting event or watching on television (O'Gunn *et al.*, 519). In its information for advertisers, Eurosport claims that sponsorship 'generates even closer association with sport', and that through sponsorship a single media source can integrate ground-level sponsorship with advertising activity (www.eurosport.com). The channel cites the example of the 'Super [motor] Racing Weekend' held at Silverstone race track in the UK in May 2001, during which on-site signage was visible for approximately 25 per cent of the total coverage of the event (www.eurosport. com). As stated earlier, this type of sponsorship-advertising works well for multilingual media, and Euronews, too, makes use of sponsorship advertising more than conventional advertising. For example, europages.com sponsors *Economica*, the business news on the channel.

The Eurosport screen as adscape

There can be fewer things more banal than the Eurosport screen. This is not the innovative, sophisticated, 'clever' approach of many of the advertisements discussed in previous chapters, advertisements that are just begging to be 'decoded'. This is the bread and butter of multilingual communication and, like the poster in the window advertising a half-price sale, it seems to work. Thus, it is important to examine how that happens and to approach it 'in a completely astonished and disconcerted way' to quote Bourdieu (1991) again, even if this is not the immediate effect. Tuning in to find motor racing being covered, the first thing that the viewer notices is that the track itself is an amalgam of advertising for various sponsors (*Motorola*, *Marlboro* and others); the on-screen clock – ostensibly part of the programme content – is also sponsored (for example by *Omega*). There is no scene in which brand names cannot be seen; the entire screen is an adscape. The channel has a manifest inter-textuality (in Fairclough's terms) all of its own, and for the casual chan-nel surfer who comes across the channel, the experience can be somewhat disconcerting. There is no 'pure' programme, and there are very few 'pure' advertisements, as the following descriptions of recorded extracts show.

For instance, watching motor racing during the day on Eurosport, global and Euro-brands are everywhere on the screen. There is no need for identification, they are self-explanatory, signifiers of knowledge common to all viewers: *CocaCola, Toyota, Marlboro, Texaco, Motorola, Budweiser, Goodyear, Toshiba*. Some are specific to motor racing, some to Eurosport. The familiar formulae of terrestrial sports programmes ('Welcome back, if you've just joined us, we're here at ...') are not given, and so it is left to the viewer to try to find out this information for him/herself. It took this particular viewer the entire programme to deduce this. The suspicion is that the broadcast is taking place 'some-where in Europe', and initially Monte Carlo seemed an appropriate Euro-location for motor sports. The only slightly disconcerting feature was the appearance of *FedEx* – more an American than a European brand, and in the end it turned out that the coverage was coming from Houston, Texas in the USA. This piece of information was, however, totally irrelevant. The fact that the coverage is coming from the USA shows how the scenery of the screen is itself self-contained, with no out-side interference. Location and geographical anchoring are seen as unimportant. So, too, is temporal grounding. Time checks are not given, since the channel broadcasts over three different ones, although Central European Time (CET) is used for programme schedules. Thus, here too is evidence of the dislocation and disorientation, in Meinhof and Richardson's terms, as discussed above.

Likewise, in the coverage of a tennis tournament there is a similarly constituted adscape, although tailored to that particular sport: *Adidas, Playstation, Perrier, Dunlop Sport*. The players, too, complement – or interfere – with the scene by bringing yet more brands to an already overcrowded screen. But, again, there are clues, given away by sponsors who have a localizing effect: for example, *Mairie de Toulouse*, which gives clues about the French location of the particular tennis tournament. Such local brands often give themselves away by virtue of the fact that they may need explanation. Using these clues, the initiated viewer can help to orientate him/herself, something that seems to be necessary, at least for the individual who has been socialized into terrestrial televi-sion. It could well be that for younger viewers of Eurosport this aspect is unimportant and they are able to navigate their way through global and Euro-locations without the need to identify and categorize them.

In some ways, it could be argued that the screen serves as a kind of message board – the viewer taking from it what s/he will. Sometimes, however, such clues can be deceptive, and the fact that they can is in some ways proof in and of itself of the creation of this Eurosport land. For example, tuning into a tennis tournament, the *Deutsche Bank* logo is reproduced on the nets, which automatically leads the viewer to believe that s/he is watching a German tournament, *Deutsche* being one of Germany's leading banking brands. Then there are some more 'local', that is less Euro brands: *Zepter*, *Marca*. Finally, it turns out that the tournament is actually taking place in Mallorca. The sponsorship by a major German financial institution of a tennis tournament on this Spanish island tells much about the European holiday industry and about the Eurosport audience, since Mallorca is a beloved holiday and retirement destination for many Germans. Interestingly, although this is a very cheap and quite effective way of advertising in a pan-national context, the sponsor is also at the mercy of the sporting event to a certain extent. Accidents and mishaps can mean that the prime sponsor's location is missed and instead the focus is on another brand. Another potential source of interference is the actual on-screen audience, the spectators. Many wear sports gear, itself a form of advertising, leading to the unintentional – on the part of the wearer – advertising of global sports brands such as *Nike* and *Fila*. This is something sponsors have no control over and which may in fact distort the adscape they are seeking to create, since crowd shots can give prominence to brands not otherwise represented on screen at the expense of paying sponsors, or they may enhance a rival sponsor's presence. Thus, despite advertisers' attempts to make the text on screen conform to their requirements, subversions can and do take place due to human factors.

The language of Eurosport advertising

In terms of the advertisements themselves that occur during the breaks in 'programmes', a feature that immediately strikes the viewer is the high degree of direct advertising. Messages in German move across the screen urging German, Austrian or Swiss-German speakers to apply for some offer and giving them the relevant number in their own country. Where the direct marketing is actually in the form of an ad, the emphasis is again on the visual, and the final part of the ad consists of a table containing the flags, country abbreviations and relevant telephone numbers. These ads contain little or no text on the screen, except for information chunks and imperatives in English (Buy! Phone!). Flags play an important role in the direct advertising, which is hardly surprising since they are an easy, non-verbal, highly visual and instantly decodifiable shorthand way of identifying the country of the viewer and, correspondingly, his/her contact for obtaining the particular product being advertised. In addition, flags can also indicate a language (German flag for German language). Whereas this kind of metonymy would not be permitted in political or journalistic discourse, commercial texts make possible or tolerable texts, associations and visuals that in another context would be impossible. So, as in the case of the Austrian or Belgian user of the MTV website discussed above, the German speaker from outside Germany has to accept membership of this language community and accept that it is represented by the German flag in order to participate in this commercial discourse.

This highlights another of the striking aspects of advertising on Eurosport: the bizarre mixture of Euro-advertising and Eurosport-specific advertising on the one hand and highly localized advertising and standardized 'cable' or 'satellite' advertising on the other. There is thus either a hyphenating or a split effect, depending on the product or sphere. The Euro-advertisements themselves use acultural music and visuals. Information is not trusted to oral communication, since in a multilingual situation this cannot be relied upon. So, simple English is used or no words at all. Places and participants are unidentified – in much the same way that a studio is never seen, presenters are not viewed on screen and are rarely identified, and accents, too, are non-specific. The images that announce the advertisements are also universal or Euro in nature: a child playing football, for example. Again, there is no location identifiable in terms of geography, culture, even surroundings. Thus, these Euro-ads complement perfectly the genre of programmes on Eurosport – the whole channel in this way creates a certain internal coherence, albeit a highly unsatisfactory one for viewers of terrestrial television.

Such advertising and programmes may be all things to all people, or they may be nothing to them. This, then, seems to be a Euro-Europe, slightly tailored to different cultures through linguistic concessions on screen or soundtracks for programmes. Sometimes, this is not even conceded. For example, advertisements for German products (for example *Hasseroder* beer and *TV Spielfilm*) often appear in their originals. Apart from these examples and concessions such as the soundtracks, the accepted *lingua franca* for Euro-communication at a basic level is English. The language is used for announcements to the Euro-public, to address the widest possible audience, where information needs to be presented textually as well as visually – for example to advertise other programmes. However, the impression given by Eurosport is that visual communication is seen as a greater guarantor of effective communication in a multilingual context. For example, the viewer knows a tennis programme is coming up next because of the visual information on the screen, and when discussing the particular tennis tournament the surface is shown, the prize money is given on screen and dates are written. Even the descriptions of competitions are given visually. Very little is trusted to verbal or textual communication alone.

Conflict and interference come in the form of the local, when the advertisements of local cable and digital operators intrude. Suddenly, the Eurosport logo disappears for the first time and the viewer is abruptly severed from this Euro-world and brought very much back to reality, for example, in the form of an advertisement for 'The Mortgage Point', which gives a local Birmingham (UK) number, without an area code even, so great is the advertiser's confidence that the target audience for this particular message is local. Following this is a standard of the British cable/satellite/digital advertising repertoire, an advertisement for 'Britain's leading psychic medium'. Equally abruptly the viewer returns to Euro-land. Thus, at one and the same time, in one consecutive advertising break, the channel can address a generic Euro-public, for example in an advertisement for the European Union and its benefits to members, and also a highly specific (in terms of geography, language, cultural knowledge) local public. So, there are two levels on which the channel communicates with the audience; the one that is missing is the 'in-between' level, the national one. 'Quality' advertisements from commercial terrestrial television are never really seen on such channels.

Apart from English, the other language most present, aurally and visually, is German. German car manufacturer *Volkswagen* has run advertisements entirely in German on the standard English-language version. The German advertisers seem content to allow their ads to be broadcast to Francophone and Anglophone countries and other countries where German is not widely known without any translation or explanation. One could argue that these advertisements are simply targeted at those Germans who opt for the standard English-language Eurosport channel. However, there is surely still some bonus for non-German-speaking viewers. Instead of telling or reminding the viewer that *Volkswagen* cars are manufactured in Germany, the Euro-consumer sees the highly visual ad showing the car and all its attributes and at the same time s/he hears the German language – rather like a specially selected and highly appropriate soundtrack – which has the association of efficiency, quality and first-class engineering (as discussed in Chapter 2). So, even though the viewer may not understand any German at all, there may still be a benefit in terms of advertising goals.

British Eurosport as a multilingual medium

It was stated above that the development of country-specific versions in the form of British Eurosport and Eurosport France was seen as an indication that pan-European broadcasting aimed at a multilingual audience could not succeed. However, watching British Eurosport is not in and of itself a fully monolingual experience either, and it is clear that the station does not position itself ethno-centrically. For example, a sponsored programme following a number of athletes preparing for the 2004 Olympics, 'Mission2Athens', highlights this lack of an ethnocentric starting point, although of course it is still Euro-centric. First of all, any national, terrestrial broadcaster – commercial or public – is, in general, primarily interested in the preparations of individuals from that country. However, on Eurosport, athletes from seven different countries are profiled, and the British athlete is not given any special attention or extra prominence in relation to his fellow Europeans. Watching this particular programme, the need to be socialized into the intertextuality of Eurosport becomes increasingly obvious. 'Mission2Athens' is certainly different to straightforward sports coverage, the mainstay of the channel. However, it is very hard to describe this and other similar texts as 'programmes' for a number of reasons, but mainly because they seem to lack the normal boundaries and conventions implicit in that term. They never seem to 'settle down'; there is a constant feeling of movement, and a very underdeveloped sense of start, middle and finish. The music, constant presence of advertising logos (international electronics brand *Samsung*, in this case), 'jerky' footage and general pace all serve to reinforce this sense.

The episodes open with the jingle or theme music of the 'programme', and the opening sequence features the names and pictures of the individuals alongside their national flags and a matchstick figure of their sport – so again, in terms of form and manifest intertextuality, there is continuity between advertising and programmes, with this visual reinforcement of verbal information using the same instruments, namely flags and matchstick graphics. This use of flags is also prevalent on Euronews, where, for instance, in the 'Presse' section which deals with headlines in particular papers across Europe, the national flag is used to identify the country-of-origin of the paper, and also on '*Economica*', the business news section, to highlight the country associated with the particular story being discussed. Coming back to the Olympic hopefuls, the profiled contenders come from France, Germany, Spain, Russia, Switzerland, Italy and Great Britain – so although there is no ethnocentric bias in national terms, there certainly is a Western European and/or 'big'-country bias. The programme consists of weekly updates on their individual progress, as well as a more in-depth feature on each one of them in different weeks.

In one episode viewed, it is the turn of the French cyclist to be featured. Not only does the cyclist speak French to his fellow athletes, coaches and others, but also to the interviewer, who responds in French and also interprets in parallel on the finished footage. Language as well as linguistic and communicative issues and difficulties are inescapable here, as is nicely illustrated by one incident in particular. The cyclist uses a French word that the interviewer does not know how to translate. The interviewer then asks the cyclist what he has said. 'You don't know this word? You never heard of it?' the cyclist replies (this is in French and is translated into English by the interviewer). Then, his fellow (French) teammates respond by saying that they do not know the word either. It seems to me that this type of communicative lapse would, on another type of channel, be erased from the final footage, again reinforcing the notion that communication happens monolingually and with ease. However, as stated earlier, Eurosport makes no attempt to plaster over the cracks caused by the multilingual nature of Europe.

Multi-voicedness in one sequence of Eurosport text

The station's coverage of the Australian Open Tennis Championship (2004) illustrates many of these issues nicely. The screen, as in all sporting events, constitutes an adscape: the dominating brand is *Kia* (motor cars), with *Heineken* (beer) and *Rado Swiss Watches* also featuring prominently. *IBM*, another sponsor, is only seen when players are getting new tennis balls or when the score is shown. Additional brand space is taken up by the players' clothing – not in written form, but visually, for example the *Nike* tick. The only local – and therefore localizing, in terms of giving the viewer a hint as to where the event is taking place – brand to feature in the adscape is the *Australia Post* newspaper. However, in order for the viewer to see this brand, a player has to complain to the umpire, or the umpire has to be shown close-up for some other reason. The adscape changes with the various changes in the choreography of the match. When the players take their rests, other brands such as *Evian* water come into view, on the bottles they are drinking from and on the coolers at the side of the court. When the crowd is show in close-up, an *Adidas* cap introduces another brand that distorts the sponsoring advertisers' intended image.

At the end of the excerpt, the *IBM* logo appears along with the www.australianopen.com logo. This is immediately followed by the appearance of the *Lacoste* (sportswear) brand on the screen, a male, non-accented voice stating in accompaniment: 'Enjoy the Australian Open with *Lacoste*.' The next visual is Eurosport's matchstick tennis players, giving information about what type of programme is running visually. Then, there is an advertisement for the *Kia Sorento* model. The advertisement features US tennis player André Agassi, the number-four tennis player in the world and last year's champion who has won the event four times previously. Agassi was seeded fourth in the tournament and made it through to the semi-finals. He steps into the car, casts a glance at a brochure on the passenger seat – the brochure's title is 'André Agassi Charitable Foundation' – and sets off, driving through rocky desert terrain, apparently showing off the various 'moves' that the car can make by doing elaborate twists and turns. Only when he emerges at his destination does the viewer realize that he has been using the tyres of the vehicle to draw out the markings of a tennis court. He then proceeds to serve the ball, which lands in the centre of *Kia*'s oval trademark. The text of the advertisement reads as follows: 'To be the best, you must strive for perfection, use every opportunity to get better. *Kia* quality comes from that dedication.' The voice is male (the type of voice associated with trailers for epic movies) and the text of course applies equally to Agassi and his striving for perfection, and all the other players in the Australian Open. The advertisement finishes with the visual message: '*Kia*, major sponsor of the Australian Open.' The matchstick tennis players then return. This is followed by the Australian Open 'jingle', which seems to feature Aboriginal dancers moving to house music. Then a ball is hit by a racket to land in the centre of the *Kia* oval trademark – in much the same way as in the Agassi advertisement – above the Australian Open logo. The aural accompaniment to this is interesting. The first part 'with *Kia*' is read in what is very obviously an 'Asian' accent; the second part, 'the car that cares', is read by a British male voice, reminiscent of many of the Eurosport commentators. Then, the viewer is back to the adscape of the tennis court, and the whole sequence starts again: the *Kia*, *Heineken* and *Rado* logos dominate, while other brands intrude every now and again, sometimes more often, other times less often, depending on what happens in the match.

The coverage ends with the *IBM* scoreboard, followed by the Australian Open jingle, the *Lacoste* ad-bite, the Eurosport matchstick tennis players, before finally, the main feature: the advertisement. The visual comprises a man in a wetsuit proudly holding up the fish he has caught for his female friend to take a photo of. The person taking the photo is not seen, but her voice is heard, and the viewer sees through her camera. She speaks English, but with a foreign, although not easily definable accent, and typically Italian music is playing. She gives him directions – 'Left a bit, right a bit, no this way, back, back more' and so on – until eventually he disappears from the picture altogether and there is only the seascape in the picture. At the same time, a British female media voice starts to read the message of the advertisement: 'In every moment of the year, Sicily is so beautiful, you won't want to see anything else.' The screen then fills with the visual of the Sicily brand and its logo in English, 'Everything else in the shade'. This is surrounded by the logos of the advertisement's various sponsors and their names in Italian: *Regione Sicilliana Ambassado Turisimo* (the Sicilian tourist board) and *Unione Europene*, the European Union. With barely a pause, the Eurosport matchstick tennis players reappear, followed by the Aboriginal dancers of the Australian Open jingle, followed by the *Kia* tennis ball ad-bite, with its split accent message.

The next break in coverage – the term 'ad break' does not really seem appropriate to use for describing Eurosport – departs from this pattern. Instead of the usual ensemble of jingles and ad bites, the logos of Eurosport (the channel), Eurosport News and the Eurosport.com website are shown as the introduction to the station's own advertising for its planned coverage of various events during the coming weekend: the Australian Open Tennis Championship finals; the Alpine Skiing World Cup; and the African Nations Football Championships. The Eurosport matchstick figures are used to represent the sports graphically on the screen to complement the written information about each sport. What is also interesting is the way in which what would on terrestrial British sports television be treated as marginal events, namely the Alpine Skiing World Cup and the African Nations, are presented as just any other event worthy of coverage. This is followed by a more general ad for sporting coverage on Eurosport in 2004 (the broadcast in question was recorded in January), which consists of a collage of sports and sporting heroes set to music. What is significant here is that there is no national bias evident in the choice of who is portrayed and which types of sport are selected. There is no re-showing of great sporting events in any nation's history in a particular sport, no overemphasis on one particular sport or on particular events and championships, no sense that the channel will be there to cover 'our own' national sporting heroes in action. Instead, there is a fairly meticulous attempt to show a variety of flags, skin colours, locations, activities and faces, not many of which are known in the mainstream media. The slogan read out, in the standard Eurosport presenter accent, at the end is 'Don't just watch sport, feel sport'. Then, without the normal signals of the various jingles and ad-bites, the tennis coverage resumes abruptly, and the viewer is back in the adscape of the tennis court.

The original pattern returns at the next break in coverage: the championship jingle, the split-accent ad-bite for *Kia* motors, and the Eurosport matchstick figures, although this time they are 'playing' different sports (martial arts and football). Then the travel theme is continued from earlier, with an advertisement for Mexico. The visual is of a middle-aged woman being driven around in the back of a taxi, where she is looking out the window as various famous sights are shown. In addition, Spanish words and Mexican place-names appear on the screen, such as '*Maya, Campeche, Chapas*, and *Yucatán*'. Then the voice of the woman is heard: 'After experiencing hundreds of years of Mayan history in Mexico, I stood in front of the mirror in my hotel room and felt so much younger.' There are two interesting things about the woman's voice: she has a (middle-class) British accent and she pronounces 'Mayan' correctly. Then the ad's slogan appears on the screen: 'Mexico: One country, a thousand worlds.' At the same time, the slogan is read by a man with an American accent. The website address (www.visitmexico.com) as well as a British freephone number appear on the screen. As in the case of the advertisement for Sicily, this 'main feature' advertisement is not familiar from the world of national broadcasting, and it looks and sounds different in intertextual terms to advertising on terrestrial television. The matchstick figures herald the end of the 'real' ad time, followed by the *Lacoste* ad-bite from earlier, and finally the Australian Open jingle launches the next band of coverage.

The three hours of coverage finally finish with a different advertising sequence. The first advertisement is for coverage of live snooker on Eurosport. This is followed by an advertisement for 'February on Eurosport', which highlights ice-skating in Budapest, winter sports in Garmisch-Partenkirchen (Germany), UEFA Champions League (football), and the African Nations Cup (football) from Tunisia. Following visuals of each sport, matchstick figures performing the various sports confirm the information given verbally and in writing on screen. What is interesting about these two advertising sequences – the first for snooker, the second for February events – is the textual interaction, both in content and form, of the local and the global. In the advertisement for the snooker coverage the voice is identifiably British, with a London accent, and the content features colloquial language and rhyming slang. However, in the 'February on Eurosport' advertisement, the voice is back to the bland, non-accented Eurosport one and the pronunciation of the foreign locations is correct. Even though this is British Eurosport, aimed predominantly at a British audience, there is none of the usual mispronunciation of foreign athletes' names and subsequent embarrassment and laughter. The commentators here pronounce French names with a French accent, German locations with a German accent, and so on. The station does not therefore tap into the general deprecation of foreign words and accents, and this attitude also complements the type of anational coverage that is the channel's differentiating feature.

Conclusion

All of the advertising texts discussed in previous chapters rely to a very great extent on external, everyday texts from the political, economic and cultural spheres. Although there is also a type of horizontal intertextuality between programmes or articles and advertisements on television and in print media, they primarily refer to intertextual links beyond the immediate context of the medium in question. However, in the case of a pan-European market and media discourse, such as that found on Eurosport, the intertextuality is primarily internal. The advertising texts link mostly with each other and are able to be understood mainly within the context of the channel itself.

For the creators of market and media discourses who are attempting to operate in a pan-European context the language issue is always there, and they have a number of options in trying to deal with it. They may simply choose, and this may be a non-choice, to ignore the issue entirely, without making any linguistic adaptation at all. There are two points to make about this. The first is that although there are some examples in German on Eurosport, this decision to ignore the language issue is generally only the case where the advertiser is operating in English. For such an advertiser, there may be no realization that language is an issue, and, even if there is such a realization, there may be an overestimation of EFL knowledge among other Europeans. On the other hand, this may be an actual choice based on the advertiser's conclusion that English is the main *lingua franca* in this context, and so the advertiser assumes that the language is a workable, usable tool for communicating Europe-wide. Whatever the motivation, however, all of these choices or non-choices become self-fulfilling: more English is seen, so more English is used; English comes to have a predominant presence in cross-cultural commercial contexts, and so becomes, for the producers of these texts and those who encounter them, more appropriate for this purpose, rendering other languages less appropriate. The language then becomes fetishized with an international, *lingua franca* association, regardless of the motivation.

Finally, what does make a difference, it seems to me, is, once English is used, how this usage is presented. Is it presented in a monolingual context in which it functions seamlessly and neutrally across the globe? Or is it, as in the case of Eurosport, presented as a compromise in a multilingual context, in hybridized multilingual sentences, phrases and texts? It makes all the difference whether a multilingual or monolingual norm is assumed in the context of the particular advertising text. The case of Eurosport shows the two competing points of view, cohabiting on one medium. On the one hand, the increasing number of individual soundtracks for various languages points to a commercial policy of parallel monolingualism; on the other, the default English-language soundtrack would seem to indicate a commercial cosmopolitan point of view; while the coming together of these two as well as the interweaving of commercial texts ensures that watching the channel cannot be a monolingual experience.

6
Creating 'Multilingual' Texts: Combating Multilingualism

The previous chapters in this book have dealt with a number of different contexts in which multilingual advertising texts are found. First of all, the largely monolingual English media context within which foreign French, German, Spanish and other words appear. Secondly, the particular case of English, with its various fetishes and associations, its use on the Internet, and its prevalence in the market discourses of Central and Eastern Europe. Thirdly, the situation of minority languages (Irish), accents and dialects (Irish-English), and their relationship to the market and market discourses. And, finally, the marketed discourse of the pan-national, multilingual context, namely Eurosport. In some cases it is the texts themselves that introduce 'multilingualism' or multi-voicedness to the context, whereas in others the texts are designed to overcome a multilingual context. Many issues emerge from this investigation of market-driven multilingualism, and the objective of this final chapter is to draw some overall conclusions from these various case studies.

The points that have come through as overarching the various chapters are discussed under two broad headings: 'creating "multilingual" texts' and 'combating multilingualism'. Although the two are by no means mutually exclusive, and, it can be argued, the same attitudes seem to underlie both the creation of 'multilingualism' by the market and its attempts to combat actual multilingualism – all in order to sell products – the distinction seems a useful one since it highlights the schizophrenic relationship advertising and market texts in general would appear to have with languages and multilingualism. Under the heading 'creating "multilingual" texts', the notions of 'linguistic colour by numbers' and 'appropriation/disenfranchisement' are discussed, while the 'language/communication dichotomy', the issue of 'English as multilingualism versus English and multilingualism' and the idea of 'fake multilingualism' are dealt with under the heading of 'combating multilingualism'.

Creating 'multilingual' texts

Looking through any 'glossy' magazine, glancing at advertisements, even at zapping pace, on television, casting a weary eye at billboards from a car or the top of a bus, using the Internet for work or leisure – it is easy to encounter any number of advertisements such as the ones discussed in the previous chapters. Greg Myers (1994) likens them to sampled bits of symphony on a pop record; however, just as in the case of symphonic samples, it is important to question what this 'linguistic sampling' does to a language. These texts may be the only contact on a daily basis with languages other than the individual's own. They work at the level of being part of the domestic linguistic landscape but also part of something foreign. They tread a very fine line between being just foreign enough and being too much, too annoying, too incomprehensible. In this context, it is worth asking what impact they have on languages, people's language awareness, and people's attitude to languages, and how they interact with this language awareness and these attitudes. These issues are addressed below under the term 'the appropriation/ disenfranchisement dichotomy'.

One of the fundamental functions of language is generally assumed to be that of facilitating contact, cooperation and understanding. However, the symbolism with which languages have been invested through linguistic fetish and other ethnocentric strategies in advertising is based on deep-seated notions of 'otherness', something that is potentially divisive. Language, in this context, is being used to differentiate and divide, in order to sell products. The stereotypes upon which linguistic fetish relies are often those that are disseminated and reinforced by institutions such as the tabloid press and which in turn link indirectly to many less 'bilious' texts, such as tourism literature. What is also noteworthy is the fact that the need to emphasize a product's origin, its 'nationality' seems greater than ever, despite, or perhaps because of, much hyped trends such as globalization or developments such as the consolidation of the European Union.

Parallel to these discourses of division, the discourse of advertising does paradoxically seem to be at one and the same time both exploiting and creating some sort of commonality. As Hugh O'Donnell (1994) has pointed out in his work on sports reporting, stereotypes of the self and of others are remarkably similar, and the very fact that linguistic fetish functions fairly easily and effectively in advertising provides proof of this. Joel Kahn (1995) argues that Enlightenment and modernist ideals of cosmopolitanism and universalism have given way to, 'the current discourse of a culturally differentiated world' (p. 172), a world in which, somewhat ironically, 'cultural difference has become global' (p. 126). One aspect of the market discourse 'of a globally differentiated world' depends, it would seem based on the examples presented and discussed in previous chapters, on a number of different language strategies and practices that can be described as a type of 'linguistic colour by numbers'. Furthermore, the fetishizing of language and the highlighting of linguistic difference in certain contexts as part of market-driven discourses takes place within a context in which foreign language learning, at least in the Anglophone world, is in decline (Phipps and Gonzalez, 2004; Bassnett, 2002), and more and more individuals choose or are forced to choose to operate monolingually.

Linguistic colour by numbers

The advertising texts presented in the book represent what can best be described as a type of paradoxical or fake multilingualism. It is one that is primarily determined from an ethnocentric base; it has little or nothing to do with real life, everyday bi- and multilingual existence; and it has to do with exploiting difference, accentuating and hyperbolizing it against a monolingual norm. This exploitation of linguistic difference for market-driven purposes results in a highly refined version of 'multilingualism', one that uses specially selected words that are deemed prototypical and even stereotypical in advertising texts. In this way, it relates perhaps most closely to Jane Hill's notion of 'Junk Spanish' (Hill, 1995, 1999), and the term 'fake multilingualism' is coined with her ideas in mind. 'Fake multilingualism' does not challenge the advertisee in any meaningful way; it does not really introduce the advertisee to new words, ideas or ways of looking at the world. It is a type of decoration or linguistic colour by numbers that has everything to do with the advertiser's and the imagined advertisee's own linguistic culture or habitus.

Since, as will be discussed below, advertisers find it rather difficult to deal with the bilingual nature of many of their markets, they opt instead to describe them in rather crude terms. Thus, it is the advertiser's perceptions of language attitudes and attitudes to difference that are presented in the advertising texts, not any realistic portrayal. However, these texts then feed into such attitudes and become part of the intertextual field within which future advertisements operate. In such a context, the term 'linguistic colour by numbers' seems more accurate than decoration, since the latter indicates some level of freedom in expression, whereas the former more accurately describes the very contained, prescribed parameters by which foreign words are used in advertisements. So, a German word or a French phrase is drawn in where it will give visual expression to a certain, very defined type of Germanness or Frenchness, the appropriate amount in the appropriate shade, but nothing more than this.

There is the valid question, however, of why there should be anything wrong with seeing 'foreign' or ethnically marked words and hearing 'foreign' or marked voices in advertisements. After all, does this not expose the public to greater diversity and enable them in some small, banal way to escape the imprisonment of monolingualism Adorno (1974) spoke of? This is one side of the argument. The other side has to do with issues of representation, always a thorny one in the sphere of advertising, and perhaps more crucially, representativeness. It is interesting to look here at the issue of representation with regard to ethnic minorities in advertising, and to see the many similarities between this and the issue of representation and representativeness for languages. As Jonathan Mildenhall points out, commenting on the lack of representation of ethnic minorities in advertising, 'it is not just the [small] number, it's the nature of the portrayals that is a problem' (cited in Benady, 2003, p. 10). His comments could just as easily apply to languages and people who are portrayed as speakers of these languages in advertising:

> Minorities are used in several ways, but they tend to be used mostly to denote ethnicity. They are never the lead character, unless they are famous, and they are never used to represent an ordinary person ... I look forward to the day when a character like Dotty[1] in the Tesco campaign could be black, not because she is selling yams or lending ethnic credibility, but because she is a person. Who just happens to be black. (Benady, 2003, p. 10)

Mildenhall also identifies different types of black people who do appear in advertisements, and again the similarities, in the case of five of them at least, with the use of 'other' languages and their speakers are revealing. The first – and probably most common – instance is when the brand wants to claim ethnic roots, and, as with linguistic fetish-type approaches, the country-of-origin concept usually has more to do with fiction than reality. Ethnic minorities are also used when the brand claims a world vision, for example *Benetton*. Another factor is to do with, as Mildenhall puts it, 'reinforcing "cool" credentials', and here he cites the example of *Levi's*. The best analogy here would be in the use of French, particularly in the sphere of cosmetics, but also in fashion. The objective may also be to undermine ethnic stereotypes – again there are examples of this in the case of *Audi*, *Continental* and *Löwenbräu* advertising, which use the German language to meet head-on stereotypes about Germany. The final case is, as Mildenhall puts it, 'when they are just people', and this, he points out, is very rare. He cites the example of a series of 12 advertisements for a new snack product '*Supernoodles*', in which one of the advertisements 'just happened to be about a black couple for no particular reason'.

This final genre, he feels, is the best way forward, in terms of improving representation and representativeness. It is, however, almost impossible to think of an example of language and/or speakers of a foreign language being used in this way. The idea of portraying someone on a street in London or in a house in Leeds speaking German, French, Urdu or some other language with no explanation, just as one randomly picked member of the greater public seems a long way off in advertising in the UK at least. Even though these are everyday occurrences in that sociolinguistic context. Thus, it is easier perhaps for advertising to continue to promote the notion of a monolingual society – something that is far from the truth in most of today's European cities – than to try to portray something that does not fit neatly into a compartmentalized view of the world in which foreign languages belong in the category of holidays, tourists, imported foods, but not in the everyday. This notion of seeing ordinary people living ordinary lives, that just happen to take place in another language, has also been highlighted by Watts (2003, p. 21), who pointed the finger at the media and their lack of representativeness for UK school pupils' waning interest in learning foreign languages.

Another important consequence of this use and abuse of multilingualism and multi-voicedness is the implications of the absence of foreign languages for the monolingual advertisee. It was noted in Chapter 2 that people are surprised to find out that *SAP*, one of the world's leading software companies, is actually German, since they expect such products to be American and by implication to be associated, symbolically and practically, with the English language. If the Anglophone advertisee is only exposed to foreignness and otherness in connection with food products, drinks, cosmetics and so on, then this, it can be argued, only adds to what could be termed the frivolous image of these foreign languages. They remain something that is part of the domain of holidays and 'funny foreigners', and they are absent from 'serious' domains such as work, computers, information technology and so forth. If these are the only encounters, then this does, it would appear, reinforce the existing notion of English as the centre, the default, the norm, for the Anglophone advertisee. And this, I would argue, is ultimately bad for the learning of languages, in that it simply compounds the idea that the real world takes place through English, similar to the effect a lack of corpus planning and a marginalization in advertising and other discourses to 'non-serious' domains has on minority languages.

The appropriation/disenfranchisement dichotomy

> German thoroughness;
> Seamless functioning;
> German effectiveness and efficiency.

At first glance, the phrases cited above look and feel like yet another ad for Europe's carmaker. In intertextual terms, the marketed discourse about German cars seems to be their field of reference, and they are reminiscent of many of the texts cited in Chapter 2. Yet, they are in fact quotes from Hannah Arendt's report on the trial of Adolf Eichmann in Jerusalem, and she is talking about the running of the concentration camps. This is a sobering thought, and I would argue that the engineering fetish associated with the German language – so beloved of those marketing German products around the world – has done much to limit the development of a more diverse, less sinister portrayal of Germanness, particularly in the UK.

In 2002, the German ambassador to the UK criticized history teaching in that country for contributing to xenophobia. His point was that while it is of course important to learn and 'know as much as possible about the Nazi period and the Holocaust ... what is equally important is the history of Germany in the past 45 years and the success story of modern German democracy', a story that is generally missing from the syllabus. As an admissions tutor for a UK university for a number of years in the 1990s, this certainly echoed my own experience. In the many personal statements written by applicants as to why they wanted to study languages, the intertextual links running through the press, education system and other media discourses, as well as the discourse of marketed country images, were obvious to see. Individuals expressed their love of French culture, food and memories of happy holidays in France, all of these prompting a desire to continue with their study of the language. The motivation to study German was almost overwhelmingly prompted by a fascination with the Nazi era: applicants were invariably involved in project work on this area, to the exclusion of other aspects of the history and culture of German-speaking countries. In fact, the Nazi period is one of the top-three favourite themes pursued by students in UK secondary schools, and British newspaper the *Guardian* has pondered, ironically, what would happen to the 'History Channel' in the UK, if there had never been a Second World War (Spiegel Online, 2002). Ofsted, the Office for Standards in Education, warned in the same year of a 'Hitlerization' of the history syllabus in English and Welsh schools, and many prominent historians argue that schoolchildren in England know more about Hitler than they do about aspects of their own history (Leffers, 2003).

It is not surprising therefore that the campaign against the UK entering the euro currency zone used a well-known British actor impersonating Hitler in a 'German' accent to convince people that the euro will be bad for British independence. The German ambassador has also singled out a more familiar target for criticism in this respect, namely the British press, with its 'repetition of clichés and ... repetition of stereotypes'. It is easy to see these comments as the expression of a collective culture that just does not see things in the same funny way that British culture does, until one discovers that his comments were a direct response to an attack on two German teenagers on an exchange in London, who were physically assaulted when a group of boys who had invited them to play football discovered that they spoke English with a German accent.

In his study of what is termed 'Inner-London Deutsch', Ben Rampton (1999) suggests that German in the UK has the status of a 'respectable, instructed and heritage-neutral' language (p. 486). His data concerned the use of German lexical items by schoolchildren outside of the classroom for tokenistic or emblematic code-switching, what he terms 'crossing' (cf. Rampton, 1995). Although he concedes that Germany 'gets a lot of mixed coverage in the mass media and has quite a historic role in the lore and language of British schoolchildren', he concludes that 'the link between Nazism and contemporary German certainly wasn't inevitable and in the contexts where adolescents switched into the German language, Germany, Germans, Nazism and racism hardly ever figured as issues mentioned or implied by the participants' (p. 486). Thus, German seems to be used by some of these schoolchildren as a playful escape from 'the poverty of monolingualism' (Adorno, 1974) – and for others to expand their linguistic repertoire.

It is, however, important to consider these conclusions in the light of events that were happening around about this time, a few miles down the road in the German School in Richmond. The German School is part of an international network of schools dedicated to teaching in German; the core of their pupils are German or have one or more German parents. In the wake of a number of assaults on pupils, the School issued guidelines to pupils and parents on how to protect themselves from attack. One guideline advised pupils not to act provocatively in public and went on to give an example of what could be interpreted as provocative behaviour: namely, speaking German in public. It seems then that there is a sociolingustic context for the German language that permits the non-native speaker to play with the language, while the native speaker dare not for fear of inciting provocation. As Jane Hill rightly points out, a problem for linguists is how to treat and assess 'crossing' in 'moral terms' (1999, p. 553). Borrowing, as Hill sees it, is problematic on a number of fronts, but mainly because it may be indicative of covert racism and because it inevitably involves appropriation of something which is unique about another culture which in turn leads to denigration (1999, p. 554).

The policy of the German School's director in the early years of a new millennium of European integration and globalization is to 'overcome hostility' to the school and its pupils, hostility prompted by the uttering and hearing of another language, by 'inviting another local school to share sports facilities and join classroom exchanges' (Vasagar, 2002). All of the sources interviewed in connection with the particular incidents of assault blame the media, tabloid headlines, war films and a never-ending supply of television documentaries, series and so on, which take the Second World War as their setting. However, in all of this discussion, the issue of advertising and market-driven discourses, is, I would argue, not given the attention it deserves, precisely because it is not as explicit – at least, generally not – as these examples, and also because it benefits the German economy. The idea that the advertising for German products works intertextually with these other media and educational texts and the notion that people may buy German products for the very same reason that they would be hostile to German-speaking children on the street are not considered in this discussion. As mentioned previously, the vast majority of advertising texts that use the German language in English language advertising are formulated in the UK. So, as in the case of 'Inner-London Deutsch', there is a situation where the language is appropriated for use by these advertisements, while at the same time speakers of the language are in reality often disenfranchised, and not allowed to use the language. People are happy to hear German in an advertisement for *Audi*, but rather less happy to hear it being spoken by people opposite them on the bus or train.

Combating multilingualism

It would seem from the previous section that multilingualism is a resource that advertisers are happy to exploit for their own purposes. While this may be the case, it also seems true that multilingualism is a problem for most advertisers, presenting them with yet another barrier to a global, homogenous message. Thus, there seems to exist a schizophrenic relationship between advertisers and multilingualism, at least in the contexts discussed in this book, whereby on the one hand multilingualism is problematized by advertising and marketing strategists, while on the other multilingualism is highlighted in order to create a differentiated image for products and brands. One such phenomenon that emerges is the language/communication dichotomy, whereby advertisers tend to downplay language and emphasize communication, as if the latter had nothing to do with the former.

The second significant issue is that of the dominance of English and the exclusion of other languages from the cross-cultural commercial context. As has been seen in previous chapters, by virtue of its presence in international marketing discourses, English comes to acquire a certain symbolic meaning or fetish beyond its communicative function, a type of credibility fetish. As pointed out in Chapter 5, however, it does seem to make a difference whether or not English is presented as part of multilingualism or whether it is seen as something separate to multilingualism.

Finally, there is in all of these trends an underlying phenomenon of what can best be described as 'fake multilingualism', which seems worth highlighting. What this means is that while companies on the one hand seem to be 'speaking people's language', in reality, everyday lived multilingualism is far too messy to be dealt with in market discourses.

The language/communication dichotomy

The key players in the creation of the globalized cultural difference discussed above are undoubtedly multinational companies, '... with global communication networks that have created a global culture of worldwide symbols and images' (de Mooij, 1994, p. 3). However, where does language come into all of this? The issue is given scant attention in textbooks on multinational marketing and media in general. For example, in Keegan (1995), language is given less than 200 words in a textbook of nearly 600 pages on global marketing, and the only issues dealt with are potentially embarrassing or ambiguous brand names. However, the question of actually *communicating* with the advertisee does not seem to be an issue at all. Instead there seems to be the idea that communication across cultures can be successful if broadcasters and media companies pay attention to cultural differences (such as religion, diet, superstitions and so on) and, only as a footnote are they reminded that they should pay attention to linguistic differences.

In a chapter entitled 'The Consumer Audience', in Wells *et al.* (2000), the following (promising) heading is found, 'Social and cultural influences on the consumer'. The text then lists and discusses all possible issues that might come under this heading: culture, norms, values, customs, social class, reference groups, family, demographics (age, gender, education, occupation, income, race and ethnicity) and geographic location – nowhere is language mentioned, even in the section on race and ethnicity. Language only features under the heading 'Language problems, in international advertising' in the index to this 562-page volume on *Advertising: Principles and Practices* (Wells *et al.*, 2000). Under the heading 'International Management', the following statement suggests ways to deal with such problems:

> The shift from national to international management requires new tools, including one language (usually English) ... English normally requires the least space in printed material or air time. The range of words (estimated at over 900,000) and the ease with which English adopts words from other languages often make it more economical than many other languages.
>
> Some languages simply do not have words equivalent to English expressions. Computer words and advertising terms are almost universally of English derivation. (*Ibid.*, p. 489)

Here, presented to the Business Studies student, potentially a future marketing/advertising professional, are completely unsupported statements that reveal a deep level of ignorance and a correspondingly worrying level of unabashed English-language chauvinism: English is more efficient; English is more economical; English is more adaptable and more open; other languages are simply not as expressive as English; English is the language of computers; English is the language of advertising.

The only particular 'cases' then alluded to, in order to exemplify the 'problems' of international advertising, are the differences between American and British English ('There are even problems translating British English to American English'), and the favourite hobbyhorse of the French-language defence policies:

> Since 1539 the French have had legislation to keep their language 'pure' and now have a government agency to prevent words, especially English words, from corrupting the French language. Marketing and weekend, unacceptable to the French government agency, are translated literally as 'study of the market' (or 'pertaining to trade') and 'end of the week', respectively. Neither quite captures the essence of the English word. (*Ibid.*)

In this worldview, then, English is not just the default, the normal state of affairs, but also the source, the ideal version, the essence of which cannot really be captured by foreign pretenders. The paragraph ends with a tokenistic, one-sentence nod to greater linguistic diversity – 'Understanding language not only prevents mishaps, but also gives advertisers a greater cultural understanding' – something totally eschewed by the authors.

Similar attitudes and sweeping assumptions prevail when the authors turn their attention to international advertising on the web. English, readers are told without any supporting evidence, 'is the dominant language on the Internet' (*ibid.*, p. 496). The topic is given a mere 90 words, and the very brief discussion is dominated by Hofstede's high-context, low-context paradigms:

> The linguistic problem is evident when Web sites are in Japanese or Chinese, languages from high-context cultures, and in English, a language from low-context cultures. English has few variations of the word yes, for instance, whereas high-context cultures may have thousands of variations. Ensuring precise, accurate communication in these situations is tough. (*Ibid.*)

And there the discussion ends. The relevance of Hofstede to the issue of linguistic differences between English and Japanese or between English and Chinese seems rather opaque. This becomes particularly pertinent when elsewhere on the page, in a discussion of CNN as a global medium, the reader learns that one downside of using this particular 'global' channel is that it broadcasts in English, 'a language understood by less than 20 per cent of the world's population' (*ibid.*). This statement, too, is unfounded and there is no attempt to overcome the apparent contradiction between this sentence and the discussion of English on the Internet, only three paragraphs beneath it. In this worldview,

English is the safe bet, the reliable, predictable, controllable language, and, venturing into the use of foreign languages is for the 'brave and trusting international director to approve copy he or she doesn't understand but is assured is right' (*ibid.*, p. 489). Although the authors are careful to take account of gender diversity, allowing for the possibility that the international creative director may be female, there is, it would appear, no need to even nod at the issue of linguistic diversity. The notion that this hypothetical international creative director might actually be, or should aspire to be, multilingual, or that they may not be a native English speaker, is not countenanced in such a statement.

It could be argued that the application of paradigms like those of Gert Hofstede (1983) has much to answer for in this regard. In Hofstede's attempt to decipher culture-specific from universal values, language (in terms of particular languages and varieties rather than organizational and bureaucratic aspects of communication) is given scant attention. As Forrester and Feely (2000) point out, 'what is missing is research specifically aimed at exploring relationships between language and business management'. This lack they see mainly as a result, not just of the problem of cross-disciplinary research, but also of the dominance of Hofstede's cultural dimensions in thinking about international marketing and advertising. The language question has, in the words of Holden (1987), attracted 'only the briefest of treatments in the broad spectrum of English-language literature on international business and management' (cited in Forrester and Feely, 2000). It does seem strange that the language question is downplayed to such an extent in the discussion of the brave new world of pan-global networks, and that language is seen as a dispensable part of communication. This language/communication dichotomy accentuates even further the differences between the monolingual advertiser who uses a linguistic colour-by-numbers approach and the 'language-as-everything' approach of ethno-marketing agencies and language ideology strategies of indigenous language advertisers. More than this, the sentiments contained in the extracts cited above also promote the idea that multilingualism is something unfamiliar and unpredictable, that has to be controlled and contained, and that is incompatible with how markets work and products are sold.

English *as* multilingualism versus English *and* multilingualism

The English language would appear to be the most successful 'foreign' language in global advertising. It can not only take on a number of different associations and fetishes (for example cosmopolitan, modern, anational), but can also function as a *lingua franca* in international advertising 'communication', and it is the default language for media that are global or pan-national operators. Corporate home pages tend to use English regardless of their domestic origin in order to cash in on its credibility bonus, to the extent that commercial credibility on the Internet seems to be about having a home page in English. As Piller (2001) puts it, 'Everyone wants to be perceived as a global player, and such as perception is best achieved through the use of English' (p. 161). Even where the presence of English is only a minimal one, in the form of a brand name or slogan, these advertising texts carry 'shards of English into other lands' (Anthony, 2000, p. 3) and change linguistic landscapes forever. The dominance of English in international commercial discourse is a self-perpetuating one: English is used in international marketing discourses, English comes to acquire a certain symbolic meaning or fetish beyond its communicative function, English comes to be connoted as the language of serious international business, and so English is used even more in international marketing discourses.

Before surrendering to the apparent hopelessness of this situation, it is important to consider that although English may be used very widely on an international basis, the way in which it is used is what is likely to affect perceptions about the language, rather than simply being exposed to the language itself. As was pointed out briefly in Chapter 5, how English is presented in multilingual advertising communication makes an enormous difference. For example, whether it is the norm or default with multilingualism being presented as something different, separate, an exception to this norm; or, whether it is seen as part of multilingualism, as one of many languages, even if its position is that of a *lingua franca*. Is the English speaker portrayed as omnipotent, confident and omniscient, or does s/he make mistakes and turn out to be linguistically lacking? Does s/he take care to pronounce foreign words correctly, rather than adopting the self-deprecating 'funny foreign word' approach? Is English portrayed as the only language needed for communication or just as a useful 'language for information', in House's (2003) terms, that many people happen to be able to use? Is the communication smooth and seamless because of English, or is English just one tool in trying to communicate in a linguistically complex situation? All of these questions need to be asked about the use of English in multilingual market-driven contexts.

It is easy, but not really very revealing to say that the hegemonic position of English is being sustained and enhanced by international commercial discourses. It is far more revealing to ask who, how, where and why questions about English when it is used. If the English language is presented in these discourses as something that is the norm, with multilingualism as the problematized, abnormal situation, then English language hegemony is assured. However, if English is portrayed as just one language within multilingualism, even where it has a privileged position, as in the case of Eurosport, it seems to me that this is driven by a rather different intention and has a rather different effect. Similarly, as in the case of Eurosport, where the company – even from within the English as *lingua franca* framework – recognizes that it is part of a multilingual world and raises the question of language as an important issue, and shows a willingness to respond to linguistic demands on the part of consumers, then an important message is sent both to the native or monolingual English speakers and the speakers of the other languages concerned.

Fake multilingualism

The discourse of marketing is all about finding and talking to the target consumer. This particular individual is necessarily a composite, an ideal: s/he is of a certain age, lives in a certain location, has a particular education and occupation, falls into a certain salary band, has certain hobbies and lives a certain lifestyle. And, speaks a certain language. It is this latter point that appears to cause advertisers working in the multilingual world a great deal of difficulty. While it seems easy enough to create age and salary bands that cover a wide variety of possibilities and allow for some difference, creating a variety of language bands or continua for this notional target consumer seems a much more difficult prospect. Thus, inevitably, language becomes a black and white matter in the world of market, audience and consumer segmentation. The advertisee is deemed to belong to this and not the other language group; the messy everyday reality of people's bi- and multilingual existence seems too complex to even attempt to describe or begin to target with an advertising text.

In his study of multilingual advertising texts in Japan, Harald Haarmann (1989) concluded that companies and brands were practising an 'impersonal bilingualism', in other words a bilingualism that had nothing to do with actual bilingualism in Japan. Numerous examples of this abound in Europe, too. For instance, a large amount of French is used in advertising texts in the UK, whereas dominant minority languages such as Urdu, Gujarati and Chinese are all absent, except within the ethnic marketing segment or where the strategy is linguistic colour by numbers to promote an 'ethnic' product. The ethnic marketing sector, too, seems unable to cope with messy bilingualism, generally preferring a monolingual strategy in the minority language. Bilingual advertising strategies may be practised by government institutions based on language-policy directives, as in the case of Irish, but these are in reality best described as parallel monolingualism: the majority language text and the minority language text side by side, rather than a text composed of a vernacular that is impure, mixed and constantly evolving. To commit such a lived bilingualism to text seems too great a leap for advertisers.

Where, despite these difficulties and the problematizing of multilingualism, brands, companies and organizations do recognize and cater for certain bilingual situations in the world, these tend to be because the consumers in question are credible ones in economic terms and/or their multilingual situation is a 'respectable' one that is politically acceptable to acknowledge, for example Quebec or Belgium. So, in these contexts brands can afford to practise a type of safe multilingualism, although again this tends to be of the segmenting kind: people in bilingual situations are deemed in market discourses to speak one language or the other, never a mixture.

Even where some sort of nod is given to localized varieties, this often tends to be symbolic rather than real. A good example here is *Microsoft Word*. At first glance, *Word is* simply a software package rather than an advertisement. However, the languages made available in the programme are, I would argue, part of *Microsoft*'s marketing discourse, and also make statements about how the brand wants to be perceived. As part of its localization strategy, Word offers a very great variety of Englishes, from Australian to Zimbabwean. One such variety offered is an 'Irish-English' language option and dictionary, and this is the one normally installed by those setting up computers in public offices, institutions and so on. However, the 'dictionary' is really only a British-English version in disguise, as this user has yet to find any material difference. For instance, everyday English in Ireland is peppered with expressions from Irish that come largely from the nomenclature adopted after independence from the UK. So, for instance, the prime minister is the *taoiseach*, a member of parliament is a TD or *teachta dáile*, the parliament is the *dáil*, and so on. In addition, there are the greeting words such as *slán* and *fáilte* and the toast *sláinte*. However, all of these words are thrown up as spelling errors by the Irish-English version of *Word*. Of course, they are not English words, they are Irish words, and *Microsoft* does provide a comprehensive language option in Irish, but a dictionary of Irish-English, prepared with a genuine understanding of the everyday mixed-up sociolinguistic context of that variety, should include these and other examples. So, the claim to reproduce the multi-voicedness of Irish-English seems more a symbolic effort, a fake multilingualism as part of a marketing effort to appeal to Irish buyers and patriot consumers rather than a genuine effort to represent that variety in a comprehensive and authentic way.

Finally, the majority of multilingual advertising texts are also a type of 'fake multilingualism' for two further important reasons. First of all, this accentuating of linguistic difference and fetishizing of foreign words in texts takes place generally within a monolingual media context that presents communication as something seamless that happens in one language. The dominant language is the norm, with very little if any attempt to be representative of any type of multilingual society. It is this type of media context that enables linguistic fetishes to work at their best: they add the colour, and they are the exception to the norm. Secondly, linguistic fetish approaches construct the advertisee as monolingual with a particular ethnocentrically based view of other and foreign languages. Such strategies disregard the many individuals who grow up speaking more than one language, and/or who acquire linguistic competence in other languages through the education system and experience in other countries. All of this linguistic diversity is subsumed under a discourse of monolingual ethnocentrism as the norm in the advertising practices of many brands and companies.

And the future ...

At the time of finishing this book (April 2004), new and different linguistic fetish approaches are appearing all the time. One interesting phenomenon is that some advertisers seem to be going further and demanding more of their audience in terms of 'tolerance' of foreign languages in advertising. So, for example, *Stella Artois* beer is using ad-sized French cinematic texts entirely in French without subtitles to advertise, and *Goodfellas* pizzas are featuring an elderly man speaking entirely in Italian with consecutive interpretation into English. A number of brands appear to be adopting a 'language as soundtrack' approach, although none of the ones I have encountered are using the language as a claim of cultural competence. *Danone* yoghurt, a 'French product', features Sumo wrestlers talking French with subtitles in English; *Heineken* beer, a Dutch product, although in reality more of a Euro brand, uses Spanish without subtitles in an advertisement showing the smuggling of *Heineken* into Mexico before it could be legally imported; and *Tennents* lager uses the landscape of Iceland and the soundscape of the Icelandic language with English subtitles to advertise its product. The last time I encountered '*Vorsprung durch Technik*' was on my concert programme a few days ago in the local concert hall in Limerick. In the top right-hand corner, those three little words were there as always, above a highly localized text. On the one hand, a reference to Ireland's current presidency of the European Union (for example '*Audi* Ireland official transport partner of the Irish EU Presidency') placed the linguistic fetish of '*Vorsprung durch Technik*' in a very particular time and place, and on the other the text was 'eventized' using the lexicon of music to tie in with the event sponsored: 'The A6 corners well in the sharps and the flats.'

Yet another change in the linguistic fetish approach was heralded by the (French) *Laboratoires Garnier* decision in 2002 to drop '*laboratoires*' from its brand name. The reasoning behind this decision was a new strategy that repositioned the brand as a 'a global player' (rather than simply a European one) and '*Laboratoires Garnier*' was seen to be 'too big and French to work on a world stage' (Cooke, 2002). The brand is now simply known as '*Garnier*'. The decision by *Garnier* to reposition itself linguistically provides just one example of how linguistic fetishes change and evolve over time.

Once linguistic fetish-type approaches become firmly rooted in the individual's experience of advertising texts, they become part of the normal, taken-for-granted assumptions and background knowledge of advertising texts and intertextuality. There is then, for the advertiser, a new challenge. If German, French or Spanish words, strange accents or exotic orthography will no longer shock, attract or entice, then additional strategies must be used for these purposes. One option then is to take language beyond traditional and recognizable boundaries in order to stand out from the mass of advertising messages.

Japanese car manufacturer *Nissan* took the issue of linguistic fetish to another dimension in an advertising campaign from 2002/03. The slogan of the campaign for the new Micra (the smallest car in the *Nissan* range) was: 'Do you speak *Micra*?' The words in the advertisement are spoken by a pair of synthetic blue glossy lips that are detached from any face or any individual. They appear suspended in space in various positions on the adscape. The lips speak the words of this brave new language or *Micra* aloud: '*Modtro*', '*Simpology*', '*Spafe*'. The voice is that of a female, it is soft, vulnerable, and there is almost a beautiful texture to it when the voice whispers. A slight accent can be detected, perhaps with hints of an Eastern European variety. There is also, however, the impression of a computer-generated or modulated voice. Each new word is followed by an explanation, which is then whispered. Thus, *Modtro* is modern and retro; *Simpology* is simple technology; *Spafe* is spontaneous and safe. The lips then ask: 'Do you speak Micra?' All the text that is spoken by the lips also appears on the screen. The final shot moves to a plain background with *Nissan* and 'shift_expectations' and the local website address given. The background to the main advertisement is a futuristic cityscape, vaguely blue and grey in colour. The figures are hazy and not well-defined. The music accompanying the lips and the scenes of the *Micra* driving around this landscape evokes the music of bands such as Portishead, which have a trance-like, futuristic quality. The ad also takes a sort of pleasure in the words, both the way in which they are spoken, the meaning and texture given to them by the lips and the voice, and the way in which they are written. They seem to fit graphically with the scene and to evolve from it. The pretext in the advertisement would seem to be the notion that language is worn out, that there are, literally, no words to describe this new car, and that the technology of the *Micra* needs a new language to reflect this.

The fact that new approaches are needed seems to suggest that the linguistic fetish strategy has become commonplace in today's advertising discourse. And, herein lies the danger. As was pointed out in Chapter 1 and in the many examples throughout the book, the symbolic value that attaches to language and languages in advertising may, through everyday encounters, come to be accepted as part of the 'natural order' and as a 'thing in and of itself', masking and obscuring the social, historical, economic, political and linguistic relations behind the process through which foreign words and other voices come to have meaning in advertising texts. All of the developments, adaptations and innovations outlined above are driven by the market; they are attempts to try to exploit language, to stretch its boundaries and possibilities even further, with the primary objective of selling products. And, once they are created and are circulating in society, these advertisements are also texts that represent some type of 'multilinguality' and that interact with other texts, contributing to shared intertextual knowledge, particularly about languages and about multilingualism.

Notes

1 Defining Multilingualism in a Market Context

1 For an overview of 'consumer socialization', see Roedder John (1999) and Moschis (1987).
2 The so-called Toubon Laws (called after the former French Minister of Culture, Jacques Toubon) came into force in 1994 in an attempt to curb the use of English in a number of spheres in French public texts, including advertising. Ager (1999) discusses this in detail.
3 Adorno (1974) used the notion of commodity fetish to apply to the appearance of foreign words in translated texts. The term 'linguistic fetish' is therefore used here in order to avoid confusion with Adorno's use of the notion of 'language fetish'.

2 Foreign Languages in Advertising Discourse

1 Bigné (2000) discusses the Spanish country-of-origin image.
2 Some of this material appeared in Kelly-Holmes (2000b).
3 The text continues: 'There shall be In that rich earth a richer dust concealed: A dust whom England bore, shaped, made aware, Gave once, her flowers to love, her ways to roam, A body of England's breathing English air Washed by the rivers, blest by the suns of home' (Rupert Brooke, 1914).
4 *Carling Black Label* (in fact a Canadian brand, but not marketed as having any particular nationality in the UK) also made this topic the focus of a campaign from the same time. All of this tapped into what was happening in the tabloid press at the time and to rivalry between the British and German soccer fans.
5 Some of this material appeared in Kelly-Holmes (2000a).
6 Which defines beer in terms of its ingredients, thus ensuring its purity (*Reinheit*). Unlike other beers, German *Bier* brewed in accordance with the *Reinheitsgebot* does not contain any additives.
7 Interestingly, this advertisement was also aired in Germany.
8 Although, ironically, as David Head (1992) points out, the reason this slogan was originally written in English was because it was imposed by Britain at the turn of the century to differentiate cheaply made and low quality produce made in Germany from their superior British counterparts.

3 The Special Case of English

1 For a discussion of issues concerning knowledge of and attitudes to English as a second or third language by speakers of other languages in Europe, see Cenoz and Jessner (2000).
2 Jürgen Habermas (1993) has talked about this in relation to East Germany.

4 Minority Languages, Accents and Dialects in Advertising

1 Niamh Hourigan (2003) discusses these issues in-depth.

2   This is followed by Chinese (2 million), French (1.6 million), German (1.4 million), Tagalog (1.2 million), Vietnamese (1 million), Italian (1 million), Korean (0.9 million), Russian (0.7 million), Polish (0.7 million) and Arabic (0.6 million) http://www.census.gov/prod/2003pubs/c2kbr-29.pdf. The main countries of origin of the Hispanic/Latino population in the USA are reported in the 2000 census as being Mexico (67%), Puerto Rico and Cuba. http://www.census.gov/prod/2003pubs/p20-545.pdf

3   For a full discussion of these issues, see Crawford (2000) and Dicker (2003).

4   Community is a problematic and unsatisfactory concept; however it is used here as a term that is generally accepted in the discourse.

5   For a comprehensive review of the position of Irish in Ireland, see Ó Riagáin (1997); Hindley (1990); Ó Laoire (1995).

6   The *Gaeltacht* consists of larger parts of counties Donegal, Mayo, Galway and Kerry on the West coast; as well as smaller areas in West Cork, Waterford and Meath. 'These are the only areas of the country where Irish is spoken as a community language and as such act as an important cornerstone for the development of a bilingual society, by providing a natural environment where the language can grow and develop' (http://gaeltacht.local.ie). The *Gaeltacht* development agency, *Údarás na Gaeltachta* is charged with economic development in these areas in order to maintain the language. (http://gaeltacht.local.ie)

7   Filppula (1999) gives a comprehensive overview of the particularities of Irish-English. See also Kallen (1994).

8   Cork is a county located on the south-west coast of Ireland. The city is the second biggest in the Republic, and the accent is characterized by a 'singing' style that rises and falls through a sentence.

9   Some of the *Brennan's Bread* material appears in Kelly-Holmes (2004), forthcoming.

10 Explanation of transcription conventions (based on Goodwin and Heritage, 1990):

(.) indicates a slight pause or delay;
↑ indicates a rise in tone/pitch; ↓ indicates a fall in tone/pitch;
° ... ° speech between degree signs is quiet or whispered;
< ... > indicates slower speech; >..< indicates faster speech;
: sound is stretched or elongated; in this transcription also indicates diphthongs;
underlining indicates stress or emphasis;
(h) indicates laughter as part of a word/phrase.
IFRV = Irish female radio voice

11 Snapper or whippersnapper – Dublin dialect item for child.

12 Plural of ma – Dublin dialect for mammy (used throughout Ireland) – mother.

13 There are four national channels in the Republic of Ireland: RTÉ 1, Network 2 (both public service), TV3 (light entertainment, commercial, owned by UK-based Granada group) and TG4 (public service, Irish language). In addition, a very large number of homes also receive the following UK channels: BBC1 and BBC2 (Northern Ireland regional version), UTV (Ulster Television, regional station of the ITV network, and Channel 4.

14 The Good Friday Agreement, concluded and signed by the British and Irish governments in Belfast in April 1998. This historic document, the result of multiparty negotiations, was seen as the way forward for Northern Ireland, as the parties to the agreement committed themselves 'to partnership, equality and mutual respect as the basis of relationships within Northern Ireland, between North and South, and between these islands'. One of the policy results of the Agreement was greater cross-border cooperation and the development of all-Ireland bodies, and Tourism Ireland is one result of these. Another result was the status given to the Irish language in Northern Ireland. For a full account of the agreement cf. http://www.nio.gov.uk/issues/agreement.htm

15 TG4, like many other minority language channels (for example the Breton channel TVBreizh), can only afford to provide a certain number of hours broadcasting in the minority language every day. The rest of the schedule is filled in with English language movies, extracts from the pan-national Euronews and other programmes. See Kelly-Holmes (2001) and Watson (2003) for a full discussion of these and other issues relating to broadcasting in Irish.

16 Williams (2000) gives a good overview of this area.

5 Multilingual Advertising in a Pan-National Media Context

1 For a review of these issues see the following: Baumann (1998); Stiglitz (2002); Boyd-Barrett and Rantanen (1998).

2 It should be noted that the BBC is relatively unique among European public-service broadcasters in this. Almost all others supplement their licence income with advertising revenues.

3 Ager (1999) provides a good discussion of the French situation.

4 This ethnocentric dilemma was addressed by Jonathan Power, newly-appointed editor to the embryonic *International Standard*, intended to be a truly anational, global, English-medium newspaper: 'The IHT [*International Herald Tribune*] speaks with an American accent. We will look at the world each morning as though from the moon, with as much detachment as a human being is capable of' (*Observer*, 1996, p. 3).

5 Since the Meinhof and Richardson study was published, the station has added Portuguese and Russian.

6 As described by, for instance, Amine (1992); Schmidt and Pioch (1996); and Price (1995).

7 'The EBU is the largest professional association of national broadcasters in the world' (www.ebu.ch). The EBU website gives a full description of activities, members, policies and so on.

8 The English version is available as part of the standard package offered by most cable, satellite and digital distributors. Individuals have to pay for the language soundtrack. German is the only other version available free, that is unencrypted.

9 Smith and Wright (1999) provide a good discussion of these issues.

10 Dariusz Galasinski, cited in Kelly-Holmes (1999b), pp. 42–3.

11 In a rather ironic twist, the channel once featured a short programme about sponsorship and how players have become marketable commodities.

The brands and sponsors being discussed, even vaguely criticized, were, however, always present on screen.

6   Creating 'Multilingual' Texts: Combating Multilingualism

1   Dotty is a fairly stereotypical elderly English lady, played by well-known actress Prunella Scales, in a campaign for British supermarket chain *Tesco*.

Bibliography

Adorno, T.W. (1974) *Notes to Literature*, Vol. 2 (New York and Oxford: Columbia University Press).

Advertising Age International (1998) 'Euronews', *Advertising Age International*, 6 August 1998, p. 9.

Advertising Age International (1999) 'Eurosport', *Advertising Age International*, 1 November 1999, p. 32.

Ager, D.E. (1999) *Sociolinguistics and Contemporary French* (Cambridge: Cambridge University Press).

Amine, L.S. (1992) 'Marketing Strategies for Europe 1992: A Portfolio Model of Consumer/Product Relationships', *Journal of Euromarketing*, 2(1), pp. 49–67.

Anderson, B. (1983) *Imagined Communities* (London: Verso).

Androutsopoulos, J. (2004) 'Towards a Typology of Language Contact in Computer Mediated Communication', Paper presented at the Sociolinguistics Symposium 15, Newcastle, UK, April 2004.

Androutsopoulos, J. (2000) *From the Streets to the Screens and Back Again: On the Mediated Diffusion of Ethnolectal Patterns in Contemporary German*, http://www.archetype.de/papers/iclavedraft.htm

Anthony, T. (2000) 'The World's Mother Tongue: As English Spreads, so do Fears of Cultural Imperialism', *Advertising Educational Foundation*, http://www.aef.com/06/news/data/1207 (4 October).

Arendt, H. (1964) *Eichmann in Jerusalem: Ein Bericht von der Banalität der Bösen*, Neuausgabe (Munich: Piper, 1986 [1964]).

Automotive News (1996) 'Nissan adds Spanish ads', *Automotive News*, 71(5683), 12 October 1996, p. 59.

Bakhtin, M.M. (1981) *The Dialogic Imagination: Four Essays by M.M. Bakhtin*, edited by Michael Holquist (Austin: University of Texas Press).

Baron, N. (2000) *Alphabet to Email: How Written English Evolved and Where It's Heading* (London: Routledge).

Barry, A. (2003) *Telephone interview with Anna Barry, TG4 Advertising Sales Executive, Posttv Dublin*, 30 September.

Barthes, R. (1981) 'Theory of the Text', in R. Young (ed.), *Untying the Text: A Poststructuralist Reader* (London: Routledge & Kegan Paul).

Barthes, R. (1977) *Image Music Text* (London: Fontana/Collins).

Barthes, R. (1972) *Mythologies* (London: Jonathan Cape).

Bassnett, S. (2002) 'A failure to Communicate', *Guardian*, http://education.guardian.co.uk/egweekly/story/0,5500,665508,00.html (12 March).

Baumann, Z. (1998) *Globalization: The Human Consequences* (Cambridge: Polity Press).

Bell, A. (1999) 'Styling the Other to Define the Self: A Study in New Zealand Identity Making', *Journal of Sociolinguistics*, 3(4) (November), pp. 523–41.

Bell, A. (1984) 'Language Style as Audience Design', *Language in Society*, 13, pp. 145–204.

Benady, A. (2003) 'Minority Retort', *The Independent Review* (3 June), p. 10.

Berners-Lee, T. (1999) *Weaving the Web: The Original Design and Ultimate Destiny of the World Wide Web* (San Francisco: Harper San Francisco).

Bhatia, T.K. (1992) 'Discourse Functions and Pragmatics of Mixing: Advertising across Cultures', *World Englishes*, 2(1), pp. 195–215.

Bigné, J.E. 'Image and Spanish Country of Origin Effect', in J. Cannon and P. Odber de Baubeta (eds), *Advertising and Identity in Europe: The I of the Beholder* (Bristol, UK: Intellect), pp. 5–17.

Billig, M. (1995) *Banal Nationalism* (London: Sage).

Bonney, B. and Wilson, H. (1990) 'Advertising and the Manufacture of Difference', in M. Alvarado and J.O. Thompson (eds), *The British Film Institute Media Reader* (London: British Film Institute), pp. 181–98.

Bourdieu, P. (1991) *Language and Symbolic Power*, edited and introduced by J.B. Thompson (Oxford: Polity Press).

Boyd-Barrett, O. and Rantanen, T (eds) (1998) *The Globalization of News* (Thousand Oaks and London: Sage).

Bundesministerium des Innern (2001) *Bericht der Unabhaengigen Kommission Zuwanderung*, http://www.bmi.bund.de/dokumente/Artikel/ix_47013.htm

Cenoz, J. and Jessner, U. (eds) (2000) *English in Europe: The Acquisition of a Third Language* (Clevedon: Multilingual Matters).

Cheshire, J. and Moser, L.-M. (1994) 'English as a Cultural Symbol: The Case of Advertisements in French-speaking Switzerland', *Journal of Multilingual and Multicultural Development*, 15(6), pp. 451–69.

Chomsky, N. (1965) *Aspects of the Theory of Syntax* (Cambridge, MA: MIT Press).

Collins, R. (1992) *Satellite Television in Western Europe* (London: John Libbey).

Cook, G. (2001) *The Discourse of Advertising*, 2nd edn (London: Routledge).

Cook, G. (1989) *Discourse* (Oxford: Oxford University Press).

Cooke, R. (2002) 'Stealing Beauty', *The Observer Review* (Sunday 31 March) pp. 1–2.

Crawford, J. (2000) *At War with Diversity. US Language Policy in an Age of Anxiety* (Clevedon: Multilingual Matters).

Crystal, D. (2001) *Language and the Internet* (Cambridge: Cambridge University Press).

Crystal, D. (1997) *A Dictionary of Linguistics and Phonetics*, 3rd edn (Oxford: Basil Blackwell).

Crystal, D. (1997) *The Cambridge Encyclopaedia of Language*, 2nd edn (Cambridge and New York: Cambridge University Press).

CSO (Central Statistics Office of Ireland) (2002) Census 2002, http://www.cso.ie/census/results.htm.

de Mooij, M. (1994) *Advertising Worldwide*, 2nd edn (New York, etc.: Prentice Hall).

Dicker, S.J. (2003) *Languages in America: A Pluralist View*, 2nd edn (Clevedon: Multilingual Matters).

Dorian, N.C. (ed.) (1992) *Investigating Obsolescence: Studies in Language Contraction and Death* (Cambridge: Cambridge University Press).

Dorian, N.C. (1991) 'Surviving the Broadcast Media in Small Language Communities', *Educational Media International*, 28, pp. 134–7.

Dotson, M.J. and Hyatt, E.M. (2000) 'A Comparison of Parents' and Children's Knowledge of Brands and Advertising Slogans in the United States: Implications for Consumer Socialization', *Journal of Marketing Communications*, 6, pp. 219–30.

Eastman, C.M. and Stein, R.F. (1993) 'Language Display: Authenticating Claims to Social Identity', *Journal of Multilingual and Multicultural Development*, 14(3), pp. 187–202.

Ebrahimi, N. (2002) 'Hosgeldiniz – Marketingexperten entdecken Deutshtürken', *Financial Times Deutschland*, http://www.ftd.de/ub/di/1031581519674 (10 September).

EBU (European Broadcasting Union) Digital Strategy Group (2000) *Media with a Purpose: Public Service Broadcasters – their place and role in the digital age. Conclusions of the EBU Digital Stretegy Group*, http://www.ebu.ch/union/publications/index.php

EBU (European Broadcasting Union) (2000) *Members Announcements: Gold Medal for Eurosport Viewers!* http://www.ebu.ch/union/publications/index.php

Economist (1992) 'Vorsprung durch Panik', *Economist*, 322(7746) (15 February) pp. 53–4.

Edwards, C. (2002) 'Branding the Nation: The British Experience', Paper presented at the Baltic Marketing Conference (Riga, April).

Edwards, J. (1985) *Language, Society and Identity* (Oxford: Basil Blackwell).

Fairclough, N. (2001) *Language and Power* (Harlow: Longman).

Fairclough, N. (1992) *Discourse and Social Change* (Cambridge: Polity Press).

Filppula, M. (1999) *The Grammar of Irish-English: Language in Hibernian Style* (London: Routledge).

Fisher, J. (2000) 'Eurosport's new way of working', *TV Broadcasting Europe*, 9(5) (May), p. 36.

Forrester, P. and Feely, A. (2000) 'Forget your Culture ... Try Bad Language Instead: An Alternative to the Hofstede Paradigm', Aston Business School Working Papers (Aston University: Birmingham, UK).

Foucault, M. (1986) *The Foucault Reader*, edited by Paul Rabinow (Penguin).

Fox, D. (2002) 'Complexity of Eurosport', *TV Broadcasting Europe*, www.tvbeurope.com (March).

Fukuyama, F. (1992) *The End of History and the Last Man* (London: Hamilton).

Geis, M. (1982) *The Language of Television Advertising* (New York: Academic Press).

Ger, G. and Belk, R.W. (1996) 'I'd Like to Buy the World a Coke: Consumptionscapes of the "less affluent" World', *Journal of Consumer Policy*, 19, pp. 271–304.

Glenny, M. (1990) *The Rebirth of History: Eastern Europe in the Age of Democracy* (London: Penguin).

Goddard, A. (2002) *The Language of Advertising*, 2nd edn (London and New York: Routledge).

Goodman, S. (1996) 'Market Forces Speak English', in S. Goodman and D. Graddol (eds), *Redesigning English: New Texts, New Identities* (London: Routledge), pp. 141–80.

Goodwin, C. and Heritage, J. (1990) 'Conversation Analysis', *Annual Review of Anthropology 1990*, 19, pp. 283–307.

Gramsci, A. (1971) *Selections from Prison Notebooks* (London: Lawrence & Wishart).

Grimshaw, C. (2002) 'Living Dangerously', *Campaign* (UK), 12(29 March), p. 35.

Grin, F. (1994) 'The Bilingual Advertising Decision', *Journal of Multilingual and Multicultural Development*, 15, pp. 269–92.

Gumperz, J.J. (1996) 'Introduction to Part IV', *Rethinking Linguistic Relativity*, edited by J.J. Gumperz and S.C. Levinson (Cambridge: Cambridge University Press), pp. 359–73.

Haarmann, H. (1989) *Symbolic Values of Foreign Language Use, From the Japanese Case to a General Sociolinguistic Perspective* (Berlin/New York: Mouton de Gruyter).

Habermas, J. (1993) 'The Second Life Fiction of the Federal Republic: We have become "normal" again', *New Left Review*, 197(Jan/Feb), pp. 58–66.

Hall, S., Critcher, C., Jefferson, T., Clarke, J. and Roberts, B. (1978) *Policing the Crisis. Mugging, the State and Law and Order* (London: Macmillan).

Halliday, M.A.K. (1985) *An Introduction to Functional Grammar* (London: Edward Arnold).

Hamstra, M. (1995) 'Transcending Translation in Spanish-language Ads', *Nation's Restaurant News*, 29(18) (1 May), p. 12.

Harris, J. (1997) 'Ireland', in J. Kallen (ed.), *Varieties of English Around the World: Focus on Ireland* (Amsterdam and Philadelphia: John Benjamins), pp. 189–205.

Harris, R. and Seldon, A. (1962) *Advertising and the Public* (London: Institute for Economic Affairs).

Harrison, B. (2002) 'McCann-Erickson Wins €10m Heineken Account with Local Knowledge and Humour', *The Irish Times* (31 October), p. 17.

Head, D. (1992) *'Made in Germany': The Corporate Identity of a Nation* (London: Hodder & Stoughton).

Hibbeler, S. (2002) 'Deutsch-Türkische Medien: Probleme und neue Dynamiken', *Istanbul Post*, 2(4) (26 January), http://www.istpost.de/02/01/04/goethe1.htm

Hill, J.H. (1999) 'Styling Locally, Styling Globally: What Does it Mean?', *Journal of Sociolinguistics*, 3(4), pp. 542–556.

Hill J.H. (1995) 'Junk Spanish, Covert Racism and the (leaky) Boundary Between Public and Private Spheres', *Pragmatics*, 5, pp. 197–212.

Hindley, R. (1990) *The Death of the Irish Language: A Qualified Obituary* (London: Routledge).

Hobsbawm, E. (2000) *The New Century*, in conversation with Antonia Polito. (London: Abacus).

Hofstede, G. (1983) 'The Cultural Relativity of Organisational Practices and Theories', *Journal of International Business Studies*, 14(2) (September), pp. 75–89.

Hollingsworth, P. (2000) 'The European Food Blender', *Food Technology*, 54(1) (January), pp. 38–40.

Hourigan, N. (2003) *Escaping the Global Village: Media, Language and Protest* (Lanham, MA: Lexington Books).

House, J. (2003) 'English as a Lingua Franca: A Threat to Multlingualism?', *Journal of Sociolinguistics*, 7(4), pp. 556–78.

Jaffe, E.D. and Nebenzahl, I.D. (2001) *National Image and Competitive Advantage: The Theory and Practice of Country-of-Origin Effect* (Copenhagen: Copenhagen Business School Press).

Jain, S.C. (1990) *International Marketing Management* (Boston: PWS-Kent).

Jameson, F. (1991) *Postmodernism, or, the Cultural Logic of Late Capitalism* (Durham, NC: Duke University Press).

Kahn, J. (1995) *Culture, Multiculture, Postculture* (London, etc.: Sage).

Kallen, J.L. (1994) 'English in Ireland', in R. Burchfield (ed.), *The Cambridge History of the English Language*, Vol. 5 (Cambridge: Cambridge University Press), pp. 148–96.

Kaplan, D. (2002) 'Mediaedge: CIA, KFC boost Hispanic focus', *Adweek Eastern Edition*, 43(3) (14 January), p. 4.

Keegan, W. (1995) *Global Marketing Management* (Englewood Cliffs, NJ: Prentice-Hall).

Kelly-Holmes, H. (2004) 'An analysis of the languages in students' repertoires and the languages they use on the Internet', *UNESCO MOST (Management of Social Transformations) International Journal on Multicultural Society, Special Issue in co-operation with the B@bel Initiative*, 6(1), pp. 29–52.

Kelly-Holmes, H. (2004 forthcoming) 'A Relevance Approach to Irish-English Advertising: The Case of Brennan's Bread', in A. Barron and K.P. Schneider (eds), *The Pragmatics of Irish English* (Berlin: Mouton de Gruyter).

Kelly-Holmes, H. (2001) (ed.), *Minority Language Broadcasting: Breton and Irish* (Clevedon: Multilingual Matters).

Kelly-Holmes, H. (2000a) 'Bier, parfum, kaas: language fetish in intercultural advertising', *European Journal of Cultural Studies*, 3(1), pp. 67–82.

Kelly-Holmes, H. (2000b) 'There is a corner that is forever Munich': Advertising and Anglo-German relations', *Debatte*, 8(1), pp. 39–54.

Kelly-Holmes, H. (1999a) 'United Consumers? Advertising Discourse and Constructions of Consumer Identity', in. P. Stevenson and J. Theobald (eds), *Relocating Germanness: Discursive Disunity in Unified Germany* (Basingstoke: Palgrave Macmillan), pp. 91–108.

Kelly-Holmes, H. (1999b) (ed.), *European Television Discourse in Transition* (Clevedon: Multilingual Matters).

Kelly-Holmes, H. (1995) *West German Banks and East German Consumers: A Study in Intercultural Advertising Communication*, PhD thesis (Birmingham UK: Aston University).

King, T. (2004) 'Witness: Secularism in France', *Prospect*, 96 (March), pp. 64–8.

Klein, N. (2001) *No Logo* (London: Flamingo).

Koranteng, J. (1999) 'TV Goes Local', *Advertising Age International* (1 November), p. 32.

Kosztolanyi, G. (1999) 'Shop till you drop', *Central Europe Review*, 1(8), http://www.ce-review.org/99/8/consume_csardas8.html (16 August).

Kottak, C.P. (2003) *Mirror for Humanity: A Concise Introduction to Cultural Anthropology*, 3rd edn (Boston: McGraw-Hill College).

Kristeva, J. (1986) *The Kristeva Reader* (Oxford: Basil Blackwell).

Kundera, M. (2003) *Ignorance* (London: Faber & Faber).

Lane, M. (2002) 'Who Puts the ooh-la-la in Lager?', *BBC News Online* (9 July).

Lang, M. (2000) 'A Beer by Any Other Name', *Advertising Age*, 21(18) (1 May), p. 86.

Lee, J.S. (2004) 'Linguistic Constructions of Modernity in Korean TV Commercials', Paper presented at the Sociolinguistics Symposium 15, Newcastle, UK, April.

Leffers, J. (2003) 'Britische Schüler: Hitler, immer wieder Hitler', http://www.spiegel.de/unispiegel/wunderbar/0,1518,226453,00.html

Leslie, D.A. (1995) 'Global Scan: The Globalization of Advertising Agencies, Concepts and Campaigns', *Economic Geography*, 71(4), pp. 402–26.

Lorin, P. (2001) *5 Giants of Advertising* (Paris: Assouline).

MacArthur, K. (2000) 'Chili's Fires up Spanish Campaign', *Advertising Age*, 71(30) (17 July), p. 28.

Marr, N.E. and Prendergast, G.P. (1992) 'Country-of-Origin Stereotyping: A Case Study in the New Zealand Motor Vehicle Industry', *European Journal of Marketing*, 26(3), pp. 37–51.

Martin, E. (2002) 'Mixing English in French Advertising', *World Englishes*, 21(3), pp. 375–402.

Marx, K. (1954) [1867] *Capital*, Vol. 1 (London: Lawrence & Wishart).

Marx, K. and Engels, F. (1959) [1894] *Capital*, Vol. 3 (London: Lawrence & Wishart).

Marx, K. and Engels, F. (1989) *Karl Marx and Friedrich Engels Selected Works in Three Volumes: Volume 1* (Moscow: Progress Publishers).

McAllister, M.P. (1996) *The Commercialization of American Culture: New Advertising, Control and Democracy* (Thousand Oaks, CA, etc.: Sage).

McLauchlin, J.E. (1993) 'Communicating to a Diverse Europe', *Business Horizons*, 36(1) (Jan/Feb), pp. 54–6.

McNair, B. (1991) *Glasnost, Perestroika and the Soviet Media* (London: Routledge).

McSweeney, G. (2003) *Email Interview with Gareth McSweeney, Brand Manager, Brennan's Bread* (14 May).

Meinhof, U.H. and Richardson, K. (1999) 'Home and Away: Television Discourse in Transition', in H. Kelly-Holmes (ed.), *European Television Discourse in Transition* (Clevedon: Multilingual Matters).

Micklethwait, J. (1990) 'Survey of the Advertising Industry', *The Economist* (9 June).

Moal, S. (2001) 'Broadcast Media in Breton: Dawn at Last?', in H. Kelly-Holmes (ed.), *Minority Language Broadcasting: Breton and Irish* (Clevedon: Multilingual Matters), pp. 31–48.

Morley, D. and Robins, K. (1995) *Spaces of Identity: Global Media, Electronic Landscapes and Cultural Boundaries* (London and New York: Routledge).

Moschis, G.P. (1987) *Consumer Socialization: A Life-cycle Perspective* (Toronto: D.C. Heath).

Multichannel News (2000) 'ESPN backs out of Eurosport', *Multichannel News*, 21(22), p. 32.

Myers, G. (1999) *Ad Worlds: Brands, Media, Audiences* (London: Hodder Arnold).

Myers, G. (1994) *Words in Ads* (London: Edward Arnold).

Newmark, P. (1988) *A Textbook of Translation* (London and New York: Prentice-Hall).

Observer (1996) 'New Global Newspaper Looks for Investors', *The Observer*, Business: 3(25 May).

O'Donnell, H. (1994) 'Mapping the Mythical: a geopolitics of national sporting stereotypes' *Discourse and Society*, 5(3), pp. 345–80.

O'Gunn, T.C., Allen, C.T. and Semenik, R.J. (2000) *Advertising*, 2nd edn. (Cincinnati etc.: South-Western College Publishing).

Ó Laoire, M. (1995) 'An historical perspective on the revival of Irish outside the Gaeltacht, 1880–1930, with reference to the revitalization of Hebrew', *Current Issues in Language and Society*, 2(3), pp. 223–35.

Ó Riagáin, P. (1997) *Language Policy and Social Reproduction: Ireland 1893–1993* (Oxford: Clarendon Press).

Olins, W. (1999) *Deutschland Europa*, http://www.jyanet.com/cap/1999/0310fe1a.htm

Özdemir, C. (2002) *Die Türken in Deutschland brauchen mehr und andere Medien*, http://www.dtsinfo.de/deutsch/p200206/Seite16.htm

Pennycook, A. (1995) *The Cultural Politics of English as an International Language* (London: Longman).

Phillipson, R. (1992) *Linguistic Imperialism* (Oxford: Oxford University Press).

Phipps, A. and Gonzalez, M. (2004) *Learning and Teaching in an International Field* (London: Sage).

Piller, I. (2001) 'Identity Constructions in Multilingual Advertising', *Language in Society*, 30(2), pp. 153–86.

Price, M. (1995) *Television, the Public Sphere and National Identity* (Oxford: Clarendon Press).

Rampton, B. (1999) 'Deutsch in Inner London and the Animation of an Instructed Foreign Language', *Journal of Sociolinguistics*, 3(4) (November), pp. 480–504.

Rampton, B. (1995) *Crossing: Language and Ethnicity among Adolescents* (London: Longman).

Richardson, K. (1997) 'Twenty First Century Commerce: The Case of QVC', *Text*, 17(2), pp. 199–223.

Richardson, K. and Meinhof, U.H. (1999) *Worlds in Common? Television Discourse in a Changing Europe* (London: Routledge).

Ritzer, G. (1998) *The McDonaldization Thesis: Explorations and Extensions* (London: Sage).

Ritzer, G. (1996) *The McDonaldization of Society: an Investigation into the Changing Character of Contemporary Social Life*, revd edn (Thousand Oaks, CA: Pine Forge Press).

Roe, K. and de Meyer, G. (2000) 'Music Television: MTV-Europe', in J. Wieten, G. Murdock and P. Dahlgren, *Television across Europe: A Comparative Introduction* (London: Sage), pp. 141–57.

Roedder, John, D. (1999) 'Consumer Socialization of Children: A Retrospective Look at Twenty-Five Years of Research', *Journal of Consumer Research*, 26(3) (December), pp. 183–213.

Russell, J.T and Lane W.R. (2002) *Kleppner's Advertising Procedure*, 15th edn (Upper Saddle River, NJ: Prentice-Hall).

Said, E.W. (1991) *Orientalism: Western Concepts of the Orient* (London: Penguin Books).

Sampson, E.E. (2003) *Celebrating the Other: A Dialogic Account of Human Nature* (Boulder, CO: Westview Press).

Schlosser, E. (2002) *Fast Food Nation. What the All-American Meal is Doing to the World* (London: Penguin).

Schlosser, H.-D. (1990) *Die deutsche Sprache in der DDR – zwischen Stalinismus und Demokratie* (Cologne: Verlag Wissenschaft und Politik).

Schmidt, R. and Pioch, E. (1996) 'Serving the Euro-consumer: A Marketing Challenge or a Case for Intervention?', *Marketing Intelligence and Planning*, 14(5), pp. 14–19.

Schooler, R.D. (1971) 'Bias Phenomenon Attendant to the Marketing of Foreign Goods in the US', *Journal of International Business Studies*, 2(1) (March), pp. 71–80.

Schreiber, K. (2000) 'Ethnisches Marketing: Graue Listen, schwarze Schafe', *Auslaender in Deutschland*, 16(1), http://www.isoplan.de/aid/2000–1/ethn_marketing.htm (31 March).

Shannon, C. and Weaver, W. (1949) *The Mathematical Theory of Communication* (Urbana: University of Illinois Press).

Shohany, E. (2003) 'Linguistic Landscape, Multilingualism and Multiculturalism: A Jewish-Arab Comparative Study', Paper given at the Third International Conference on Third Language Acquisition and Trilingualism (Tralee, September).

Shore, C. (1997) 'Governing Europe: European Union Audiovisual Policy and the Politics of Identity', in C. Shore and S. Wright (eds), *Anthropology of Policy: Critical Perspectives on Governance and Power* (London: Routledge), pp. 165–92.

Smith, A. (1998) 'Introduction', in A. Smith (ed.), *Television: An International History*, 2nd edn (Oxford: Oxford University Press), pp. 1–6.

Smith, A.D. (1991) *National Identity* (Reno: University of Nevada Press).

Smith, D. and Wright, S.M. (eds) (1999) *Whose Europe? The Turn Towards Democracy* (Oxford and Boston: Basil Blackwell).

Smith, R.N. (1982) 'A Functional View of the Linguistics of Advertising', in R.J. di Petro (ed.), *Linguistics and the Professions – Vol. 8 of Advances in Discourse Processes* (New Jersey: Ablex Publishing), pp. 189–99.

Solomon, M., Bamossy, G. and Askegaard, S. (1999) *Consumer Behaviour: A European Perspective* (Harlow: Prentice-Hall).

Speer, L. (2000) 'Eurosport News Pitches for Instant Loyalty', *Advertising Age Global*, 1(1), p. 16.

Sperber, D. and Wilson, D. (1986) *Relevance: Communication and Cognition* (Oxford: Basil Blackwell).

Spiegel Online (2002) 'Briten testen ihr Deutschlandwissen: "We want to beat you Fritz!" ' http://www.spiegel.de/unispiegel/wunderbar/0,1518,226453,00.html

Sredl, K.C. (2003) *Advertising and the Development of a Consumer Society*, http://www.irex.org/programs/iaro/research/Sredl.pdf

Steiner, G. (1975) *After Babel: Aspects of Language and Translation* (London: Oxford University Press).

Stiglitz, J.E. (2002) *Globalization and its Discontents* (London: Allen Lane).

Stock, J. (2002) 'EBU Members Announcements: Jean Stock, Honorary President of TV5', http://www.ebu.ch/news/press_archive/press_news_1901.html. Trim, R. (2002). 'The Lexicon in European Languages Today: Unification or Diversification?', in M. Holt and P. Gubbins (eds), *Beyond Boundaries: Language and Identity in Contemporary Europe* (Clevedon: Multilingual Matters), pp. 35–45.

Tuominen, K. (2002) 'Monologue or Dialogue in the Web Environment? The Role of Networked Library and Information Services in the Future'. Paper presented at the 66th International Federation of Library Associations and Institutions Council and General Conference (Jerusalem, August).

Twitchell, J. (1999) *Lead us not into Temptation: The Triumph of American Materialism* (New York: Columbia University Press).

Van Dijk, T. (1998) *Ideology* (London: Sage).

Vasagar, J. (2002) 'History Teaching in UK Stokes Xenophobia, Says German Envoy', *The Guardian* (9 December).

Venuti, L. (1994) 'Translation and the Formation of Cultural Identities and Preliminary Remarks to the Debate', *Current Issues in Language and Society*, 1(3), pp. 201–24.

Vestergaard, T. and Schroder, K. (1985) *The Language of Advertising* (Oxford: Basil Blackwell).

Watson, I. (2003) *Broadcasting in Irish: Minority Languages, Radio, Television and Identity* (Dublin: Four Courts Press).

Watts, C.J. (2003) *Decline in the Take-up of Modern Languages at Degree Level* (London: Anglo-German Foundation for the Study of Industrial Society).

Wellmer, A. (1981) 'Critique of Marx's Positivism', in T. Bottomore (ed.), *Modern Interpretations of Marx* (Oxford: Basil Blackwell), pp. 56–67.

Wells, W., Burnett, J. and Moriarty, S. (2000) *Advertising Principles and Practice*, 5th edn (Upper Saddle River, NJ: Prentice-Hall).

Wentz, L. and Schnuer, J. (2001) 'Census Eases Pain for Media: Performance Beats General Market', *Advertising Age*, 72(37) (10 September), p. 21.

West, D. (1999) '¿Que Pasa? Spanglish Ads Anger Some, Confuse Others', *Pharmaceutical Executive*, 19(4) (April), p. 10.

Williams, H.C. (2000) (ed.) *Language Revitalization: Policy and Planning in Wales* (Cardiff: University of Wales Press).

Williams, R. (1981) *Culture* (London: Fontana).

Wright, S.M. (2000) *Community and Communication* (Clevedon: Multilingual Matters).

Zbar, J. (1998) 'Spanish-language TV Upgrades Program Fare', *Advertising Age*, 69(34) (24 August), p. 18.

Websites and Internet publications cited

http://djurdjevic.com/Bulletins/emerging/96–32.htm

http://www.archi-web.com/unileverromania/rom.htm

http://www.bizsites.com/2004/January/article.asp?id = 543

http://www.carpages.co.uk/renault/renault_england_rugby_stars_score_with_renault_07_12_03.asp)

http://www.carpages.co.uk/renault/renault_thierry_and_animal_explain_meaning_of_va_va_voom_25_10_03.asp)

http://www.mmdcee.com/

www.acento.com

www.adamericas.com

www.archi-web.com

www.australianopen.com

www.benetton.com

www.cairdeschoilecaillte.ie

www.carpages.com

www.census.gov/prod/2003pubs/c2kbr-29.pdf

www.census.gov/prod/2003pubs/p20–545.pdf

www.coislife.ie

www.design.bg

www.dunnesstores.ie

www.ebu.ch

www.esljobfind.com

www.euronews.net

www.eurosport.com

www.fiat.com

www.fiosfeasa.com

www.gaelscoileanna.ie

www.gaeltacht.local.ie

www.google.com

www.google.ie

www.gti.ro

www.hertz.com

www.ikea.co.uk
www.ikea.de
www.litriocht.com
www.lostschoolfriends.ie
www.mango.es
www.nio.gov.uk/issues/agreement.htm
www.nivea.co.uk
www.nuacht.com
www.renault.com
www.seat.co.uk
www.seat.com
www.siveco.ro
www.smaointe.com
www.tourismireland.com
www.toyota.com
www.visitmexico.com
www.volkswagen.de
www.vw.com
www.webbery.ie
www.wella.co.uk

Index

Printed in the United States
134944LV00001B/24/P